Counterfeit Kingdom

The Dangers of
New Revelation,
New Prophets,
and New Age Practices
in the Church

HOLLY PIVEC *and* R. DOUGLAS GEIVETT

PUBLISHING
BRENTWOOD, TENNESSEE

Published by B&H Publishing Group
Brentwood, Tennessee

Dewey Decimal Classification: 289.9
Subject Heading: NEW APOSTOLIC
REFORMATION / CULTS / SECTS

Cover design by B&H Publishing Group. Illustration by duncan1890/
gettyimages. Interior illustration by Old Books Images/Alamy.

4 5 6 7 8 9 • 27 26 25 24 23

To the handsome stranger I met at Starbucks. (See chapter 2.)
—Holly

To my father, Howard, and my mother, Dixie
—Doug

Acknowledgments

Many people have helped us in various ways with the completion of this manuscript—with research, critique, and encouragement. Of course, their assistance, whatever form it has taken, in no way implies endorsement of our book or agreement with its conclusions. Those who assisted us include Alisa Childers, Aaron Mapes, Jennifer Stoll, Teasi Cannon, Greg Koukl, Natasha Crain, Mike Heiser, Brandon Kimber, Keith Gibson, Monique Duson, Kevin Lewis, Paul Carden, Simon Brace, Rudy Boshoff, Todd Johnson, Doreen Virtue, Mike Winger, Marcia Montenegro, Alan Gomes, Cheryl Sackett, Mitch and Melody Flynn, Greg and Kerry Pippin, Doug Wubbena, Alan Kurschner, Richard Moore, K. L. Marshall, Bart McCurdy, Alison Townsend, Lakshmi Mehta, Belinda Clark, Tara Pauls, Mary Beth Osborn, Dianne Geivett, Erin and Forrest McBride, Howard and Kris Geivett, Dixie and Frank Smith, Debbie and Larry Stout, Brenda Sandeno, Stephanie England, Kimberly Larson, Jon Griswold, Peter Everett, Adam Pivec, Daniel Peters, Linda Peters, Kate Pivec, Lizzie Pivec, Sherina Anderson, Kara Beck, Jon and Lacey McBride, John Tebay, and the members of Holly's church small group.

We are very grateful to our agent, Bill Jensen, for his deep concern for contending for the faith, his encouragement, and his extraordinary expertise. And we have been blessed to partner with Taylor Combs, Ashley Gorman, and the rest of the team at B&H Publishing.

Contents

Foreword

I will never forget the feeling of walking into a brand-new church, still timid and guarded from my last experience. I'd been burned by a church family who went from singing *In Christ Alone* on Easter Sunday to apologizing for the lyrics to *Amazing Grace* within a year. Our church had fallen into progressive Christianity, and it nearly took my faith with it. Now, just weeks after walking out the door for the last time, I was stepping foot into the fold of a new flock that would become our church family for the next seven years. I was instantly put at ease when the worship started. It was dynamic. It felt electric and alive. I was sure this was a safe place because although I was still walking with a spiritual limp, the passionate worshipers were boldly "storming the gates of heaven," and that made me feel safe. I spent a couple of years sitting on the back row of the balcony recovering from an injurious faith crisis. Then I slowly got involved. First, I volunteered in the nursery. Then I joined the worship team. Then I became involved with teaching apologetics to the women and youth. I was all in.

This community of believers was slightly charismatic but gospel-focused and balanced. Then things started to change. To this day I'm not sure if *they* changed or if I just became more discerning as I studied apologetics and theology with vigor. Then it happened. Our pastor invited a well-known New Apostolic Reformation (NAR) prophet to speak on a Saturday night and the following Sunday morning.

Around this time, I discovered the work of Holly Pivec and Doug Geivett. They had already researched and written in great detail what I ended up witnessing in real life: the process and subsequent fallout of what happens when the teachings and practices of the NAR come to a church. I have personally witnessed the devastation of the many wounded people left in its wake. I've watched unsuspecting Christians who are hungry for revival become swept up in a movement that promises unity, renewal, and even miracles only to deliver confusion, empty promises, and manipulation.

Maybe you haven't heard of the NAR, but if you are a Christian who goes to church, there is an almost 100 percent chance you have sung one of their songs in a worship service. This is why it's so vital that every Christian, and in particular, every Christian *pastor* read this book.

It's my prayer that the careful research, gentle tone, and truthful observations found in this book will help shield many churches that may be drifting into the theology and practices of the NAR. I pray it serves to help many churches make critical course corrections as they pursue authentic Christianity in spirit and in truth.

Alisa Childers
Bestselling author of *Another Gospel? A Lifelong Christian Seeks Truth in Response to Progressive Christianity*

Authors' Note

In this book we share memories of our personal past experiences. We have retold events to the best of our memories and after carefully reviewing our own recorded observations. We also share stories of individuals who have been damaged by the New Apostolic Reformation movement, as those stories have been shared with us. Where possible, we obtained permission to share those stories; otherwise, we removed personally identifying details to protect individual privacy. We also changed the names of some individuals. There were other stories we very much wished to include but did not because the parents who shared them with us were nervous about possible repercussions if their adult children—who have become followers of the "apostles" and "prophets" and have broken off communication with them—were to learn that they spoke with us. These parents feared that their already fractured relationships would be broken beyond repair. Their fear sends a strong signal about the destructive effect of the movement we write about.

This book focuses especially on the *practices* of the New Apostolic Reformation movement—the concrete ways it is showing up in churches, ministries, and music. We have written other academic books that take a deeper dive into the theology, and they are heavily documented. They are *A New Apostolic Reformation? A Biblical Response to a Worldwide Movement*, and the condensed version of that book, *God's Super-Apostles: Encountering the Worldwide Prophets and Apostles Movement* (both published by

Lexham Press). While writing *Counterfeit Kingdom*, we completed another academic manuscript focusing on the theology of Bethel Church in Redding, California. Forthcoming with Cascade/ Wipf & Stock, it is titled *Reckless Christianity: The Destructive New Teachings and Practices of Bill Johnson, Bethel Church, and the Global Movement of Apostles and Prophets*. If you have questions that are not answered by this book, we refer you to these other books and to Holly's blog at www.HollyPivec.com.

We also wish to note that when we refer to teachings of NAR leaders in this book, we do not mean to imply that every apostle, prophet, or teacher in this movement holds to all of the same beliefs or agrees on every point of theology and practice. But the practices and teachings we highlight here are those promoted by influential leaders in this movement and, for that reason, have gained entrance into a growing number of churches. We've welcomed every opportunity for direct dialogue with leaders of the movement.

*I appeal to you, brothers, to watch out
for those who cause divisions and create
obstacles contrary to the doctrine that
you have been taught; avoid them.*
—Romans 16:17

CHAPTER 1

Wake Up, Olive

*It's a church that quite frankly messes with
you: your theology, your way of doing church
and your view of your walk with Jesus.*
—*Premier Christianity* article
about Bethel Church[1]

With more than 780,000 Instagram followers, Bethel Church in Redding, California, is one of the best-known churches in America and around the world. A major reason for this is their music. Bethel Music (with a staggering 1.7 million Instagram followers) has produced many of the most popular songs sung in churches and streamed online, including "No Longer Slaves," "You Make Me Brave," and "Reckless Love." The pastors, including Bill Johnson and Kris Vallotton, have written numerous bestselling books, like *When Heaven Invades Earth* and *Supernatural Ways of Royalty.*

Obviously, many Christians know *of* Bethel Church. But do they *really* know what goes on there, and do they know what the church's leaders actually teach?

Sure, they might know that the church is charismatic. But while that type of theology is not every Christian's cup of tea, there are plenty of faithful charismatic Christians. So maybe Bethel's beliefs aren't too far out there. Or are they?

Let us give you some revealing snapshots of Bethel behind the scenes, and you can judge for yourself.

Wake Up, Olive

The story is heartbreaking. Readers will no doubt empathize with those who walked through this tragedy, especially if they've ever been through something similar. But what Bethel did afterward shocked and disturbed Christians around the world, including many Pentecostal and charismatic Christians who expect God to perform miracles of healing sick people, but did not approve of Bethel's actions.

On December 14, 2019, two-year-old Olive Heiligenthal was sleeping in her bed and suddenly stopped breathing. When this was discovered, her family called 911, and paramedics rushed her to the hospital. But it was too late. Little Olive had died.

A senseless tragedy. Every parent's deepest fear. The hollow ache of helplessness with a funeral sure to follow.

But maybe not, this time around.

Most grieving parents would have planned a funeral. But not Olive's parents. Her mother, Kalley—a worship leader at Bethel—and her father, Andrew, refused to accept her death. Based on their peculiar understanding of the Bible—taught to them by Bethel Church leaders—they appeared 100 percent convinced that God would raise Olive from the dead. So they kept her body at the local morgue—just for a bit—while they waited for her to come back to life.

Through social media, Bethel leaders urged Christians around the world to join the parents in "declaring" a resurrection because they believed their spoken words, as children of God, had the power to bring Olive back. The hashtag #wakeupolive went viral. Tens of thousands across the globe joined the chorus of "declarations" posted to Facebook and Instagram.

> "Praying, and declaring resurrection Life for Olive . . . Little Olive, arise, in Jesus's name!"
>
> "Father, in Jesus's name we decree and declare Spirit of life come back into Olive!"
>
> "Awake little Olive, we release resurrection power into your body in the name of Jesus."[2]

Even well-known worship leaders from other churches, including Hillsong's Taya Gaukrodger and Brooke Ligertwood, joined the Instagram chorus. American singer and songwriter Kari Jobe made what must have been a startling announcement to her one million followers: "We're still standing in faith for Olive to wake up."[3]

The story was picked up by national news. The *Washington Post*, the *Daily Mail, USA Today, Slate,* and *BuzzFeed* were among the many high-profile media outlets that covered it. *BuzzFeed* used words like *heartbreaking* and *horrifying* in this description of the church's attempts to raise Olive.

> This week, an Instagram plea from a mom who is a prominent figure in an influential yet controversial Christian church has gone viral. Her request is both heartbreaking and horrifying: She is asking her church and believers across social media to pray for her child, who died suddenly

> over the weekend, to be raised from the dead. . . .
> Thousands of people are rallying around the
> idea that the power of prayer, and spreading it
> through social media, can literally "breathe life"
> back into a child.[4]

Riveted by these reports, people around the world watched the story unfold.

One day passed.

No resurrection.

Two days.

Nothing.

Three days. Surely this would be the day. After all, Jesus was raised three days after His death. So Bethel's followers reasoned.

Still nothing.

But the story was not yet over. They persisted. "Day 4 is a really good day for resurrection," Kalley wrote on Instagram.[5] Later that night, the couple stood on the church's stage, singing at the top of their lungs: "Olive, come out of that grave, come out of that grave in Jesus's name!"[6] The congregation joined with them, dancing, raising their arms in the air above their heads, and commanding Olive to come back to life.

The next day, Kalley repeated the same words, "Day 5 is a really good day for resurrection."[7]

Finally, after six days, the church suddenly gave up. USA Today declared: "Olive Hasn't Been Raised: After Praying for a Miracle, Girl's Family Now Plans Memorial." Many other news organizations ran similar headlines.

The conclusion to the dramatic events of the previous week was anticlimactic. Bethel leaders sent out a press release announcing that the family had begun planning a memorial service. Their attempts to raise her had been loud and took place very much in the public eye. In contrast, the service was planned quietly and held behind the scenes. Almost as if they were hoping to draw as little attention as possible to the funeral—and their failure to raise Olive.

What Bethel saw as bold Christian faith, other Christians viewed as foolishness. The declarations, feverish dancing, and denial had come to an end. Olive's parents were left with nothing but a hole in their hearts and promises from a church that didn't pan out.

What would become of Olive's parents? concerned onlookers wondered aloud. *Would their faith survive? What about the church's followers throughout the world who truly believed Olive would be raised? Would they be so disillusioned that they'd give up on church— or even worse, on God?*

Many worried that Bethel's "crazy" antics would taint the way non-churched people think about all Christians and damage their witness to a watching world. Sadly, they were right. One popular atheist blogger, who has more than half a million Facebook followers, saw an opportunity to take a jab at *all* religious beliefs, not just Bethel's. Hemant Mehta—who goes by the pen name "The Friendly Atheist"—wrote:

> My heart goes out to the family. I don't know what they're going through. But the church needs to rethink its own theology because it's downright cruel to tell people their dead loved ones might come back *if only they pray hard enough*. It takes religion to add a second layer of misery on top of already unthinkable grief.[8]

No doubt many of the Friendly Atheist's followers felt confirmed in their belief that Christians are unreasoning buffoons.

Another blogger suggested that Bethel exploited the case of little Olive by releasing a Bethel Music song titled "Come Out of That Grave (Resurrection Power)." The album debuted within six months of her death.[9]

Of course, some still defend Bethel for trying to raise Olive. Maybe the church's beliefs are bizarre—they say—but the people meant well, and that's what matters. But regardless of their good intentions, there's no denying the devastating consequences of their actions and their message.

Grave Sucking

It's not just activities taking place at the church that have raised eyebrows. So have the "field trips."

What would possess a bunch of college-age students to hang around a graveyard? The desire for miraculous powers.

Some were sprawled on their backs on the tops of grave markers. Others lay face down on the grass before the headstones. One was curled up in a fetal position in front of a tombstone, as though nourishing herself on the corpse's still-living spiritual power. Bethelites call this power the "anointing."

Turns out the students were from the Bethel School of Supernatural Ministry (BSSM), and they were taking part in a practice called "grave sucking" or "grave soaking." They would visit the gravesites of well-known "miracle-workers"—such as the British faith healer Smith Wigglesworth and the American "healing" evangelist Kathryn Kuhlman—and try to "suck" (or "soak") up the dead miracle workers' powers. What reason did they give for their ghoulish goings-on? They pointed to a little-known Bible verse, 2 Kings 13:21. It's the story of when a dead man's body came into contact with Elisha's bones and the man came to life.

Controversy erupted. Bethel denied that its leaders ever promoted it. But former BSSM students say they absolutely promoted it.[10] And pictures and videos—still available through a quick Google search—suggest a different story. A YouTube video shows Bethel pastor and BSSM graduate Ben Fitzgerald taking part in it.[11] And even Beni Johnson, wife of Bill Johnson and a senior pastor herself, can be seen, in different pictures, lying on her back on a grave and tightly embracing a tombstone. When questioned about her reasons for this, she said, "Remember Elisha and his bones?"[12]

Grave sucking soon became a PR problem, and Bethel has since shut down the practice. But the cat is out of the bag, and grave sucking has heightened concern about the way people at Bethel are taught to read the Bible—by cherry-picking verses and misusing them to invent strange new practices for Christians.

Angelic Slumber

We're betting you didn't know that angels can get bored sometimes. At least, that's what they teach at Bethel. On her blog, Beni Johnson shares two stories about angels who were so bored they fell asleep. In the first, a student in the Bethel School of Supernatural Ministry claims God told her to go to Moriah Chapel, a prayer chapel in Wales, and shout "wakey, wakey." She did and, to her surprise, she awakened an angel who had taken up residence in the chapel. Here is Beni Johnson's account of what happened:

> She then stood there that day and yelled at the top of her lungs, "WAKEY WAKEY!!!" Nothing happened for about five minutes, so she turned around to cross the road to go over to a shop. As she turned around, she felt the ground begin to shake and heard this huge yawn. She looked back

at the chapel, and a huge angel stepped out. All she could see were his feet because he was that large. She asked him who he was, and he turned to her and said, "I am the angel from the 1904 revival and you just woke me up." She asked him, "Why have you been asleep?" The angel answered and said, "Because no one has been calling out for revival anymore."[13]

Beni Johnson was so inspired by her student's story that she now makes a regular practice of waking up angels. Here's another of her stories.

In the last couple of months, I personally have become aware of the angelic activity in this realm. One of those times was when we were on a prayer trip to Arizona. A group of us had decided that it was time for us to take a prayer trip down to Sedona to release more of God's Kingdom. In doing so, we rented an RV and drove from Redding, California, (where we live) all the way down to Sedona, Arizona. Along the way, we would stop and pray if we felt impressed to do so.

One morning as we were driving up over Tehachapi Pass and coming down into the Mojave Desert, I began to feel angels. The closer we got, the stronger the impression felt. I could see them everywhere! Whenever there are angels present, I get very animated and excited, knowing that God is up to something big. I announced this to the group and said, "We have got to stop! We have to stop somewhere." We found an exit, took it, and drove into this little town. We didn't really know what to do or where to go. We just knew that something was going on and we needed to find out what. As we drove around a corner I said, "I think that we are going to wake up some angels here." No sooner had I said that than we drove past a hotel to our left and, no joke, the name of the store was Mariah Country Inn. When I saw that sign, we immediately remembered the wakey story from Wales. We knew we were to turn around, get out of the RV and wake up the angels. I wish I could convey to you the energy and the quickness of how God was working. We jumped out of the RV, I blew the shofar [a trumpet made from a ram's horn] and rang the bell, and we yelled, "WAKEY." We got back into the RV and drove off. As we drove off, hilarious laughter broke out! We were stunned at the speed at which this all took place and were spinning from the adventure and the angelic activity. What in the world has just happened?! Heaven collided with earth. Woo hoo!!"[14]

Beni Johnson wrote that, since that time, there has been a stirring in her to awaken angels. In her public ministry, she often leads people to cry out, "Wakey!"

The idea of sleeping angels may seem a little unusual. But one of the most irreverent statements about angels was made by a senior worship pastor at the church. Jenn Johnson is Bill and Beni Johnson's daughter-in-law. While teaching at a woman's conference, she described a scene from the Bible, in the book of Revelation, where angels surround the throne of God. There they worship Him, crying out, "Holy, Holy, Holy." Jenn Johnson said she was thinking about this worshipful scene when she imagined ways the angels probably laugh and goof off when they're circling the throne. These thoughts came to her mind: "I bet they text each other. I bet they have farting contests."[15]

The women attending the Bethel conference laughed hysterically at her talk of angel flatulence. But beyond the walls of Bethel, many were not amused. Taken together with Beni Johnson's depiction of dozing angels, a disturbing picture emerges. At Bethel, holy things appear to be treated as commonplace and trite.[16]

"Thou Shall Not Pass"

What in "Middle Earth" is going on at Bethel? That's what many people wondered when they saw the video on Facebook. It showed the church's senior pastor, Bill Johnson, with two other well-known "apostles" taking part in a bizarre *Lord of the Rings* reenactment.[17]

The "prophetic" reenactment—held at Bethel and broadcast on Bethel.TV—was based on an iconic *Lord of the Rings* scene, where the wizard Gandalf confronts the demonic monster Balrog in a high-stakes standoff. But, unlike the movie, the apostles weren't doing battle against the Balrog. They were there to cast out a powerful and demonic "spirit of racism" from the global church. As apostles, they claimed to have extraordinary authority from God to make the so-called "apostolic decree."

Led by a prophetess dressed in a white cape—imitating the role of Gandalf—the apostles and a few others assembled in the middle of the stage. They gripped a long wooden staff with their hands. The audience was instructed to stand in agreement with the "historic" prophetic act about to take place.

"We decree and declare that racism will end. It's over . . . from this night forward, in Jesus's mighty name," apostle Ché

Ahn declared. The rest of the apostles, in a release of supernatural power, banged the staff loudly on the stage floor.

Next, the wizard-woman, using nearly identical words to Gandalf in the movie, shouted, "Thou shall not pass." Imitating Gandalf, she commanded the audience to repeat the phrase with her three times.

With the reenactment over, the demon of racism was allegedly defeated. The apostles clapped, and the audience erupted into cheers.

Just checking—does anybody think that worked?

If your idea of Christianity doesn't involve apostle-wizards driving their staffs into the ground to ward off powerful demons, you're not alone. But apparently, it's the Bethel way. And other than the occultic elements, what's especially significant is that the apostles weren't just play-acting. In their worldview, this was serious business—the heaviest type of spiritual warfare that can be waged by followers of Christ—with profound implications for the church.

Glory Cloud

The chaos at Bethel Church first came to the public's attention in 2011. It was not well known among many Christians until it burst onto the church scene in a Cloud of Glory—literally, so they say.

In 2011 a mysterious, glittery, gold substance began materializing during the church's worship services. It appeared twenty-six times over eighteen months, according to church leaders. They named it the "Glory Cloud" and celebrated it as a sign of God's special presence in the auditorium. One eyewitness described the Glory Cloud like this:

Up from the floor it rises up out of nowhere, out
of thin air. Standing underneath the source you
could feel it going through your body, touching
your skin, or getting in your eyes. It would also
stick onto anything. Those who had sickness and
disease were told to go under the cloud, and some
were healed within minutes.[18]

Others described the cloud as not rising from the floor but
descending from the ceiling. Some people made videos and posted
them to YouTube, catapulting the church into the limelight. In
the videos, people are seen staring up at the floating substance and
yelling, "Whoa," and catching some in their hands and exclaim-
ing, "Isn't that crazy? Look at it!" Many people made the trip to
Redding, hoping to witness the phenomenon.

Years later, people continue to debate what really happened
at Bethel. Some say it was all a publicity stunt perpetrated by the
church's leaders. They say the sparkling substance was merely
glitter, purposely placed into the church air conditioning vents.
Rumors are that some people even collected the substance and
took it to gemologists for analysis. It was determined not to be gold
or anything else of value. In other words, it was a trick.

Others suggest a scientific explanation—perhaps it was merely
an effect created by the bright overhead lights as they shown
through dust particles, or sweat droplets, in the air. Still others
insist that the Glory Cloud was the real deal, and nothing will
change their minds.

Of all the things to have happened at Bethel, the Glory
Cloud is still one of the most talked about—even more than the
"angel feathers" that reportedly fluttered down from above during
church meetings and the inexplicable, indoor gusts of wind. Bill
Johnson has defended the Glory Cloud—and the feathers and

wind—against the critics, calling them miraculous "signs that make you wonder."[19] Others say they're not genuine miracles: they're a bunch of hype—more than likely hoaxes—and that they distract from the real worship of God based on the truth of Scripture.

And that's Bethel Church—lots of razzle-dazzle winning over many fans of the church, while leaving many others uneasy and uncertain about what to make of it all.

The Bethel Church Movement

These are only a few of the many strange stories coming out of Bethel. We didn't mention the "purple bubble" of protection. The church's chief prophet, Kris Vallotton, said that God releases this bubble over Bethel students to make them "impervious" to bullets, bombs, abductions, rapes, and murders.[20] Nor have we described the church's "trips to heaven." The "prophet" Bob Jones claimed to take the entire Bethel congregation to visit Jesus and God the Father in heaven, during a church service, when he led them through a series of deep breathing and visualization techniques designed to result in an out-of-body experience. He told them they could use the same techniques he taught them to travel to heaven as often as they choose.[21] In Bethel's children's classes, kids also have been taken by leaders on "trips to heaven" and they are taught to raise the dead by being wrapped in toilet paper, like mummies.[22] In the following pages, we share other equally wild stories.

You might think these bizarre stories are too ridiculous to be taken seriously, but you'd be wrong. Through media, music, and savvy marketing, Bethel has gone global, in turn fueling a massive movement known as the "New Apostolic Reformation," or NAR for short (pronounced NAHR). In the United States alone, more than 3.5 million people attend NAR churches that are governed by modern-day "apostles" and "prophets."[23] Many millions more worldwide attend churches that look to NAR apostles and prophets, including those at Bethel, to provide "anointed" teaching.

It is striking that many of Bethel's followers attend more traditional Christian churches. These people believe their churches are missing something crucial. So they show up to their own services on Sunday mornings. During the week, they seek the teachings of Bethel Church because they consider its leaders to be genuine apostles and prophets with miraculous powers and a direct pipeline to God. Many believe that, without Bill Johnson and Kris Vallotton's new revelations, they cannot experience intimacy with God, defeat demonic strongholds in their lives, or fulfill their divinely appointed destinies. These are no small matters.

More than 11,000 people call Bethel Church "home," but it's also become a Christian "Mecca," where thousands of people from around the world travel each year, seeking a personal "word" from God or healing from a sickness or disease. Others come to attend Bethel conferences for men, women, youth, and Christian leaders.

If people can't travel all the way to Redding, no worries. Bethel leaders will come to you. They travel frequently throughout the world and are regularly invited to speak—by small churches in tiny towns (places like Iowa and Alaska) and the very biggest churches in the largest cities (like Houston and Sydney).

Many churches also send their young people to Bethel School of Supernatural Ministry—a center for training miracle-workers—with more than 2,600 students and 13,000 alumni from more than 100 nations. And pastors—seeking to remake their own churches in Bethel's image—join the Bethel Leaders Network. The Bethel Leaders Network is an "apostolic" network—meaning that it's overseen by an apostle (Johnson) working together with a prophet (Vallotton). By joining the network, pastors agree to submit to their spiritual authority.

Why would pastors ever agree to submit to the authority of an apostle or prophet? To get a blessing. In a nutshell: there's a divine chain of command. And if they are not under the authority of an apostle and prophet, they're rebelling against God's revealed will for the church. So, the psychological and spiritual pressure for them to submit to Bethel's apostles and prophets (or the apostles and prophets from another church) is intense.

> **Why would pastors ever agree to submit to the authority of an apostle or prophet? To get a blessing.**

If the stories you've read in this chapter give you concern, know they concern us too. We've been contacted by countless people from around the world sharing their own stories of how they, their families, and their churches have been damaged by Bethel teachings and the teachings of other NAR churches.

This is why we've written this book—to give their stories a voice. It's meant to expose the movement and its practices. Along the way, we reveal the dangers of NAR teachings, the harm they're doing, and the ways they're compromising the gospel.

The truth is, even though Bethel is the leading church in a global movement that has influenced thousands of churches, it hasn't been on the radar for many Christians. Perhaps even your own beliefs have been influenced by Bethel and NAR, without your awareness. But no longer. In the rest of this book, you'll see behind the curtain so that you can become part of the resistance, for the sake of the gospel.

CHAPTER 2

Who Are the New Apostles and Prophets?

More, God. More! I must have
more of You at any cost!
—The "apostle" Bill Johnson

Who are the mysterious men and women behind the movement that has transformed churches around the world and influenced the beliefs of millions of Christians? In this chapter, we take a close-up look at two of the most influential "apostles" and "prophets"—the apostle Bill Johnson and his right-hand man, the prophet Kris Vallotton, both from the popular and polarizing Bethel Church in Redding, California.

We'll show who these men are, how they rose from obscurity to become the leaders of a worldwide movement, and what drives them. We'll also say a little about ourselves so you will understand what drives us in our own mission to unmask these leaders who seek to redefine the Christian faith.

Who Is Bill Johnson?

Bill Johnson, a fifth-generation pastor, is the senior leader of Bethel Church and is obsessed with "revival"—or expanding God's kingdom. As Bethel likes to say, "Bethel's mission is revival—the personal, regional, and global expansion of God's kingdom through His manifest presence." And the expansion of the kingdom, Johnson believes, is accomplished through miracles. He claims to work miracles himself, most notably, prophesying and healing the sick. He credits his own miraculous powers, in large part, to a supernatural experience he had in 1995, when he made a bargain with God.

That experience happened the year before he arrived at Bethel while he was pastoring a church in the nearby town of Weaverville, California. For months he had been pleading with God, day and night, to give him "more of Him." In the middle of the night, God answered his prayer, though not in a way he had expected. Here's what happened, in Johnson's own words:

> I went from a dead sleep to being wide-awake in a moment. Unexplainable power began to pulsate through my body, seemingly just shy of electro-cution. It was as though I had been plugged into a wall socket with a thousand volts of electricity flowing through my body. My arms and legs shot out in silent explosions as if something was released through my hands and feet. The more I tried to stop it, the worse it got. . . . It was raw power . . . *it* was God.[1]

At first, Johnson was embarrassed, even though no one else could see what was happening to him. He then had a "mental picture" of himself in front of his congregation preaching. Suddenly, his arms and legs began flailing around. The "picture" changed: he was now walking down the main street of his town when, again, he lost control of his arms and legs. He didn't think anyone would believe that God was responsible for what was happening to him. That made him think of Jacob, the Old Testament patriarch, and how he walked with a limp for the rest of his life after his encounter with the Lord. Johnson also thought of Mary, the mother of Jesus, and how even her own fiancé did not at first believe that the child within her was conceived by God.

> It was becoming clear; the favor of God sometimes looks different from the perspective of earth than from heaven. My request for more of God carried a price. . . . At the forefront was the realization that God wanted to make an exchange—His increased presence for my dignity. . . . In the midst of the tears came a point of no return. I gladly yielded, crying, *More, God. More! I must have more of You at any cost! If I lose respectability and get You in the exchange, I'll gladly make that trade. Just give me more of You!*[2]

His encounter with God energizes Johnson to this day. As a result of it, he drives Bethel Church to "host" God's presence and "bring heaven to earth" through miraculous signs and wonders. His personal vision is for all believers to experience God's presence and to work miracles. But he and other Bethel leaders believe that God is especially present at Bethel Church and that miracles and healings occur regularly there.

Under his leadership, Bethel Church left the Assemblies of God denomination and became an independent church—freeing its leaders to pursue Johnson's controversial view of revival through miracle-working. Though half of the 2,000-member congregation left when he took the helm, the church has since grown to more than 11,000 people. He also travels the world, speaking at conferences and sharing the stage with other well-known "apostles," "prophets," and leaders of NAR-influenced organizations (for instance, Benny Hinn, Brian Houston, Randy Clark, Ché Ahn, Mike Bickle, and Heidi Baker).

Who Is Kris Vallotton?

Partnering with Bill Johnson is Kris Vallotton, the senior associate leader at Bethel and the church's chief "prophet." Unlike an apostle, who calls the shots in a NAR church and has the final say in all important decisions, the prophet's job is to receive direct revelation from God and share it with the apostle. Thus, an apostle and prophet will often team up, as Johnson and Vallotton have done. These two claim to have formed a special "covenant" relationship that is intended to be lifelong and allows them to tap into each other's miraculous gifts and anointings.

Like Johnson, Vallotton claims to have had remarkable encounters with God. During one encounter in 1985, God told him that he had a special calling on his life.

> Jesus walked into my bathroom amid my evening bath and told me, "I have called you to be a prophet to the nations. You will speak before kings and queens. You will influence prime ministers and presidents. I will open doors for you to talk to mayors, governors, ambassadors, and government officials all around the world."[3]

Vallotton believes he has been called as a "prophet to the nations"—though, as we'll show in this book, his prophetic track record is lackluster, to say the least.

In 1998, Vallotton was invited by Johnson to join him at Bethel and start the Bethel School of Supernatural Ministry. Vallotton writes:

> That same year, I was lying on the floor and praying one morning when the Lord spoke to me so clearly that it stunned me. He said, *There is a new epoch season emerging in this hour. Much like the Protestant Reformation, there is another reformation coming that will unearth the very foundation of Christianity. This move of the Spirit will absolutely redefine your ideologies and philosophies concerning what the Church is and how she should function.* I asked Him, *What will this transition look like?* He said, *My Church is moving from denominationalism to apostleships.*[4]

Vallotton has since become a bestselling author. Under his leadership, Bethel School of Supernatural Ministry—a three-year, full-time program—has grown from an annual enrollment of just thirty-seven students to more than 2,600. And his rising reputation as a prophet landed Vallotton a meeting with the Pope.

Together, Johnson and Vallotton are regarded as apostle and prophet, not only at Bethel in Redding, but over the international Bethel Church movement. They also claim to be giving new "revelations" to the global church, critical truths the church once had and later lost. These lost truths are now being restored by Johnson, Vallotton, and other "apostles" and "prophets" so that all Christians can develop miraculous powers. Though the pair do not readily admit this, they are part of a larger movement of "apostles" and "prophets" known as the New Apostolic Reformation. These prophets and apostles started rising up in churches in the United States in the 1980s and 1990s.[5] Like Johnson and Vallotton, they claim to have received their own divine encounters, face-to-face visits with Jesus and angels, and even to have made trips to the courtroom of heaven.[6]

Who Are Holly and Doug?

You might wonder, *Why do these two care so much about this movement? Do they just have a bee in their theological bonnet?* Quite the opposite. Our approach is to love and help, not to nitpick, and both of us have personal reasons for doing so.

Holly's Story: Why She Cares

My introduction to the New Apostolic Reformation was a bit mundane. There was no visitation from God. It started with an e-mail from someone I didn't know.

I was working at Biola University, a Christian university in Southern California. As the managing editor of *Biola Magazine*, I regularly received e-mails and letters from readers. One day in 2002, a reader sent an e-mail describing a movement of apostles and prophets that she said was taking over churches in her U.S. city. She was very concerned. She was hoping to find a professor who might write a book showing the dangers of the movement's unbiblical teachings.

I had never heard of NAR. But a simple Google search revealed that this was indeed a large and influential movement. Further digging revealed NAR's extreme teachings. This movement's prime agenda is to bring governing apostles and prophets back to the church. It's led by men and women who call themselves apostles and prophets and have amassed followers in churches throughout the United States and around the world. They claim that God has given them strategies for raising up a miracle-working army and establishing God's kingdom on earth.

To this end, Christians everywhere must develop supernatural powers. Prophesying and healing the sick are most urgently needed. In other words, if you follow these apostles and prophets, you'll be privy to God's special favor and become a player in His end-time plans and purposes for the world. And if you don't follow them? You'll sit on the sidelines as a mere spectator.

These teachings go far afield of what other Christians believe—including "continuationists" (those who believe that all the gifts of the Holy Spirit granted during the apostolic age in church history are active today, including the miraculous gifts, such as speaking in tongues, healing, and prophesying). This explains why even many Pentecostals, charismatics, and other continuationists are concerned about NAR.

Yet when I was first learning about this movement and started having concerns, I didn't know anybody who was involved with it. Or so I thought.

I had always been interested in learning about cults and offkey religious groups. While working at Biola, I was simultaneously earning my master's degree in Christian apologetics, in part to be better equipped to explain what sets apart Christianity from the counterfeits. So, initially, my interest in this movement of apostles and prophets was a mix of curiosity and a desire to become more knowledgeable. Here was a new group with unusual beliefs I had never heard of, and that seemed dangerous. It should make for some interesting research.

But what began as an academic pursuit quickly turned personal. I started learning the teachings of the movement and its particular lingo close to the same time I met a handsome stranger at a Starbucks coffee shop, reading his Bible.

I found out that he (Adam) was a Christian and, not too long after our first meeting at Starbucks, we started dating and getting to know one another.

I would never consider dating someone who did not share something as important to me as my belief in Christ. Yet I knew his theology differed from mine, though I couldn't pinpoint it. At first, I pegged him as a charismatic who happened to put more emphasis on the miraculous gifts (like speaking in tongues, healing, and prophesying) than the other spiritual gifts. But while I was researching his church online—trying to learn more about his beliefs—I was startled to recognize some of the lingo and teachings. I read words like "apostle" and "prophet" in the description of the church's leaders. I put two and two together, and the light went on. That was it! He was part of the New Apostolic Reformation.

Our dates included walks on the beach, many more cups of coffee, and (since we had both been English majors in college) games of competitive Scrabble. When we were not together, I was spending much of my free time trying to learn everything I could about this movement so I could better discuss it with him.

When I finally got up the courage to broach the topic with him, his indignant response was, "Movement? My church isn't part of any movement." (That was the first, but definitely not the last time I've heard that response over the years when people are confronted about their church's NAR teachings. Even many people who have embraced its teachings are not aware they've done so.)

I'll cut a long story short. We dated for two delightful years. During that time, we had many, sometimes tense, theological discussions.

> Me: *Where does the Bible support your pastor's claim to be an apostle?*

> Him: (Shows me two passages in the Bible from the book of Ephesians) *Read these verses.*

Me: *Yes, those verses talk about apostles, but they're being cited out of their context.*

During another conversation:

Me: *Have you seen what the prophets your church promotes teach?* (I hand him pages and pages of information I printed off the internet.)

Him: *I've never heard them say anything like that.*

And on and on it went. I wondered, how could someone so intelligent—someone who obviously held God's Word in high regard—not see that he was deceived?

We couldn't even attend church together because I disagreed so strongly with the teachings at his church, and he viewed my Bible-teaching church as a half-dead, spiritually sleeping church because it didn't have apostles and prophets and wasn't waging true "spiritual warfare." It seemed so wrong to me that two people who both loved Jesus didn't have enough theological common ground.

"God, please open his eyes. Please." It was a prayer I prayed innumerable times. I didn't want to let this one go. But I knew that, sadly, our relationship could not lead to marriage when apostles and prophets stood between us.

Yet, in the end, his eyes were opened. God answered my desperate prayers. Adam's high regard for Scripture won out.

Over time at his church, he began to observe abuses of authority by the apostle, shady "prophets" brought in to speak, and a failure by the leaders to correct serious doctrinal error. His own observations meshed with my warnings. He realized that he had, indeed, been swept up in a dangerous movement. The divisive, false beliefs began to quickly shed off. We were able to find a new sound church to attend together, and it felt so good to worship next to him.

Some of his relatives, though, remained a part of this movement, and not all of them were thrilled the day he married the woman they blamed for taking him away from a more "awakened" form of Christianity. One of those relatives clung to promises from apostles and prophets that she would be healed of cancer if only she believed hard enough. Sadly, she was not healed. But you can see why this movement, for me, is no longer theoretical. It has hit close to home. I've experienced firsthand the needless division it creates among Christians, even within families. I've seen the pain that is caused to family members when a dying loved one insists that they aren't really sick, and they demand that everyone around them pretend they aren't sick—lest others' "lack of faith" prevents them from receiving their healing.

The day I received the e-mail from a *Biola Magazine* reader seeking someone to write a book responding to NAR, I had no idea that I would be the person writing that book—and eventually multiple books. I've written them together with my coauthor, Doug Geivett, a Biola professor I persuaded to team up with me. We both desire to warn people about the ways Bethel and other NAR churches have distorted the Christian message and damaged the church's witness.

Doug's Story: Why He Cares

I first learned of the New Apostolic Reformation from Holly. She had already researched the movement, and she had compiled a manuscript documenting her findings. She invited me to read her evaluation of NAR. It was illuminating and disturbing. We talked about collaborating on a book that would alert readers to the many problems with NAR teaching.

The *two* books we later wrote clearly struck a nerve. They sold well. Holly's website exploded with new readers. Correspondence poured in from people who were feeling frazzled by their experiences in NAR churches and organizations. In my conference speaking I discovered that talks on NAR-related topics were especially popular. Copies of the books sold out.

I discovered that the appetite for biblical assessment of NAR was strong around the world. I was drawn into conversations about NAR while lecturing in Australia, Ukraine, and South Africa. I learned that Kyiv is home to one of the largest NAR churches in the world, just a few miles from the seminary where I was lecturing on Christian apologetics. A few of my experiences overseas starkly demonstrate the impact of NAR globally.

A group organized a speaking tour for me in South Africa. The national leader in charge of my calendar told me that people were asking for talks about the New Apostolic Reformation. At the time, he wasn't sure what that was, but he was agreeable. One meeting was in the Cape Town home of his in-laws where I was staying.

The idea was to have an informal gathering where I would just outline some of the themes and problems, then allow time for discussion. Two women who came that night were very familiar with the New Apostolic Reformation and had lots of questions. This was the first they had heard a thorough discussion of critical problems that had them worried. After everyone cleared out, my host told me he now understood something that hadn't made sense before. His own brother was involved in NAR, and he didn't realize it.

One of the last events of my time there was at that national leader's home. A young woman, who partners with him and his wife in ministry to university students, was there for dinner. I asked her about her journey as a believer. She talked about how she came to be involved in outreach to university students, and how she first had to wean herself from her home church that had taken to teaching strange things. She recounted her experience of being active in a NAR church, why she felt compelled to leave, and the painful consequences of that decision. I had to know—*How did she discover the dangers of NAR?* She said, "I found some helpful materials online. Holly Pivec is my hero."

"Why don't we see if we can get Holly on the phone?" I asked. (Unfortunately, we had a time zone issue, and we couldn't make it happen.)

My speaking tour in South Africa concluded with a lengthy radio interview for South African Theological Seminary about the New Apostolic Reformation. Rudy Boshoff peppered me with well-informed questions—about miracles, prophecy, the purpose of the church, apostles. He described the scope of the NAR movement in his country.

At every step along the way, I've discovered that core problems with NAR intersect directly with long-standing themes in my own study, teaching, and scholarship. As a university and seminary professor with advanced degrees in Bible, theology, and philosophy, I write and lecture extensively on issues related to the nature of Christian belief and why it is reasonable to believe the message of Jesus. I get concerned when the message is garbled, and more so when it is completely distorted.

Many Stories, The Path Ahead

We never would have imagined that the unusual life stories of people calling themselves "apostles" and "prophets," including Bill Johnson and Kris Vallotton, would intersect with our own. Yet our stories of interaction with NAR provide only part of the picture.

Throughout this book, we will share experiences of others as these have been passed along to us. Some are truly heartbreaking.

But first, Holly will share another story of direct personal encounter with NAR—specifically, the startling things she saw during a visit to Bethel Church. In the next chapter, we'll also clue you in on the dangerous NAR practices that have entered many churches—some of which bear a remarkable resemblance to New Age and occultic practices.

CHAPTER 3

Hogwarts for Christians

*It's the first day of Prophecy Week at the Bethel
School of Supernatural Ministry. Or, as students
here like to call the place, Christian Hogwarts.*
—The opening sentences of a *BuzzFeed*
article about Bethel Church[1]

"There are only three rules in this class," the teacher began. *"Rule 1:
Get drunk. Rule 2: Stay drunk. Rule 3: Get other people drunk."*

Not words you expect to hear in church, and certainly not
from the leader at the start of a Sunday school class. But this
wasn't at *just any* church, and this wasn't *just any* Sunday school
class. I [Holly] was smack-dab in the middle of Bethel Church's
Firestarters class—a 12-week course designed to create "modern-
day revivalists." And boy, was I in for a few surprises.

My Eye-Opening Visit to Bethel Church

I quickly realized this was not to be a typical Sunday school class, like one at my own church, where we might study a Scripture passage or a book from the Bible. The Firestarter action got started even before class did. Outside the classroom and from down the hallway, a commotion could be heard. I peeked inside a room where about a dozen round tables had been set up. Behind the tables, in some empty space near the back, a couple of people were laying stone still, flat on their backs, surrounded by a circle of about a dozen people standing over them. Some had their arms raised, some were walking around touching each other on the shoulders and shouting "More!", and some speaking in tongues (using words that some Christians believe are a spiritual language given to them by the Holy Spirit, but that others think sound like gibberish).[2]

The speaking-in-tongues part didn't surprise me. Tongues-speaking (or "glossolalia") is practiced by many Christians, particularly in Pentecostal and charismatic churches. While Christians debate whether tongues-speaking is a legitimate gift of the Holy Spirit for today—or just meaningless babble—it's not that unusual. Many were also laughing uncontrollably. I knew this was an exhibition of "laughter in the Spirit" or "holy laughter." What was striking was the bedlam. The scene was one of utter chaos.

This spectacle set the tone for the entire class. Once everyone was seated at the tables, the teacher set forth his drinking rules. This elicited cheers from the students. I knew that the plan was to "get drunk" on the Holy Spirit—a popular practice in more extreme charismatic circles and in churches led by modern-day "apostles" and "prophets," including Bethel. Presentation of the rules was followed by hysterical laughter, much staggering about, and a few people falling to the ground. Some students moved about the room, giggling and placing their hands firmly on the shoulders of those who were seated, so as to impart to others their experience of "holy laughter."

Calling for a semblance of order, the teacher asked everyone to stand up and place their hands in front of them, fingers flexed as if gripping a huge bottle. "Drink it dry," he urged. "It's heavenly wine." More laughter rippled through the room. He led the students in reciting an invitation: "Come, Holy Spirit. We welcome you here."

Inviting the "Holy" Spirit to join the pandemonium was weirdly disorienting. The behavior in the room had seemed so *unholy* up to that point. But this was their party; I was just there to observe.

Periodically, the teacher would sense it was time for another drink. He would urge the group to take another swig of their heavenly wine. One middle-aged woman near me lay back against her chair, as if passed out, for much of the class. *Was it possible to get too much of the Spirit?*

After the students were loosened up by the generously flowing heavenly wine, the lesson portion of the class began. On this particular day, the class was being taught how to prophesy—how to receive personal messages from God to give to other people. That's right: they believed that a supernatural ability to speak for God was something they could learn to do in a classroom setting. And they believed that they were all now ready and primed to do just that.

Now I was wondering, how could someone *learn* to prophesy? The idea that people could learn how to prophesy or develop any other supernatural powers—like healing sick people (the topic of another Firestarters class)—was completely foreign to me. During my many years growing up in church, I had never even heard of such a thing. I had been taught that God gives spiritual gifts, and you either have been given a specific gift or you haven't. While you could learn to grow in the use of your gift, you couldn't learn how to acquire a gift you didn't already have. Now here I was, about to see first-hand how prophetic powers could be learned. And while the feigned "drunkenness" had taken me aback, what followed was jaw-dropping.

Prophesying 101

Four volunteers who had never publicly prophesied before were called to the platform to be "activated." In churches like Bethel, "activation exercises" are used to trigger unused supernatural gifts that dwell deep within a Christian. Each volunteer was told to select from the people in the room someone they didn't know. They were then to prophesy to that person. All they had to do was say whatever words popped into their minds. "If you don't know what to say, just start talking and you'll get there," the teacher told them. During the exercise, students were assured that they need not be afraid of making mistakes when learning to prophesy. Missing it was part of the process. At one point, my table leader led a smaller group discussion. He told those seated at the table with me, "If you're right, you're right. If you're wrong, who cares?"

Whoa! Wait a minute. What did he just say? That it doesn't matter if they give a prophecy to someone that turns out to be wrong? I wondered how that could possibly be so, given the many warnings in Scripture about false prophets and the importance of testing all prophecies to know whether they are truly from God.

Eventually, one of the volunteers began her first-ever attempt to prophesy. She said she felt that God had given her two pieces of information that would identify the person God would have her prophesy to. He gave her the name "Anthony" and the date "July 17." "Does that name mean anything to anybody?" she said, looking around the room of about sixty or seventy people.

Only awkward silence.

After a few moments, a young man spoke up. "My birthday is July 17."

From somewhere in the room someone called out the question we all were thinking. "Is your name Anthony?"

"No, it's Xavier."

How many synonyms are there for "oops"? His name wasn't even close to Anthony.

Undaunted by this "miss," the young woman said, "Let's take July 17." She then gave Xavier a message that she had, so she believed, received from God.

I no longer recall the exact words she gave him. Here's what I do remember: they were "positive" and "life-affirming." The students had been instructed to give only such messages. No negative words, no judgmental words, no words of correction. The class notes we had been given stated: "True prophecy calls out the gold in people."[3] In other words, it doesn't expose a person's sin, or reveal any troubles that may lie ahead for them. Rather, it speaks only uplifting and encouraging words.

This restriction, what you might call the "golden" rule for prophesying at Bethel, differs dramatically from so much of the "negative" messages doled out by the Bible's prophets. Blue-sky prophecies were a problem in Jeremiah's day. Speaking through him, the Lord warned against prophets who gave false assurances of good things: "They dress the wound of my people as though it were not serious. 'Peace, peace,' they say, when there is no peace" (Jer. 6:14 NIV).

In fact, hard-hitting judgment reverberates throughout the book of Jeremiah. For the first twenty-five chapters, the "weeping prophet" *wails* against Jerusalem and the whole of Judah. And chapters 46–51 are filled with oracles against the foreign nations. You could also say that the themes of doom and gloom pervade the pages of Jeremiah's shorter book called, wouldn't you know it, "Lamentations."

In 2 Kings 17:13, we have a summary statement of a core aspect of the prophet's ministry in the Old Testament: "Yet the LORD warned Israel and Judah by every prophet and every seer, saying, 'Turn from your evil ways and keep my commandments and my statutes, in accordance with all the Law that I commanded your fathers, and that I sent to you by my servants the prophets.'" Warning and rebuke were a big part of their job description.

The New Testament prophet Agabus warned of a famine that was about to descend upon the Roman world (Acts 11:27–30), a message that so concerned the believing community at Antioch that they pooled their resources to send relief to their fellows living in Judea. Agabus also foretold the apostle Paul's impending arrest (Acts 21:10–14). This sent those who were present into near panic. Failing to talk Paul out of journeying to Jerusalem, they gave up the attempt and declared, "Let the will of the Lord be done."

Real downers, those prophecies. They were not all sunshine and rainbows like the prophecies given at the Bethel class.[4] But among this group of budding prophets, no scary use of prophecy was allowed.

Uncanny Similarities

What especially caught my attention that day, what really troubled me, in fact, were the techniques used by these novice prophets and their trainers. The activation of their supernatural gifts fits a disturbing pattern. Bethel's teachings on how to activate prophetic gifts resembles the New Age attempts to "awaken" psychic powers.[5] For that matter, they are the same techniques used by mentalists—entertainers who, though they do not claim to have any psychic powers, awe their audiences with "cold readings" of complete strangers. Mentalists make educated guesses about their audience, based on close observations and probabilities, so that when they have a "hit" they seem to know things they couldn't possibly have known about those people. And they become skilled at reading body language.[6] That strategy of reading reactions has been taught to people at Bethel Church by Beni Johnson, Bill Johnson's wife, who advises: "Keep your eyes open when you're praying for somebody. I know that sounds strange, but it really does work." She says, "If you close your eyes when you're praying for somebody, you're going to miss it. . . . You may say one word and that may be a trigger for them, and they just lose it, or they'll begin to cry. And if you're looking at them, you'll be able to say, 'Oh, we've hit something here. Let's go after this.'"[7]

In no way did the prophesying I saw at Bethel resemble prophesying found in the Bible. You will search in vain for a place in the Bible where a prophet of God shouted out some disconnected name or date—plucked from thin air—got it wrong, and called it "Close enough!"[8] That's something you would expect from a John Edward TV special, not a Sunday morning church class.[9]

During my Bethel visit, I observed that the activation of supernatural gifts in individuals has more in common with New Age occult practices than with biblical Christianity.[10] As we'll show, that's just one of their occult-like practices. These practices are not confined to a single church in California. Through the influence of Bethel and many other churches that share Bethel's NAR theology, these practices—and the teachings that undergird them—are taught at countless churches throughout the United States and around the world.

In this chapter, we'll look at other activities and practices—including some that are downright spooky. But first let's see what the Bible *does* say about miraculous gifts—including a gift of prophesying—and compare that with New Age practices.

The Bible's Teachings about Miraculous Gifts vs. New Age Teachings

Most Christians believe that the Holy Spirit has bestowed one or more spiritual gifts to every Christian.[11] In the Bible, four lists of these gifts can be found (Rom. 12:6–8; 1 Cor. 12:8–10, 28–30; and Eph. 4:11), which, together, name nineteen gifts: administration, apostleship, discernment, evangelism, exhortation, faith, giving, healing, interpretation of tongues, knowledge, leadership, mercy, miracles, pastoring or shepherding [overseer], prophecy, service, teaching, tongues, and wisdom.

Some of these gifts stand out as especially "miraculous" (though it must be understood that each type of gift is imparted by the Holy Spirit at His discretion and is thus, in some sense, a supernatural endowment). Many Christians believe these gifts are still given by God to Christians today, though others disagree.[12] But for the most part, Christians have not suggested that the Spirit's gifts—including even the miraculous ones—are powers that can be "activated" in any Christian who desires them. Rather, they are *charismata* (to use the Greek word), or "grace-endowments," given by the Holy Spirit to individuals as He alone decides (1 Cor. 12:11).

So, God has given Christians gifts to serve others and help the church flourish. However, the Bible warns against occult practices—such as fortune-telling and communicating with the dead—which are very different than miraculous gifts given by the Holy Spirit. These occult practices seek to obtain supernatural power and secret knowledge—about the past, present, or future—by making contact with the spirit world, including contact with the dead, or by using various tools and techniques of "divination." These practices are expressly forbidden by God in Scripture.

"When you come into the land that the LORD your God is giving you, you shall not learn to follow the abominable practices of those nations. There shall not be found among you anyone who burns his son or his daughter as an offering, anyone who practices divination or tells fortunes or interprets omens, or a sorcerer or a charmer or a medium or a necromancer or one who inquires of the dead, for whoever does these things is an abomination to the LORD. And because of these abominations the LORD your God is driving them out before you." (Deut. 18:9–12)

One reason they are forbidden is that occult practices—which are associated in Scripture with the activity of demons—open people up to demonic influence (Deut. 32:17; Ps. 106:34–43; Acts 16:16–18; 1 Cor. 10:19–21; Rev. 9:20–21).

Occult practices are openly and enthusiastically promoted today. Books and websites abound offering to teach people how to "unlock," "awaken," and "activate" latent psychic powers within themselves. Notable examples include *The Secrets to Unlocking Your Psychic Ability* (2020), written by television star and best-selling author Matt Fraser, and *Spirited: Unlock Your Psychic Self and Change Your Life* (2011), written by the medium-to-celebrities Rebecca Rosen.

Biblical teachings about miraculous gifts and New Age occult practices are worlds apart. We think that NAR talk of activating the miraculous gifts bears a closer resemblance to New Age practice than to the way Scripture speaks of how the gifts are bestowed by the Holy Spirit. Talk of activation is a NAR invention with no historical precedent. But here's a shocker: NAR leaders acknowledge that some of their practices look a lot like those of psychics and occult practitioners They claim that New Agers have stolen these practices from Christians. And they openly call for reclaiming them for the global church. But, of course, the global church has never taught activation.

Bethel and the New Age

A revealing book, titled *The Physics of Heaven*, is sold in the Bethel Church bookstore. It includes chapters written by Bill and Beni Johnson and a foreword written by Kris Vallotton. According to the book's coeditor, Ellyn Davis, all the leaders who contributed to the book agree "that there are precious truths hidden in the New Age that belong to us as Christians and need to be extracted from the worthless."[13]

What are these truths? In one of the chapters, author Jonathan Welton provides a list of things that "actually belong to the church, but they have been stolen and cleverly repackaged," including "spirit guide, trances, meditation, auras, power objects, clairvoyance, clairaudience, and more."[14]

Another Bethel-endorsed book promotes practices that have historically been associated with the occult. *Moving in Glory Realms*, by Joshua Mills, includes a foreword written by Bill Johnson. This book teaches that Christians can have "encounters" with dead Christians, and it promotes "spirit travel"—when a person's body remains in one physical location, but their spirit travels to heaven or to other nations on earth, and can even travel to events in the past or future. Johnson enthusiastically writes, "It is a book I highly recommend."

And Beni Johnson's own bestselling book, *The Happy Intercessor*, claims that Christians must travel to specific cities and attempt to open "portals"—or "spiritual gates"—so they can access the "heavenly realm." Seeking to locate and open "spiritual portals" as a way to interact with the spirit realm is a known New Age occult practice.[15]

In short, many NAR leaders believe many occult practices must be redeemed and reclaimed by Christians because they are important tools for advancing God's kingdom. These astonishing teachings explain why New Age–type practices can be found at Bethel Church. And Bethel School of Supernatural Ministry is ground zero for teaching and disseminating them.

Levitation and Teleportation

Perhaps it's no surprise that a generation growing up with Harry Potter would be drawn to the Bethel School of Supernatural Ministry (BSSM)—a place students have fondly likened to the Hogwarts School of Witchcraft and Wizardry featured in J. K. Rowling's book series.[16] In true Hogwarts fashion, BSSM students have attempted to levitate coins and guitar picks and walk through walls.[17]

When speaking to the media about the students' odd attempts at levitating objects and walking through walls, Bethel leaders have laughed them off and admitted that they're "a little out there."[18] They have also implied that the students' activities were not officially sanctioned or taught by the school.

What could possibly be the point, you ask? Why even attempt to do such things? These activities fall in line with BSSM's goal of training miracle-workers who can prophesy, heal sick people, and raise the dead. And they are merely the tip of the iceberg of occult-like practices emanating from Bethel School of Supernatural Ministry.

Psychic Fairs and "Spirit Readings"

After BSSM students are activated with a prophetic gift, they are sent out to the Redding community to "prophesy" to strangers. One way they do this is by going undercover to psychic fairs, where they set up booths, masquerade as psychics, and offer "dream interpretations" and "spirit readings."[19]

Their so-called "spirit readings" are actually "prophetic words" they give to fairgoers using the techniques for prophesying they have learned at Bethel, but they are very careful not to call them "prophetic words," or to use any other terminology that might identify them as Christians. Why? They want to blend in with the New Age crowd. They also don't want to say anything "religious" that might be offensive. So they refer to God as the "Spirit of Creation."

The students claim they're involved in a creative and unique form of evangelism that will reach New Agers with the gospel. But we have to ask, how can they possibly be sharing the gospel when they deliberately avoid mentioning the name of Jesus? What "gospel" are they sharing? They claim that those who come to their tent eventually figure out that they are Christians and that one young man ended up "giving his life to Jesus." But one must wonder what, exactly, they mean when they say he gave his life to Jesus? Did he truly understand the gospel, the means by which one is saved? It's impossible to imagine Jesus's apostles avoiding using Jesus's name during their own evangelism.

In the early days of the church, when the high priests of Jerusalem demanded to know "by what power or by what name" Peter and John had healed a lame man, the rulers could have asked any of the eyewitnesses, or the thousands who had heard and believed their message. Peter had plainly said to the man, "In the name of Jesus Christ of Nazareth, rise up and walk." To the gathering crowd, Peter had asked, "Men of Israel, why do you wonder at this, or why do you stare at us, as though by our own power or piety we have made him walk?" And then he declared that it was the name of Jesus, and faith in that name, that had made the man whole.

In his later speech, Peter had gone on to proclaim "in Jesus the resurrection from the dead." It was their unmistakable proclamation of salvation in the name of Jesus that got Peter and John arrested. Still, when they were set before the tribunal of interrogators, in the presence of Annas the high priest, and were called upon to identify the source of their power, Peter was bold to answer. He said, "by the name of Jesus Christ of Nazareth . . . this man is standing before you well. . . . And there is salvation in no one else, for there is no other name under heaven given among men by which we must be saved." In response, the council charged these model evangelists "not to speak or teach at all in the name of Jesus." But Peter and John replied, "Whether it is right in the sight of God to listen to you rather than to God, you must judge, *for we cannot but speak of what we have seen and heard.*"[20]

Peter and John were fearless. They healed in the name of Jesus and they preached Him and His resurrection. Take Jesus out of the equation, and there is no gospel. And they were not about to disguise their message with vague and misleading language. They were compelled to speak of what they had seen and heard, to speak as witnesses *of Jesus*. Their opponents thought to shut them up by forbidding them to speak or teach in the name of Jesus. This they would not do. And no real disciple of Jesus can.

> Take Jesus out of the equation, and there is no gospel.

Destiny Cards

At these psychic events, many BSSM students have used Christianized versions of tarot cards, called "Destiny Cards," to aid in their readings. Tarot cards are decks of cards used by fortune tellers to seek hidden knowledge about a person's past, present, or future. They are a tool for divination.

Destiny Cards, designed by a Christian organization named Christalignment, have been likened to tarot cards by team leaders at Christalignment. The card images of angels, animals, and nature scenes are produced by "prophetic artists and photographers," as they are called on their webpage. The pictures have symbolic meanings and function much like tarot in the hands of prophetic readers. A supernaturally gifted "reader" provides a card's interpretation. Through Christalignment readings, "clients" have received answers to questions like, "Have I chosen the right career for me?" and "Will I have any more children?"[21] The following description of one deck of Destiny Cards appeared on an early version of Christalignment's website:

> Psalm readings are similar to tarot in that cards
> are counted out according to your birth date date
> & year [sic]. Only three cards are used and these
> will represent your past, present and future.[22]

In testimonials shared in social media by Christalignment, clients describe "encounters" with Jesus. One woman—who had been suffering from stress—said Jesus appeared to her as a surfer and danced with her.[23] Another woman claimed that Jesus gave her "physical affection and touch" that she had been longing for and that he "pet" her while she was fully naked.[24] These are disturbing images.

Controversy erupted in 2017, when it came to light that many BSSM students had joined Christalignment teams over the years and had given Destiny Card readings. Bethel Church prophet Kris Vallotton and Theresa Dedmon, another pastoral staff member, published statements online defending Ken and Jenny Hodge (the founders of Christalignment) and their Destiny Cards.[25] Bethel Church also released a formal statement about Christalignment, saying that Bethel has no formal affiliation with the organization.[26] However, Bethel supports Christalignment's outreach to the New Age community and denies that their Destiny Cards have been used like tarot cards. This despite all evidence to the contrary, including the evidence of Christalignment's own words on their website. (It is noteworthy that Christalignment removed all references to tarot cards after the controversy broke out. The original site can still be viewed on The Internet Archive.[27])

Contrary to what Bethel leaders say, Destiny Cards are being used like tarot—in an attempt to discover hidden knowledge outside of God's ordained means. Even if some Christians today do have a genuine gift from the Holy Spirit for prophesying—as in the early days of the church—they must never attempt to control the Holy Spirit, or seek vainly to discern the testimony of the Holy Spirit, through card reading or any other tool of divination.

Telepathy

You've no doubt heard of mind reading or telepathy. It's an occult attempt to communicate with others without using words or any forms of physical communication. Astoundingly, it was taught to parents by Bethel's former, longtime children's pastor, Seth Dahl (himself a graduate of the Bethel School of Supernatural Ministry and coauthor with Bill Johnson of the children's book, *God Is Really Good*). Of course, Dahl did not refer to the practice as telepathy. He called it "communicating spiritually with our children."

In a video he posted to Facebook in 2017, Dahl told parents that the practice is helpful with children who are very young or sick and have trouble verbalizing their needs.[28] He also said he had used it successfully with his own children. In one instance, his son, who was a-year-and-a-half at the time, could not fall asleep. Dahl said they communicated with each other spiritually, and his son psychically messaged him to stay near his crib and rub his back. According to Dahl, his son fell asleep within minutes.

Experienced parents will wonder, *Who needs telepathy for that? It's common sense.* But Dahl is promoting an occult method of communication that he believes to be a source of useful information that you might not otherwise have access to. It is a "spiritual" process for channeling messages between persons.

Seeing Dead People

An even creepier, more sinister form of communication has been promoted by Bethel leaders—communication with the dead, also known as necromancy. In a recorded message given at the church, Ben Armstrong (the church's Prophetic Ministry Director), shared stories about Christians who have seen and talked with dead people.[29] The deceased people they encountered were Christian "revivalists"—including the faith healers Maria Woodworth-Etter and Kathryn Kuhlman.

Armstrong may have anticipated an objection from his audience—some of whom must have known that necromancy is prohibited by God. "What we need to get away from is this thing of talking to the dead," he says. He explains that Christians should not be opposed to talking with dead Christians, since they are, after all, part of the "great cloud of witnesses" that Scripture speaks of (referring to Heb. 12:1).[30] So these folks aren't actually dead. Rather, they live outside of time, in heaven. It's okay to communicate with dead revivalists and prophets because they were Christians and are still alive spiritually.

This flatly contradicts Scripture's unqualified prohibition against consulting the dead (Deut. 18:9–12; compare Gal. 5:19–20; Acts 19:19). Things did not go well for Saul when he asked a medium to summon the spirit of Samuel—even though Samuel had been a prophet of God! Saul knew necromancy was banned by God, and it was a brazenly disobedient act. Not so coincidentally, he died in battle the very next day. (For the whole story, including the gruesome details, see 1 Samuel 28–31.)

Ben Armstrong's sermon is noteworthy for the wacky justification he gives for speaking with deceased saints. But his presentation is outdone by Shawn Bolz's performance while speaking at Bethel Church for a leadership conference. While he was on stage, Bolz announced that he had, in that very moment, "tapped into Bob Jones prophesying" from heaven to Bill Johnson—who was sitting in the audience.[31] Bob Jones, an influential "prophet," had died nine months earlier. Bolz claimed to see Bob Jones in heaven talking with Bill Johnson's deceased father, Melvin Earl Johnson, and hanging out with some of Bill Johnson's other deceased family members, who were all singing in a heavenly choir. And Jones's message for Bill Johnson, through Shawn Bolz, included these words: "Your next installment's coming." The "installment," Bolz explained, referred to money that people would soon entrust to Johnson.

To head off any concerns among those listening, Bolz said, "This isn't necromancy or anything; I'm not, like, calling on the dead." But he didn't explain how the communication he claims to have received from Jones is any different than necromancy. And he has suggested that other Christians should expect to have communications with deceased believers, as God will be making more such "connections" in the days ahead.[32]

The Dangers of Bethel's Occult Practices

The practice of "activating" people in a prophetic gift is one of many that Bethel Church shares in common with the New

Age idea of "awakening" occult abilities. And it's not just Bethel. We regularly receive first-hand reports about occult-like practices invading churches.

Is it any wonder that occult-like practices are spreading rapidly among Christians? More than 13,000 students have graduated from the Bethel School of Supernatural Ministry and taken these practices back to their home churches around the world. Some well-known BSSM graduates have taken their training back to influential organizations where they hold leadership roles.[33] And hundreds of churches have started their own schools of super-natural ministry—many utilizing BSSM curriculum with assistance from BSSM School Planting.[34] Through these supernatural schools, these practices have been introduced to Christians in small towns and large cities throughout the United States and the world. That's not to mention the many churches, independent of Bethel, that have already been promoting similar occult-like practices for many years.

These practices are not harmless; they threaten grave spiritual danger. Young Christians and recent converts are especially at risk, as they have not yet had time to grow in discernment. Former New Age participants who are now Christians report—with con-cern—that many New Agers who have come to Christ are getting drawn back into occult practices through the teachings of Bethel and Bethel-influenced churches.[35] We urge readers to join us in warning Christians about these dangerous practices before they gain traction in more churches.

CHAPTER 4

Jesus's Overlooked Warning

Beware of false prophets.
—Jesus

Most people know Jesus's teachings about forgiveness, giving to the needy, and loving your enemies. But there is one teaching many have overlooked. "Beware of false prophets," He said, "who come to you in sheep's clothing but inwardly are ravenous wolves" (Matt. 7:15).

This was not His only warning about false prophets. When speaking about the end time, Jesus said, "For false christs and false prophets will arise and perform great signs and wonders, so as to lead astray, if possible, even the elect" (Matt. 24:24). Taken together, His teachings show that the threat of false prophets is always present, especially in the final days leading up to His return. False prophets will disguise themselves as true believers, and they will appear to work miracles that are so amazing that even believers are in danger of being deceived.

The Bible contains many other warnings about false prophets, false apostles, and false teachers, including this from the apostle John: "Beloved, do not believe every spirit, but test the spirits to see whether they are from God, for many false prophets have gone out into the world" (1 John 4:1). John's words suggest that some people who claim to be prophets of God are actually operating under the influence of deceiving demonic spirits.

These sober warnings underscore the urgent need for believers to be on alert for false prophets. Of course, false prophets won't always look like false prophets—they don't come with warning labels tatted to their foreheads.

If Jesus warned that false prophets wear clever disguises, how can you tell whether an alleged prophet is the real deal or an imposter? The Bible gives us three *negative* tests: the Orthodoxy Test (do their prophecies line up with Scripture?), the Lifestyle Test (are they greedy and lustful?), and the Fulfillment Test (did they get it right?). We call these negative tests because, if a "prophet" fails any one of them, you must not accept the prophet's claims; they are automatically disqualified. However, they are not *positive* tests for truth. In other words, if a "prophet" passes these negative tests, it doesn't guarantee that the person is a genuine prophet. For one thing, a "prophet" may pass one test (they may give a prophecy that lines up with Scripture), but fail another test (they may live an immoral lifestyle). For another thing, a "prophet" may pass all three tests and still not be a genuine prophet of God! They may give a prophecy that lines up with Scripture, they may be a decently moral person, and they may get lucky and make a prediction that happens to come true. But passing these tests is not a green light to believe someone is a prophet. They must also offer positive evidence.

The first two negative tests are critical, and we apply them elsewhere in this book.[1] In this chapter, we focus on the third negative test, the Fulfillment Test: did they get it right? But before we explain this test, we must focus on a more fundamental question: Is there any special reason why I should accept a particular "prophet's" claim to be a prophet, in the first place? What is the positive evidence for that claim? We come, then, to the burden of proof.

The Burden of Proof

We believe that Christians often make a basic mistake when they encounter prophets who call themselves Christians. They give the speaker the benefit of the doubt and simply assume that he or she is a prophet and speaks with God's authority. You should never accept a prophetic word without evidence that the speaker is a true prophet of God. This requirement is a game-changer. The principle is, *evidence first, then belief.*

In other words, the burden of proof is on the person claiming to be a prophet to demonstrate that he or she is indeed a prophet. But to determine whether they've met this burden you do not simply test a specific prophecy. You must test the whole pattern of a prophet's teaching practice and look for supernatural evidence of their special authority. How do you do that?

> You must test the whole pattern of a prophet's teaching practice and look for supernatural evidence of their special authority.

Here an initial basic guideline is found in their use of Scripture. Is the person a skilled student and teacher of the "word of truth," the Scriptures (2 Tim. 2:15)? A prophet of God will take special care to interpret the Bible by proper rules of interpretation and teach it accordingly. And it should be clear at all times that

Scripture is the central control on all that he or she judges to be of God. This is a methodology test. How does the person handle the Bible, in personal study and teaching?[2] Of course, the person's teaching must be sound—it must line up with the Word of truth. This is a results test, clearly connected to the methodology test. Paul counseled Timothy, "Pay close attention to yourself and to your teaching; persevere in these things, for as you do this you will ensure salvation both for yourself and for those who hear you" (1 Tim. 4:16 NASB1995).

Never trust a "prophet" who can't interpret the Bible responsibly. Do not trust a "prophet" who plays fast and loose with the meaning of Scripture. Reckless use of Scripture creates a credibility gap for any would-be prophet.

God is jealous of His reputation, and He does not wink at anyone—certainly not "prophets"—who misrepresent His words (Deut. 18:20; Jer. 23:28–32; Titus 1:9; 2 Pet. 3:16; Rev. 22:18). So if "prophets" are careless in their use of Scripture, you can disregard their claims, even if they seem to pass the other tests. They have shown by their treatment of Scripture that they cannot be trusted as prophets of God.[3]

In addition, the performance of authentic miracles would lend greater weight to a person's claim to be a prophet. For example, if they have given some detailed prophecy that has been fulfilled with spectacular accuracy or if they have worked other bona fide miracles with clear demonstration of their miraculous nature, that would help to confirm their status as authoritative spokespersons for God.

When God commissioned Moses to go to Pharaoh and demand the release of His people, He instructed Moses in a method for establishing his authority to speak for God. He was to bring forth positive evidence of his status as God's spokesman. "When you go back to Egypt, see that you do before Pharaoh all the miracles that I have put in your power" (Exod. 4:21; see also Exod. 7:3). That method included a demonstration of superior power over Pharoah's own clever magicians who tried to fake a miracle (Exod. 7:8–12), and the forecasting and execution of ten increasingly horrific plagues of judgment on the land and people of Egypt (Exod. 7:14–11:10). John the Baptist fulfilled specific prophecies of Scripture (Isa. 40:3–5; Mal. 3:1). Jesus did too, of course, and He performed various incontrovertible miracles and rose from the dead, the ultimate confirmation of His authoritative status (Rom. 1:4). We see in the book of Acts how the apostles demonstrated their authority to teach new truth by performing great signs and wonders.[4] But they also had the benefit of receiving a direct commission from Jesus to perform their authoritative role (Matt. 10:1–7; 28:16–20; Acts 26:12–16; Rom. 1:5, 14–15). The two witnesses of Revelation 11 will prophesy, they will be miraculously protected from severe persecution, and they will be quite dramatically raised from the dead to corroborate their authority (Rev. 11:3–13).

The point is that prophets must give adequate evidence of their prophetic authority. They cannot expect anyone to simply take their word for it. And God is quite able to ensure that a true prophet's claims are backed up with suitable evidence.

If, and only if, a prophet has first met the burden of proof, should you even concern yourself with the Fulfillment Test.

The Fulfillment Test

According to this test, any prediction made by a prophet must come true—otherwise the individual is not a genuine prophet of God. This test is set forth in Deuteronomy 18:20–22.

> "'But the prophet who presumes to speak a word
> in my name that I have not commanded him to
> speak, or who speaks in the name of other gods,
> that same prophet shall die.' And if you say in
> your heart, 'How may we know the word that the
> LORD has not spoken?'—when a prophet speaks
> in the name of the LORD, if the word does not
> come to pass or come true, that is a word that the
> LORD has not spoken; the prophet has spoken it
> presumptuously. You need not be afraid of him."

Notice the importance of verse 20 for understanding the full force of the Fulfillment Test. This verse is clear about the penalty for getting it wrong. Once is enough. "That same prophet shall die."[5]

NAR leaders don't like this test, for they recognize that their track record of prophesying accurately is pretty sketchy. To deflect application of this test to themselves, they play games with Scripture. They acknowledge that the Fulfillment Test applied to prophets in the Old Testament, but they conveniently deny that it applies to today's prophets. And while things aren't exactly the same in the New Testament as in the Old (under the Old Covenant, death was the consequence for false prophecy; under the New Covenant, no precise penalty is stipulated), they make a grave mistake to assume there's no real threat to them on the other side of false prophecy. God provided the Israelites—and us—one clear way of identifying imposters: see whether their predictions come to pass.

Do well-known NAR prophets pass this test? No, they do not. We will show you what we mean by taking a look at the three types of prophecies they commonly give: Fails, Fortune Cookie Prophecies, and Fraudulent Prophecies. Pay close attention: once you learn about these faux types of prophecy, you will be able to spot them for yourself.

Fails

Fails are predictions made by NAR prophets that prove to be flat-out wrong. Here are two recent examples of failed predictions that were highly publicized and garnered national media attention.

The "Trump Prophecies"

Many high-profile prophets and apostles predicted that Donald Trump would be reelected to a second term in the 2020 U.S. presidential race. One Baylor University professor counted at least forty.[6] Among them were Kris Vallotton, Jeremiah Johnson, Mark Taylor, Shawn Bolz, Johnny Enlow, Kat Kerr, Curt Landry, and Paula White. Here's what Vallotton said while delivering a message at Bethel Church on December 8, 2019:

> I believe that the Lord's gonna step into the impeachment process. . . . This is decreed. The Lord is gonna step in sovereignly. . . . And I believe the Lord's gonna give him another term . . . because the Lord wants it.[7]

But on November 7, 2020—four days after the election— Vallotton posted a video apology to Facebook, admitting he was wrong.

> I really want to apologize, sincerely apologize, for missing the prophecy about Donald Trump. . . . I was completely wrong. I take full responsibility for being wrong. There's no excuse for it. I think it doesn't make me a false prophet, but it does actually create a credibility gap.[8]

Vallotton's eager followers advised him that his apology was premature, since the election results were still being contested. So he removed the apology. He then reposted it on January 8, 2021—the day following congressional certification of the election results.[9]

Other prophets (though not all) issued their own apologies, including Jeremiah Johnson and Shawn Bolz.[10] And a number of well-known prophets and other Christian leaders who believe there are modern-day prophets scrambled to do damage control. They released a document called the Prophetic Standards Statement.[11] Initially signed by more than ninety prophets, apostles, and other leaders including prominent continuationists, it calls for prophets to make public apologies when their publicly delivered predictions fail.

But all this was too little, too late. The damage had been done. The failed predictions caught the attention of major news outlets. They published headlines including "The Christian Prophets Who Say Trump Is Coming Again" (*Politico*) and "Life After Proclaiming a Trump Reelection as Divinely Ordained" (*New York Times*).[12] And an atheist with a very large following, Hemant Mehta (a.k.a. "The Friendly Atheist" previously mentioned in chapter 1), linked to a video compilation of the botched predictions in an article titled "Here Are 12 Christian Preachers Who Wrongly Predicted Trump's Re-Election."[13] As a result of these false prophecies, media pundits mocked all Christians (especially Pentecostals and charismatics), and atheists gained more arguments for their arsenal to use against them. Failed prophecies regarding the election brought shame to the church, injured its witness to the world, and undermined the faith of believers.

The End of the Covid-19 Pandemic (or Not)

Interestingly, no NAR prophets foresaw Covid-19. So you may wonder, as we do—*What good are prophets who failed to predict such a significant event in recent world history?*

Not a single prophet saw Covid coming. But soon after its arrival, a speedy recovery was predicted by multiple NAR prophets of note.[14] One of these was Shawn Bolz, a prophet who is closely associated with Bethel Church and who often speaks there. He is also the founding pastor of Expression58 Church in Los Angeles.

On February 27–29, 2020, near the start of the pandemic— while he was speaking in South Africa at a conference with Bill Johnson—Bolz prophesied the end of Covid-19. He said, "I just felt like the tide is turning shortly—whether it's two weeks or two months—God cares about this."[15] And on Facebook, February 28, 2020, he posted: "The Lord is saying, 'I am removing the threat of this.' Within a short amount of time, the extreme threat will feel like it is in the way past." Days later he told *Fox News*, "We're going to see it come to an end. It's not going to be the pandemic that people are afraid of."[16] That, of course, was not to be—he made these predictions right as the virus became a global threat, showing his prophecy to be quite different from what happened.

You may be surprised that Vallotton and Bolz consider themselves to be true prophets despite their very public and very false predictions. But the idea that a true prophet of God can make mistakes is common in NAR. Most NAR leaders agree to this. They don't believe the Fulfillment Test applies to them or other contemporary prophets. They believe it applied only to prophets of the Old Testament, such as Moses, Isaiah, and Jeremiah. Mike Bickle makes the point with crystal clarity and stunning dogmatism in his bestselling book *Growing in the Prophetic*:

> Unlike the Old Testament ground rules for
> prophets, where 100 percent accuracy was
> required upon the penalty of death, the New
> Testament doesn't require the same standard of
> its prophets.[17]

But this test surely does apply to both Old Testament and New Testament prophets. The *penalty* may be different, but the standard has not changed. There is no indication in Scripture that the test was ever cancelled. No new understanding of genuine authoritative prophets who can make mistakes is anywhere defined, described, or exhibited and condoned in the New Testament. Even if it could be shown from Scripture that people with the spiritual gift of prophecy can sometimes make mistakes in their prophesying, as believed by many continuationists (those who believe in present-day miraculous gifts), it does not follow that NAR leaders who claim to be authoritative prophets (and hold the formal *office* of prophet) can be mistaken.[18] We will explain what NAR leaders teach about the office of prophet (and the office of apostle) in the next chapter. But for now, it is important to understand that those who hold these church offices possess tremendous authority. Because they possess such great authority, they should not claim to be exempt from the Old Testament test for prophecy. So the burden of proof is on them to show that the Fulfillment Test was cancelled, a burden none of the NAR prophets have met.

In addition, if a prophet's record is inaccurate, he has no practical authority as a prophet of any kind. And how could he? You would never know what to believe or how to act in response to any prophetic word if it is fallible. If a prophecy is fallible, it is not reliable.

NAR prophets are actually inconsistent in their teaching. They expect people to believe that they are genuine prophets when their prophecies "come true." But when they do not come true, they assert that this does not mean they are false prophets. They want it both ways. Confirmation when they get things right; no disconfirmation when they get things wrong. But this is a deception, on the same level as their demonstrably false prophecies. We are expected to take their word for it that they are true prophets, but they deny one biblical test of their authority—a test that is fully sufficient for identifying false prophets (recall Deut. 18:20). And even if all their prophecies were to "come true," this would not confirm their claim to be prophets because they must also pass the other tests (the Orthodoxy Test and Lifestyle Test).

NAR leaders deny the application of the Fulfillment Test because they have a dismal track record. Their denials notwithstanding, issuing a false prophecy is a sure mark that someone is a false prophet. They throw out the most obvious test, and they offer no other reliable way for testing prophecy—no *positive* test.[19] But clearly, if we are to *test* the spirits, God must have provided appropriate means for testing them.

Loophole Prophecies

NAR leaders also often attempt to explain away their failed predictions by giving what we call "Loophole Prophecies." We are referring to the many excuses that are given for why a prophet's prediction has not come to pass. Those excuses may be that the people who received the prophecy did not believe the prophetic word with all their heart, or they failed to make enough "prayer declarations" for that prophecy to come to pass, or there was some other requirement by God that they failed to meet.

For example, during the year-end message Bill Johnson preached at Bethel Church's Sunday morning service on December 26, 2021, he told the Bethel congregation that, in the early hours of that morning, he had sensed God telling him that the prophetic words of personal promise that the people in the room (several hundred of them) had received in 2021 would still be fulfilled. Preaching from 1 Samuel 30, Johnson explained why the 2021 promises had not come to pass during that year. The Lord first wanted the people to "strengthen" their hearts in the Lord by abandoning themselves in worship and getting into God's Word.[20] Surely someone in the congregation that morning must have wondered, "Do you mean that God wanted something else of me before He would keep His promises to me? Why am I just now finding this out?" Apparently, a new condition for the fulfillment of past promises had been revealed to Bill Johnson during the wee hours that morning.

It is true that God sometimes did give conditional prophecies through the prophets in Scripture—meaning that their fulfillment depended on the obedience or disobedience of the people who received the prophecies (Lev. 26; Jonah 3). But when fulfillment of a prophecy depended on meeting certain conditions, the conditions were directly stated or implied in the prophecy. However, on December 26, when Johnson announced the condition for the eventual fulfillment of God's 2021 promises, it was dropped on the people by surprise, out of nowhere, literally at the last minute (the final Sunday of the year). It was as if God had been given a year-long extension on the fulfillment of His 2021 promises! But now, based on Johnson's application of 1 Samuel 30, the promised blessing was boosted to a "double recovery." In other words, despite the delay, there would be more blessing than originally envisioned, if the newly revealed conditions are met.

We stress that there is no point to stipulating conditions if they are not specified on the front end when a promise is given, especially if its fulfillment depends on the actions of recipients of the prophecy. But NAR leaders imply—by their frequent use of loopholes—that virtually all prophetic words given today are conditional. Loophole Prophecies are another means for getting around the Fulfillment Test.

But if the Fulfillment Test is to have any practical value, NAR prophecies must be actual predictions, not just pleasing platitudes posing as predictions. This leads us to consider another very common type of NAR prophecy that appears to make predictions—but only on the surface.

Fortune Cookie Prophecies

Many so-called predictions made by NAR prophets are so vague there would be no way to know if they came true or not—much like the words found inside a fortune cookie.

We'll show you what we mean by "Fortune Cookie Prophecies" with three examples of predictions made by the Apostolic Council of Prophetic Elders. This council consists of twenty to thirty high-profile prophets who meet together once a year to collectively receive revelation for the global church.[21] Recent members include Cindy Jacobs (Generals International), James Goll (God Encounters Ministries), Stacey Campbell (founder of the Canadian Prophetic Council), Bill Hamon (Christian International), the late Harry Jackson Jr. (Hope Christian Church in Beltsville, Maryland, and spiritual advisor to President Donald Trump), Matt Sorger (Matt Sorger Ministries), and Sharon Stone (Christian International Europe). Here are excerpts from a document containing their revelations, called the "Word of the Lord for 2020."[22] Notice how the words are encouraging, inspiring, and uplifting, but also virtually meaningless.

- "2020 is significant in that it is literally a new era. One of the words God has given is that we're going to grow into our own skin. . . .

We're going to grow into the purpose of God that He has for us."

- "Of course, it will be a challenging season as well. Any time you're going to a new level—we used to say, 'New levels, new devils'—there will be some resistance. . . . If you're going into your Promised Land (your purpose, your destiny, what God has for you), and you're not having any pushback (there are no giants in the land), then you're not going in the right direction. There will be Jerichos to take, so there will be battles, but it's going to be exciting."

- "And finally, for now, it is a year of reset. This is the day when we will be anointed for reset. This reset will bring a breakthrough for relations, for families, for the nation. God is going to turn impossible situations around."

"Reset." "Breakthrough." The reversal of "impossible situations." Any of those words could be found in a fortune cookie or a daily horoscope. But what do those things even mean? And how would anyone know if, when, or how the things they "predicted" had occurred?

Without knowing what their prophecies refer to specifically, they can be made to mean anything—whatever the prophets' followers want them to mean. And that means they are *unfalsifiable* and *untestable*. But if you can't apply the Fulfillment Test to a prophecy that claims to predict the future, then that prophecy fails the test the moment it's uttered.

Variations of the Fortune Cookie Prophecy—which are unspecific and untestable—include Archetype Prophecies and Broad Fishing Net Prophecies.

Archetype Prophecies

Have you ever heard a prophet tell someone that they are a "modern-day Esther" or a "modern-day David" or a "modern-day Deborah"? If you've spent any time in NAR circles, then you almost certainly have encountered these prophecies. And the recipients of these prophecies usually take great encouragement from being likened to one of those (or any of the other) heroes of the Jewish and Christian faiths.

For example, consider this prophetic word that was given by a woman from Bethel Church during a "Prophetic Zoom Session" to a man named Jonathan. (Anyone can sign up on the Bethel Redding website for a Prophetic Zoom Session.) At the start of the session, the woman went straight for delivering an archetype prophecy, seizing on Jonathan's name.

> Jonathan, before we even called you I had, like, an image, I would say, of the Jonathan that's in the Bible. What the Lord was pointing out through your name is the strength that Jonathan had. He wasn't afraid to go and fight for the army of the Lord, just him and his armor bearer. That he had courage, he had strength, and he was, like, victorious. So, the Lord was just saying that those are the qualities that you carry. You have strength, you have courage, and He declares you to be victorious.[23]

The problem with "Archetype Prophecies," like this one, is that they are quite vague and subjective. (And they generally work by free association—as in this case, playing off the fellow's name.) What does it mean, exactly, that a man is a modern-day Jonathan? He is courageous (how?), strong (in what sense?), and will be victorious (victorious in what?). The Bethel "prophets" could only offer generic statements and speak in hazy metaphors. They did not make any concrete predictions.[24]

And what does it mean that a woman is an "Esther"? What trait of Queen Esther is the prophet alluding to? Do they mean that she is influential? Do they mean she is brave and self-sacrificing? Do they mean she's beautiful? Is a modern-day David someone who vanquishes (symbolic) giants with a slingshot? Someone who plays an instrument with skill? Someone who worships God with his whole heart (and maybe writes music)? Someone God is going to use despite grave sins committed in his past?

These prophecies "work" because many things can come to mind when someone thinks of a particular Bible hero. So all recipients of the same "prophecy" would likely be able to identify something in themselves that they see to be similar to that Bible character. Like the next variety of Fortune Cookie Prophecies, they are unspecific and, therefore, untestable. But we guess that doesn't diminish how wonderful you may feel about being compared to a hero of the Bible.

Broad Fishing Net Prophecies

Many NAR predictions about current events are so broad and encompassing that they will be correct simply because the odds are tremendously in their favor. That's why we call this variety "Broad Fishing Net Prophecies"—they're bound to catch something.

Here's an example of such a prediction made by Brian Carn, founder of Kingdom City Church (in Charlotte, NC; Jackson, FL; and Houston, TX). It's a prediction from his "Word for the

Lord for 2020": "A famous 1980s star dies in 2020 who was a big name."[25]

It doesn't take a prophet to make a successful prediction like this. It's safe to assume that at least one movie star who was performing sometime during the 1980s would die in the year 2020. And given that People.com identified 210 celebrity deaths that year, he surely got that one right.[26] Carns made many similar predictions for 2020.

- "A shocking discovery by the end of August to reveal a great secret that will create a stir."
- "A famous preacher has heart problems in 2020 and will take a break from ministry."
- "A rapid amount of children overdosing on prescription drugs."
- "A New York City problem that will be found to reshape the way people view real estate."
- "A famous class action lawsuit begins in 2020."

These headlines could be used year in and year out, with equal effectiveness time after time. These Broad Fishing Net predictions—similar to the other varieties of Fortune Cookie Prophecies—are too vague to be meaningfully predictive. With all of these "prophecies," something generic is cast out there. All you have to do is fill in the details and imagine a pattern of fulfillment—to your own amazement.

The Real Deal

Clearly, in resorting to such vague, broad, and outright silly prophecies, the NAR prophets have put a large distance between themselves and the biblical prophets, who made detailed predictions, often long in advance of their fulfillment. They were awe-inspiringly accurate.

An example is the prediction made by an unnamed biblical prophet who foretold the rise of a king named Josiah (1 Kings 13:2). The prophet not only revealed the rise of this future king—including even the king's name—but he also predicted that King Josiah would sacrifice idolatrous priests on an altar and burn human bones on that altar. Though the fulfillment of the prophet's prediction took nearly 300 years, every detail of the prophecy was fulfilled to the letter (2 Kings 23:15–20). And many more examples could be given.

- Joshua's prediction that anyone who attempted to rebuild the demolished city of Jericho would do so at the cost of the lives of their oldest and youngest sons (Josh. 6:26; 1 Kings 16:34).
- Isaiah's prediction *by name* of the pagan ruler, Cyrus, who would arise and liberate the Jewish people (Isa. 44:26–28; 45:1; 2 Chron. 36:22–23; Ezra 1:1–4).
- Daniel's prediction about the rise and fall of four major kingdoms (Babylon, Medo-Persia, Greece, and Rome), including strikingly precise details about Alexander the Great revealed by Daniel some 200 years before Alexander's rise to power (Dan. 2:1–45; 7; 8:5–22; 11)!
- Elisha's prediction of the miraculous end of a famine in a single day (2 Kings 7:1). His prediction included the exact prices of flour and barley. (Though he made his prediction

only one day prior to its fulfillment, it was contrary to what everyone else anticipated.)

These are just some of the astonishingly accurate predictions made by prophets in the Bible. We could add the numerous detailed predictions about the coming Messiah, Jesus Christ, including His virgin birth (Isa. 7:14; Luke 1:35), the town of His birth (Mic. 5:2; Matt. 2:4–6), and His arrival to Jerusalem on a donkey (Zech. 9:9; Matt. 21:8–10; Mark 11:1–10), as well as details concerning His suffering and death (for example, Isa. 53; Zech. 11:12–13 with Matt. 27:6–10; Exod. 12:46 and Ps. 34:20 with John 19:31–36; Ps. 22:16–18 with Luke 24:39–40 and John 19:23–24, 33–37). When NAR prophets' predictions are held up next to the predictions of biblical prophets, there simply is no comparison.

The fact that NAR prophets cannot accurately predict the future is very telling. It shows that the source of their predictions is not God, who alone knows and controls the future. As God said through the prophet Isaiah, "For I am God, and there is no other; I am God, and there is none like me, *declaring the end from the beginning and from ancient times things not yet done,* saying, 'My counsel shall stand, and I will accomplish all my purpose'" (Isa. 46:9–10).[27] Only a prophet who has truly heard from God can accurately predict the future. All else is pseudo-prophecy.

Without hearing from God, NAR prophets are left making predictions that are inaccurate ("Fails") or so vague they are not truly predictions ("Fortune Cookie Prophecies"). But there is still one more type of prophecy that NAR leaders give—sham prophecies.

Fraudulent Prophecies

Two varieties of sham "prophecies" are extremely accurate . . . but only because the "prophets" got a little (or a lot of) outside help.

Headline Prophecies

One common variety of NAR prophecy appears, misleadingly, to predict tomorrow's news headlines today. Many NAR prophets claim to predict tomorrow's events *supernaturally*—by receiving revelation directly from God—but there's nothing supernatural about their predictions. The events are ones anyone could foretell if they merely watch the news and pay attention to what's going on in the world.

A perfect example of this can be seen in a "prediction" given by the prophet James Goll about the U.S. Supreme Court. Goll is one of the most highly respected prophets in NAR today. But one of his public predictions did not survive the scrutiny of YouTuber Mike Winger, who provided an analysis of Goll's prediction. Here's what Winger found.

On September 13, 2019, Goll publicly declared that God visited him and told him there would be another vacancy on the Supreme Court and a woman would be appointed by then-President Donald Trump. She would be a "modern-day Esther," she would be pro-life (against abortion), and she would tip the scales of the court toward "true constitutional conservatism."[28]

Just over a year after Goll made this prediction, Justice Ruth Bader Ginsburg died (on September 18, 2020) and President Trump appointed Amy Coney Barrett to replace her. This seemed to some like an amazing fulfillment of Goll's prophecy. But everything specific he predicted came straight from the headlines of the time. The news outlets had been reporting that Ginsburg, who was then eighty-six years old, had pancreatic cancer. Her retirement was believed to be imminent. And Barrett had already been identified as being President's Trump's most likely choice to replace Ginsburg.[29] A leak from the White House—reported by *Axios*, *Fox News*, and the *New York Post*—revealed that Trump had been saving Ginsburg's seat specifically for Barrett.[30] And even if he had chosen not to appoint her, most of Trump's other top choices were also women and constitutional conservatives. Thus, Goll's prediction—that the new Supreme Court justice would be a pro-life woman and a constitutional conservative—did not appear to be the result of any true prophetic powers. Why would God bother to tell him something the media had long known and been reporting? His prediction appeared instead to be merely plausible prognostication, based on common knowledge of the time, which Goll passed off as a prophecy.

Hot-Reading Prophecies

Some NAR prophets who give "words of knowledge" about people at major public events have been accused of cheating, since they seem to be employing a practice used by phony psychics known as "hot reading." This allegation deserves some consideration.

What is a hot reading? As we explained in chapter 3, a "cold reading" is a technique used by phony psychics or mentalists (entertainers who do not claim to have any physic powers) who pretend to know things about a person in the audience that they couldn't know by ordinary means. In a *cold* reading, they are merely making educated guesses based on their observations about the person's age, attitude, demeanor, clothing, etc. For example, the presence or absence of a wedding ring is evidence of a person's marital status, and this can be useful information for making further successful guesses about a person.

In contrast, during a *hot* reading, a psychic or "prophet"
obtains information about a person *before* a live event, through
research of some kind, then pretends to receive that information during the event, directly from God or another supernatural
source, or by the psychic's own paranormal abilities. There is
evidence that Shawn Bolz—known for his incredibly accurate
prophecies—engages in hot reading and has done so while standing on the stage with other influential "apostles" and "prophets,"
including Lou Engle, Todd White, Heidi Baker, and Benny Hinn.

Some of this evidence is exhibited in a video posted to
YouTube, which alleges that Bolz engaged in hot reading during
"The Send" conference, held in Orlando, Florida, February 23,
2019.[31] During the conference, which was aired on Bethel TV,
Bolz spoke on a stage in a stadium filled with a reported 70,000
people. While speaking, he claimed to receive information (or
"words of knowledge") from God about someone specific in the
audience. Bolz—raising his hand to shield his eyes from the stage
lights and scanning the crowd—said:

> I'm looking for a Dennis, who you're either from
> the Ukraine or your parents were, and you moved
> to America, and, I think, to Washington state or
> Washington, D.C. . . . Help me out here: Is there
> a Dennis? We've only done this in stadiums this
> big a few times. It's a little hard.

Within several seconds, a man named Dennis raised his hands
in the air to identify himself, and those seated near him in the
stadium started pointing excitedly at him. Bolz, acting surprised,
said, "We have somebody. Thank God." He went on to reveal
more details about Dennis's life, including his troubled youth, his
parents' divorce, and the new ministry he was presently launching
in Pennsylvania. Dennis's jaw dropped, he alternated raising his

hands in the air and placing them on his head, and, at one point, he jerked spastically. He was clearly stunned by Bolz's accurate description about himself, and his reactions caused the crowd to erupt into wild cheers and applause. Bolz's "words of knowledge" for Dennis caused such a stir that *Charisma Magazine* shared a link to a video of them.[32]

The video exposé suggests that Dennis was being scammed. It explains that everyone who attended the conference had to register in advance and provide their email addresses. As it happens, all the information given about Dennis could be found on his social media accounts and personal website—sources that fake psychics are known to mine for information about people in their audiences. For example, the exposé video shows how a YouTuber named Jack Vale can amaze total strangers simply by sharing information he discovered about them on Facebook, Instagram, and Twitter. Likewise, anyone could have discovered where Dennis lived simply by reviewing his public profile on his Facebook page. And they could learn the more intimate details of his life from a video testimony about his life found on his ministry website—including information about his Ukrainian background, his parents' divorce, and his teenage drug use and time in the juvenile justice system. It's all there.

As the video critique of Bolz's technique says, "If you have a smart phone and some social media accounts, your life is an open book and anyone can 'read' you."

Investigation of the Send incident is not the only time Bolz has been accused of engaging in hot reading. During an appearance on the Sid Roth *It's Supernatural!* television program, Bolz appeared to be reading information about individuals right off of his tablet—as those individuals watched on—yet the people were still awed by the information he knew about them.[33] Sometimes you don't even have to be subtle to be convincing, especially if people want to believe your message.

That Bolz engages in hot reading seems to be a plausible explanation for his exploits. Since it's clearly possible that Bolz has consulted social media sources for details about individuals in his audience, it isn't at all obvious that he has received a word from God. So why do "apostles" and "prophets," including Todd White, Lou Engle, and Heidi Baker, look on with seeming approval? Why does Bethel TV air Bolz's performance? And why does Sid Roth call Bolz "the most amazingly detailed prophet he has ever known"?[34] This implicates White, Engle, and Baker in his fraud and casts doubt on their own claims to be prophets.

Others have been suspected of hot reading to feign prophecy. William Branham—one of NAR's most revered prophets—also allegedly engaged in this practice long before the internet was invented. He could not, of course, have relied on social media accounts. Instead, Branham reportedly obtained personal information about people from the "prayer cards" they were urged to submit at his meetings.[35]

The words of knowledge that NAR prophets like Bolz claim to receive about people aren't limited to predictions about the future, but sometimes they purport to be revelations of accurate information about the present. Thus, these words can and should be examined in light of the "Fulfillment Test." But this test is not very useful if fulfillment by natural means (like using social media accounts) is a reasonable possibility.

Even if prophetic power cannot be completely ruled out in this case, it definitely looks like it was a stunt. This is suggested by the showmanship, characteristic of mentalist performers—the formulaic language Bolz uses, the way he plays the audience for effect, etc. In addition, though it may seem to put a prophet today at a disadvantage, the mere availability of a plausible alternative explanation defeats the value of the prophecy. Because technology may very easily be used to accomplish these feats, a true prophet must be capable of offering something more demonstrably compelling than what Bolz does here, *if he is to be trusted as a prophet*. The point is not that a fellow must be a pseudo-prophet if it can be established that he *could have* used social media to acquire the knowledge he exhibits; rather, the point is that the audience is *not rationally justified* in believing that he is a prophet, if all they have to go on is this kind of evidence, since it could be produced (and hence explained) another way. Because this knowledge could be so easily obtained via social media, all bets are off as to whether it was revealed to Bolz directly by God.

We should add that if it can be established that Bolz has cheated (lied) in this case, then he should henceforth be blacklisted and should no longer be favored within NAR ranks. If it cannot be established that he cheated, all NAR leaders (Bolz himself included) should at least acknowledge that his gift of prophecy has not yet been established or confirmed by the evidence turned up during these events. They should affirm the wisdom of withholding judgment about his prophetic powers until the right sort of evidence is made available. Their prudence as leaders is doubtful if they cannot acknowledge this.

NAR prophets also frequently use their "words of knowledge"—and the trust they gain from people by seeming to know so much about them—as a launch pad to make predictions about a person's future. For example, after Bolz wowed Dennis with all the details he so clearly knew about his life, he prophesied to Dennis that God is calling him to lead a "movement" and is "commissioning" him to go to Ukraine and Eastern Europe. "It's your time, brother," Bolz told Dennis, "It's your time." But how could Dennis know that he wasn't being duped?

Fool Me Twice . . .

If certain prophets make predictions that do not come to pass (a "Fail"), you can be sure that they have not been sent by God. And if they make "predictions" that are so vague they are untestable ("Fortune Cookie Prophecies"), you can safely ignore them because they are not truly predictions. Be on the alert for "Headline Prophecies" and "Hot-Reading Prophecies" given by bogus prophets and con artists. But the first order of business is always to be sure that an alleged prophet has met the burden of proof by establishing on suitably strong grounds that he or she is a genuine prophet of God.

CHAPTER 5

The Apostolic Takeover
and Spiritual Abuse

*The whole movement rests on the giant claim
that God Himself is restoring the offices of
apostle and prophet and the entire body of Christ
must submit to their authority or else miss out
completely in the "new" move of God. If that
claim is false, the entire movement crumbles.*
—"Dean," a full-time missionary whose
ministry was overtaken by NAR[1]

NAR apostles and prophets claim great authority in the church—
and beyond the church. And because of the powerful position they
supposedly occupy between heaven and earth, their authority can
wreak powerful havoc in the lives of those who submit to them.

Bruce and Sheila were one such couple. They were fooled for
fifteen years by their church leader—a man who called himself
an "apostle." At the time, they had no idea they were attending

a NAR church, which advertised itself as nondenominational. While there, they took part in NAR practices. They frequently engaged in NAR-style "spiritual warfare." They commanded demons. They commanded angels. And the couple did not feel free to make decisions—to move, change jobs, have children, or even discipline their children—without consulting a prophet or the apostle himself. Bruce also worked loyally for the apostle, without pay, the entire time. If he ever questioned the apostle's interpretation of Scripture, he was told he had "misunderstood" the apostle. This gaslighting happened so often that he stopped questioning. The apostle would "correct, humiliate, and call out" Bruce in front of the whole church. He used guilt and fear to control Bruce and Sheila. But they remained at the church because they truly believed the man was an apostle who heard from God.

Church services lasted between four to six hours and, after years of showing steadfast loyalty to the apostle and serving the church, the couple began to burn out. Bruce begged for a break because he was depressed and struggling, but the apostle wouldn't grant it. The couple grew disenchanted and pulled back. They decided to leave the church. Bruce's exit meeting was cruel. "The apostle told him that he'd never work in ministry again," Sheila recalled. Nobody at the church asked them why they left. (Questions like that are often discouraged in NAR churches.) But a few higher-ups from the church knew why they left, and some of them claimed to have had "visions" from God of their return. Sheila now sees that the church's shameless leader doesn't pass the test for being an apostle. When Sheila reached out to us, they were still reeling from the spiritual abuse. But she said she was finally feeling freedom for the first time in her Christian life.

Spiritual abuse can happen in any church. It happens in churches that aren't led by apostles and prophets. But the potential for abuse is much greater in NAR churches because apostles and prophets not only claim to speak directly for God, they also claim much greater authority than pastors (pastors must submit to them) and because they often do not oversee a single church (like most pastors do), but multiple churches (as many churches are in their network—sometimes thousands!).[2] So the authority of NAR apostles and prophets runs both deep and wide.

Why do people succumb to manipulative and controlling spiritual leaders? In this chapter, we explain how NAR leaders catch their followers and we describe the tactics they use to keep them in their grip. We also offer advice for battered and broken spirits who have left NAR churches and seek healing.

How "Apostles" and "Prophets" Catch Their Followers

"Apostles" and "prophets" lure their followers with the promise of blessings. Blessings are the bait. They claim they have something no other church leaders have. Pastors teach the written Word of God and nurture their flocks. But apostles and prophets have the new revelations their followers need to develop miraculous powers, bring God's kingdom, and fulfill His will on earth.

The Blessing Brokers

Followers become dependent on the apostles and prophets for everything. They're convinced they need them to experience intimacy with God, know His will for their lives, receive physical and emotional healing, learn to work miracles, and protect themselves from demons who would hinder them from fulfilling their destinies. There's an inherent authority structure that lends itself to spiritual abuse. Apostles and prophets hold the keys to the kingdom.

Do you desire to be spiritually great and lead a life of significance? If so, you must go through them. They are the gatekeepers, the movers and the shakers, the friends in high places who will give you a special "in" with God. They have what you need for being all you can be and maximizing everything God wants to give you, including your dream job, financial prosperity, and a happy marriage and family.

To illustrate the uniqueness of the "anointing" (or miraculous powers) possessed by the apostles and prophets, the "prophet" Kris Vallotton offers the following analogy. He tells his followers at Bethel Church to think of the different types of church leaders as flavors in a soda fountain. "They all have one thing in common; they all have soda water. But if I want Coke, I can't come to the 7UP fountain because the fountain determines the flavor."[3]

What he says plainly, though not quite directly, is that going to a pastor won't cut it when someone needs what only an apostle or prophet can give—namely, the apostolic or prophetic flavor. And there is a reason Vallotton's soda foundation has *five* flavors. It has to do with a key NAR teaching known as the "fivefold ministry."

The Fivefold Ministry

According to this doctrine, Christ, at His ascension into heaven, gave five offices for governing, or authoritatively directing, the church: *apostles*, *prophets*, *evangelists*, *pastors* ("shepherds"), and *teachers*.[4] Churches that desire to operate as Christ intended must have a government that includes all five offices.[5] That belief is displayed on the website of Bethel Church, which states: "We embrace the biblical government of apostles, prophets, evangelists, pastors and teachers."[6] And Bill Johnson called the five offices, working together, the "secret sauce" for the church to transform the world.[7] Those churches that don't have apostles or prophets of their own often join an apostolic network or affiliate with a church like Bethel Church.

We pause here to ask: Does your church have apostles and prophets in leadership, or does it defer to apostles or prophets in some larger network? Or does it instead recognize only pastors/ elders as the ultimate church leaders?

If your church recognizes only pastors/elders, you're not alone. Most of today's churches are governed by pastors/elders, not apostles and prophets. And even churches that believe there are people today with the gift of prophecy—most notably, Pentecostal and charismatic churches—do not usually believe that those prophets must *govern* the church.[8] But if NAR leaders are right, the majority of churches are missing two pivotal offices—the only offices that are authorized by God to bring critical new revelation to the church.[9]

According to NAR leaders, these two offices must be recovered if the church is to be complete and operate in supernatural power. And how will that power be manifested? Kris Vallotton claims that God told him the restoration of the fivefold ministry would result in "increased angelic activity manifested by extraordinary miracles rarely witnessed in the history of the planet."[10] The reason for such a flurry of angelic activity is that apostles (and, by extension, their followers) have the authority to make "prayer declarations" that the angels must carry out. Imagine that! Having angels at your beck and call.[11] But the authority to make declarations that angels must obey is granted only to those who submit to apostles, according to Vallotton. He cautions: "We can only declare a word of the Lord that commissions and sends the angels if we are under authority and therefore have authority."[12] He also offers this tantalizing promise: "When we come into submission to God's apostolic leaders, we are known in heaven and feared in hell. True heavenly authority causes angels to help us and causes demons to respect our influence."[13] Such are the benefits of restoring apostles and prophets to church government.

Control Tactics

NAR leaders have adopted tactics for exercising control over their followers. Here are several of them.

Tactic No. 1: Twisted Scriptures

The "apostles" and "prophets" are skilled at twisting Scripture verses to bolster their teachings and boost their own authority in the eyes of their followers. The apostle Peter warned the first-century Christians about false teachers who "twist" Scriptures (2 Pet. 3:16).

Ephesians 4:11

NAR leaders say their fivefold doctrine is taught clearly in Ephesians 4:11, which states: "And he [Christ] gave the apostles, the prophets, the evangelists, the shepherds (pastors) and teachers." But this verse merely lists five types of gifted leaders that Christ has given the church. It does not teach that He has given the church a hierarchical leadership structure made up of five formal governing offices. It doesn't say anything at all about offices. Thus, it does not support the NAR fivefold ministry teaching.

Ephesians 2:20 and 1 Corinthians 12:28

We've seen that apostles and prophets must hold governing offices in the church. Since they are the ones who receive new revelation, they must hold the *highest* offices, and all who are neither apostles nor prophets must submit to them. That includes pastors and elders.

To support this teaching, they turn to two verses, Ephesians 2:20 and 1 Corinthians 12:18. Ephesians 2:20 states that the church is "built on the foundation of the apostles and prophets, with Christ Jesus himself as the chief cornerstone." And 1 Corinthians 12:28 states, "And God has appointed in the church first apostles, second prophets, third teachers, then miracles, then gifts of healing, helping, administrating, and various kinds of tongues."

See, NAR leaders reason, *it says right in those verses that the church "rests on the foundation or leadership of the apostles and prophets"* (to use the words of Danny Silk, a senior leader at Bethel Church) *and that when it comes to church governance apostles and prophets are first and second in God's "order of priority"* (Silk's words, again).[14] So that settles it—apostles and prophets must take the driver's seat.

But these verses are quoted out of their context. Ephesians 2:20 refers back to the beginnings of the church. It does not teach that God intended a new batch of apostles and prophets to provide top-level leadership for the church in each generation. It teaches that a foundation has already been laid, not that each generation is to re-lay the foundation. And 1 Corinthians 12:28 provides a list of spiritual gifts, not church offices. That is clear in the larger context of the twelfth chapter, where the entire focus is on spiritual gifts. These verses simply do not teach that apostles and prophets hold the two highest church offices.

Other than the apostles of Christ (most notably, the Twelve and Paul, who held an exclusive office in the early church), the only two churches offices that are clearly identified in the New Testament are elders/overseers (what many churches refer to today as "pastors") and deacons.[15] And there isn't the slightest hint that the prophets spoken of in the New Testament held church offices. Most Protestant churches today are governed by pastors/

elders, assisted by deacons. Except for a few groups on the fringes, Christians have not believed that apostles and prophets should be included in church government. The ground began shifting with the arrival of the New Apostolic Reformation at the turn of the twenty-first century (a development anticipated by its shorter-lived, less influential predecessor, the Latter Rain Movement of the late 1940s and early 1950s).[16]

It is shockingly pretentious and condescending for NAR leaders to teach that, for the past 2,000 years, the vast majority of churches have gone off the rails—neglecting the form of government that Christ Himself established—and that only today's NAR churches have gotten it right. How odd that Christ should allow such a major slip-up during the course of church history!

The idea that apostles and prophets must hold the highest offices in the church is an audacious claim. And because it is controversial, NAR leaders typically do not state it so explicitly. Instead, they employ euphemisms to make their teachings seem more palatable and defensible.

Tactic No. 2: Euphemisms or "Word Games"

A *euphemism*, according to *Merriam-Webster*'s dictionary, is "the substitution of an agreeable or inoffensive expression for one that may offend or suggest something unpleasant."[17] In other words, it's a roundabout way of saying something that many people would find unacceptable. And when it comes to NAR, it's a softer, gentler, less direct way to deliver a contentious teaching.

NAR leaders make abundant use of euphemisms. Many NAR euphemisms are designed to cushion the blow of their teaching that all Christians must submit to the authority of today's "apostles" and "prophets." Here are seven common expressions to listen for:

- "Alignment": The word *alignment* is code for *submission*. NAR leaders teach frequently about the need for all Christians, including pastors, to be properly "aligned" with—or submitted to—the fivefold ministry leaders, especially the apostles and prophets. For example, Kris Vallotton writes that, to experience spiritual victory, believers must be sure they are in proper alignment with apostles and prophets: "If we don't understand how to recognize and align ourselves under true spiritual authority, we may build bigger armies, develop better strategies and buy more powerful weapons, but we will still lose."[18] And the apostle Ché Ahn says, "I encourage you to get as close as you can to the apostle with whom you are aligned. What do I mean by being close? . . . submitting to his authority. The closer you are with your apostle, the more you will receive the blessing of the corresponding grace and favor that comes with the alignment."[19] Pastors align with apostles and prophets by joining one of the many apostolic networks, such as the Bethel Leaders Network, Harvest International Ministry, or Global Awakening. Or they invite apostles and prophets into their churches to teach and prophesy. The rest of God's people align with apostles and prophets by attending a church where the senior leaders are apostles and prophets or a church where the senior leaders have voluntarily submitted to apostles and prophets.[20]

- "Spiritual covering": A spiritual covering is NAR code for the blessings and protection that come to a believer who has aligned with (or submitted to) the authority of an "anointed" church leader. The highest level of covering is provided by an apostle and is known as an "apostolic covering." A spiritual covering has been described as a "spiritual force field" because it supposedly brings in "good things" (God's blessings) and blocks "bad things" (demonic attacks).[21]

- "Spiritual fathers and mothers": This phrase is NAR code for "apostles" and "prophets."[22] Many NAR leaders are careful not to speak of themselves explicitly as "apostles" and "prophets" (though they don't prevent others from referring to them by such titles). And they don't always refer to other NAR leaders by these titles, either. They know that using the titles is controversial and will raise eyebrows, so they play coy and speak of themselves and each other as "spiritual fathers" and "spiritual mothers." Those who come under their authority are "sons" and "daughters." An information packet for the Bethel Leaders Network states, "We believe spiritual covering is accessed as individuals position themselves as sons and daughters to receive from spiritual fathers and mothers."[23] It is clear from this statement that "spiritual fathers and mothers" stands for figures with special authority in the group. *Access to spiritual covering* comes through these leaders. You must "position yourself" in the submissive role of a son or a daughter to gain access.

- "Gift," "Grace gift," or "Function": In a more recent development, some NAR leaders have moved away from using the word "offices" when referring to apostles and prophets and instead refer to "gifts," "grace gifts" or "functions." They have done this because they know the term "office" is controversial and draws too much direct attention to differences between themselves and other continuationists who believe there are apostles and prophets today but do not believe that those apostles and prophets govern or hold formal offices. When they want to distract attention from those differences, they use this other language.

- "Covenant relationships": NAR leaders teach of the need for all Christians to be in a "covenant relationship," which is code for a relationship that entails spiritual accountability and submission to another wiser believer, spiritual leader, or a local church congregation. These relationships are ideally lifelong. And they are essential for believers if they are to fulfill their destinies.[24] For example, Kris Vallotton writes, "Everyone needs these deep covenant connections—not primarily because they keep us from failing, but because they inspire us to reach for the high call of God that rests on each of our lives."[25] An ordinary believer need not be in covenant relationship with an apostle or prophet—in their case, a wiser believer will do. But forming a covenant relationship with an apostle or prophet has added perks because those who are in "covenant relationship" with an apostle or prophet can do everything that the apostle or prophet can do, according to Vallotton.[26] This means they can access an apostle's or prophet's miraculous power. And the language of "covenant" is telling. It invokes the notion of a pledge or promise. If you enter into a covenant relationship with a NAR apostle or prophet, you pledge your support for and accountability to them, and they exercise the power and authority in the relationship. It is a lop-sided relationship.

- "Culture of honor": Bethel leaders celebrate what they refer to as a "culture of honor" at their church. This is NAR code for "honor everyone, but especially the apostles and prophets." One of Bethel's senior leaders, Danny Silk, has a book titled *Culture of Honor: Sustaining a Supernatural Environment*. This book is required reading for students in the Bethel School of Supernatural Ministry. Silk writes, "The Principle of Honor states that: accurately acknowledging who people are will position us to give them what they deserve and to receive the gift of who they are in our lives."[27] That is, believers must show proper honor to the apostles and prophets as a condition for receiving rewards from them, including miraculous giftings and supernatural empowerment.

- "Relational leadership": NAR leaders like to use this language to insinuate that today's apostles are not heavy-handed and authoritarian. Rather, they are collegial and "lead from consensus," choosing to build leadership teams around themselves with whom they govern and receive input from. The "apostle" Randy Clark clearly employs this euphemism.[28] But this disguises the way that relational dynamics can actually be exploited for authoritarian purposes, and it ignores the fact that apostles and prophets do exercise unique authority. So stressing the relational aspect does nothing to alleviate concerns about the presumed authority of an apostle.

As you can see, NAR leaders don't always state candidly their most controversial teachings. Rather, they rely on insinuation, implication, and innuendo. Nevertheless, the message is clear to NAR insiders, those "in the know": if you want to be blessed, show honor and submit to the apostles and prophets.

Tactic No. 3: Brainstoppers

Another go-to control tactic is the use of what we refer to as "brainstoppers." These are catchphrases used by NAR leaders to desensitize their followers to legitimate concerns about NAR teachings and practices. Use of brainstoppers gets their followers to shut off their minds so they don't critically evaluate NAR claims and teachings. Here are four examples:

- *"Eat the meat and spit out the bones."* This popular catchphrase means that if you hear a teacher give a questionable teaching—something you don't understand or that seems off somehow—you can ignore that particular teaching, but you shouldn't stop listening to their other teachings. Or if you are part of a "revival" and it comes to light that the "apostle" or "prophet" leading that revival has a secret immoral lifestyle (such as the healing evangelist Todd Bentley, leader of the 2008 Lakeland Revival in Lakeland, Florida), you should still believe God was working through that "unclean" person and that they led a genuine "move of God."[29] Bill Johnson preached an entire sermon promoting this idea.[30] But as we know, when it comes to responding to false teaching or immoral church leaders, this maxim doesn't have the support of Scripture. For example, the apostle Paul told the Romans to "watch out for those who cause divisions and put obstacles in your way that are contrary to the teaching you have learned" and to "keep away from them" (Rom. 16:17 NIV). And Jesus said that false prophets will be recognized "by their fruits" (Matt. 7:16), which includes their immoral lifestyles. The maxim is also a faulty metaphor. When eating fish, you can easily pick out the bones, and there's no real danger. But what if, instead of eating fish, you were drinking a milkshake and it had been laced with poison? In that case, it would be ridiculous to advise someone to just "drink the milkshake and spit out the poison." Such a task would be impossible. In a similar way, dangerous teachings, even when mixed with some good teachings, are so corrupting that following a teacher who engages in them is too risky.

• *"You should trust God's ability to protect you from being deceived more than you trust Satan's ability to deceive you."* NAR leaders often recite this catchphrase to dispel people's fears of being deceived by false apostles and false prophets. Bill Johnson has delivered it in the form of a rhetorical question: "What do I trust most, my ability to be deceived or His ability to keep me?"[31] But the idea that Christians need not worry about being deceived goes against the many warnings in Scripture about guarding against false teachings (Matt. 7:15–20; 16:11–12; Acts 20:28–30; 1 Tim. 1:19; 4:16; 1 John 4:1–6; 2 Pet. 2; 3:16–17). God is certainly able to protect us from deception, just as He is able to protect us from falling into sin; but just as we, too, have a responsibility to avoid sin, so we have a responsibility to use the tools He has given us to protect ourselves from deception! These tools include Scripture, sound teaching, and the use of our God-given intellect.

- *"God offends the mind to reveal the heart."* This catchphrase means that God works through "prophets" who seem bizarre and do things people don't understand, or may even find offensive. He does this to show what is in people's hearts. If they refuse to listen to those so-called prophets, that is a sign of an evil, hard heart. This phrase is often deployed when someone questions unusual manifestations that are occurring in a church gathering, such as when people are "drunk" in the Holy Spirit" or overtaken by "holy laughter."[32] Mike Bickle (founder of the International House of Prayer in Kansas City) devotes an entire chapter to promoting this catchphrase in his bestselling book *Growing in the Prophetic: A Practical, Biblical Guide to Dreams, Visions, and Spiritual Gifts.* He writes, "My introduction to prophetic ministry was difficult because I despised the weirdness of some of the people God used. I was also bothered by some of their bizarre methods that were foreign to everything in my evangelical background."[33] Likewise, the apostle Chuck Pierce (founder of Global Spheres in Corinth, Texas) teaches, "If you're going to walk with God, you're going to have to accept some things you don't understand because God will confound the mind to test the heart. That means He will do things you do not understand just to see if you will love Him and trust Him anyway."[34] The problem with this catchphrase is that it basically tells people to not think critically. And it warns that if you do get concerned or alarmed by disturbing things taking place, the problem is not with the so-called "prophet" promoting those things, but with you and your bad heart. This is a brainstopper with a sinister twist. It is dangerous to tell people to ignore the sense they have that something occurring in a meeting is wrong. That sense may well be their biblical discernment kicking in. And it is pernicious to accuse a person of wrongdoing when he or she is only trying to use their mind to evaluate activities that may or may not be of God.

- *"God is bigger than His book."* This is a very common catchphrase used by NAR leaders. A closely related catchphrase is "Don't put God in a box." If you are in NAR any length of time, you will likely hear these mantras deployed, usually in defense of supernatural experiences reported by "apostles" and "prophets" that cannot be found in Scripture. That is the way Bill Johnson uses "God is bigger than His book," in the title to a subsection of one of his books. He writes: "Revival is mixed with many such dilemmas—God doing what we've never seen Him do before."[35] It is certainly true that we cannot control God or place limits on what He

can do. Yet it is also true that He will always
act in accordance with what He has revealed
of Himself in Scripture.[36]

Tactic No. 4: Book Ban

Another tactic NAR leaders have used to stifle criticism is
what we refer to as a "book ban." Bill Johnson strongly warns
his followers not to read books that are critical of NAR teachings
about healing and miracles. He does this in his popular book
When Heaven Invades Earth: A Practical Guide to a Life of Miracles.
Here are his words: "Be childlike and read the works of those who
have succeeded in the healing ministry. Stay away from the books
and tapes of those who say it shouldn't or can't be done. If the
author doesn't walk in power, don't listen, no matter how profi-
cient they may be in another field."[37] It's always a red flag when
someone, especially a church leader, warns you to stay away from
books or teachers who are critical of their teachings. That tactic
has been used for years by the cults of Christianity, such as the
Jehovah's Witnesses and the Church of Jesus Christ of Latter-day
Saints (formerly known as the Mormons). But the problem goes
deeper. It presumes that the authors Johnson favors, including
himself, are "walking in power." Why should anyone think that?
How can that be tested?

Tactic No. 5: Name-Calling

Name-calling is one of the most effective tactics NAR leaders use to inoculate their followers against criticism of themselves.
Instead of responding to legitimate challenges, "apostles" or
"prophets" often resort to slapping their critics with disparag-
ing labels. The labels they've given their critics are numerous:
*mean-spirited, heresy hunters, judgmental, Jezebel, Pharisee, legalist,
unspiritual,* and *unanointed*—to name a few. They also frequently

accuse them of being under the influence of a demonic "religious spirit." Even influential "apostles," including Bill Johnson, are not above using this tactic.[38]

This tactic is effective because their followers start to believe that everyone who questions an "apostle" or "prophet" is evil or unspiritual. They readily dismiss any criticism of their leader, without ever determining whether there is merit in the criticism. Many followers of these "apostles" and "prophets" have responded to our books and articles in this way. One comment we've received is that we're just "jealous" of the success of the ministries we've critiqued. This is classic name-calling. If someone's favorite teacher is challenged, a better response is to show where the critic is wrong and respond to specific evidence the critic has presented.

Tactic No. 6: Threats

When other tactics fail to silence their critics, NAR leaders resort to threats. One example is pious repetition of the warning "Touch not the Lord's anointed." When someone dares to challenge a NAR prophet or apostle, they are often met with those ominous words, as if from God Himself. They are adapted from Psalm 105:15 and 1 Chronicles 16:22, which declare, "Touch not my anointed ones, do my prophets no harm!"

When quoting these verses, NAR leaders insinuate that it is a sin to raise a hand against (metaphorically, to speak critically about) a so-called prophet or apostle. But they are misapplying the passages. In Psalm 105:15 and 1 Chronicles 16:22, the warning not to harm God's prophets applied to *all* His "anointed ones," which meant God's specially chosen people, the Israelites. God was warning the surrounding peoples not to oppress them. And the New Testament teaches that *all* Christians are the Lord's anointed (or chosen ones); the designation is not reserved for "apostles," "prophets" or teachers (see 2 Cor. 1:21–22; 1 John 2:20, 27). First John

2:18–29 addresses a situation where certain teachers were falsely claiming that they had a special anointing that set them apart from other Christians—the very thing NAR leaders are claiming today. Oddly enough, this threat is reinforced in the recent Prophetic Standards Statement. It may sound like the statement is revoking use of the catchphrase "touch not the Lord's anointed." In truth, it actually reinforces its use. The statement says:

> **WE BELIEVE** it is essential that all spiritual leaders, including prophetic leaders, have a presbytery of peers and seasoned spiritual leaders who can hold them accountable regarding their life and ministry. In keeping with this, we reject the notion that to judge a prophet's words is a violation of Psalm 105:15 (where God exhorted the ancient nations not to touch the patriarchs or harm His prophets). Prophets who err must be willing to receive correction from peer leaders with whom they are in accountable relationship. Those refusing such accountability should not be welcomed for ministry.[39]

The statement does allow that a prophet's words may be "judged," but only by a member of the prophet's inner circle. Only a peer leader in an accountability relationship is at liberty to judge. In other words, no one else may touch the Lord's anointed.

Again, we see how Scripture is wielded as a weapon to intimidate those who question NAR leaders' unproven claims to authority.

Recovering from NAR

We've described several ways that so-called apostles and prophets attract their followers and keep them. We realize that some who read this book will have experienced spiritual abuse under NAR leadership. If you are in that situation, how can you break free from your painful church past and move forward in your walk with God? What should your next steps be? Here are our suggestions.

Learn to Read the Bible Better

Many people tell us that they don't trust themselves to read Scripture accurately, since the "apostles" and "prophets" have propped themselves up by modeling faulty methods of interpretation and claiming to have special revelation into the "deeper meaning" of passages. The answer is to learn a new and responsible way with Scripture. A simple acronym may be a helpful reminder for how to read the Bible well. The acronym is BOD: broadly, often, and deeply (because we all need to get our "spiritual bods" into shape). We do this by reading Scripture *broadly*, by reading it *often*, and by reading it *deeply*.

To read Scripture broadly requires reading the entire Scripture, all sixty-six books of the Old and New Testaments (not just our favorite, go-to books, such as the Gospels or Psalms). As the apostle Paul told the young pastor, Timothy, "*All* Scripture is breathed out by God and profitable for teaching, for reproof, for correction, and for training in righteousness" (2 Tim. 3:16).[40] This means there is value to be gained from every book of the Bible. Also, when you are not acquainted with the whole Bible, you are at risk. NAR teachers tend to exploit the lesser-read books to promote their bizarre notions and practices. For example, recall from chapter 1 how "grave soaking" has been defended by appealing to a little-known Bible verse, 2 Kings 13:21. Bear in mind that whole-Bible reading provides a broader grasp of context for interpreting the Bible.[41]

To read Scripture often requires reading it every day (as far as that is possible). And it requires actually reading Scripture itself—the meat and potatoes. Carefully selected devotional books are good as supplements to our own Scripture reading. But they are not a substitute. If we settle for small spoon-fed doses of Scripture that are interpreted for us by someone else, we're in danger of being deceived. We must read and wrestle with Scripture for ourselves. The best way to accomplish this is to plan for it; a plan of daily reading keeps you tuned to Scripture all the days of your life.

To read Scripture deeply requires really digging into Scripture and making sure we are reading it in full consideration of its context—not snatching verses out of their surrounding passages and attributing to them some meaning the author never intended. A verse removed from its context can be made to support almost any teaching—as NAR practices have shown us time and again. In 2 Timothy 2:15, Paul tells Timothy to be one who correctly handles the word of truth (Scripture). To assist you with this task, we recommend that you use a good study Bible, one that provides commentary from reputable Christian scholars on the background information you need to know. And here's another tip: the best study Bibles have notes compiled by multiple scholars providing commentary in their respective areas of expertise. For example, some scholars are experts on the book of Isaiah, while others are experts on Matthew or Romans. The ESV Study Bible, the NIV Study Bible, and the CSB Study Bible all offer contributions from multiple scholars.

But studying the Bible deeply is more than learning to interpret verses accurately. It also involves taking the time to meditate on Scripture. By meditation, we don't mean the mystical or New

Age close-your-eyes-and-shut-off-your-mind type of thing; we are referring to a biblical sense of meditation, where you think about, reflect on, and delight in the Word, where you hide it in your heart (by memorizing it), talk about it with other Christians, and apply it to your life by obeying it. Read Psalm 119 to see an inspiring description of this type of meditation.

Better Bible reading involves several practices: broad reading through the whole of Scripture (daily and as often as once a year), close study of select books, meditation, and memorization of key passages.

Find a Good Church

Many of our readers tell us that after leaving their NAR churches, they struggle to get plugged into a new church because they are afraid of being duped again. You, too, may be jaded by past experiences and tempted to stay away from church. But merely listening to sermons online will not provide you with the support of other Christians who are committed to growing in their discernment and maturing in their faith—something that is pivotal to keeping your own walk with God on track. Nothing can substitute for the specific quality of fellowship and service that is available through participation in the life of a healthy local church (Heb. 10:24–25). To find a biblically sound church, take a look at their doctrinal statement. That statement often can be found on the church website, along with any position papers the church has adopted (stating their positions on controversial theological issues, such as abortion, same-sex marriage, and the miraculous gifts). The statement should reflect a high regard for Scripture, containing words such as these found in the Lausanne Covenant: "We affirm the divine inspiration, truthfulness and authority of both Old and New Testament Scriptures in their entirety as the only written word of God, without error in all that it affirms, and the only infallible rule of faith and practice."[42] If a church website does not provide a detailed doctrinal statement, that may be a red flag that the church does not place much importance on its beliefs, or is even hiding them.

A word of warning: a church publishing a sound doctrinal statement is no guarantee that the church is doctrinally sound. Make sure they practice what they preach. Many NAR churches publish doctrinal statements that make them appear sound on paper, artfully neglecting to mention their NAR beliefs in those statements. So, there is much you can learn about a church's beliefs only by visiting and listening well.

Pay close attention to the pastor's sermons. They should be expository and exegetical. This means that the pastor preaches from an actual text of Scripture (expository) and interprets it in context (exegetical). The biblical preacher shows considerable evidence of careful study of the text, and explains how you can apply it to your life. It is good practice for you to mentally ask questions of interpretation and application as you follow along with the sermon. Think about whether the sermon addresses those questions and how well it does so. An expository preacher does not just share a bunch of random thoughts, personal opinions, and feelings about a passage. Always feel free to approach the pastor later with any questions you have.

Learn about Spiritual Abuse

Learning about spiritual abuse and the tactics used by spiritual abusers has been immensely helpful to many people on their path to healing. It will also help you steer clear of domineering churches in the future. One such book is *Twisted Scriptures: Breaking Free from Churches That Abuse*, by Mary Alice Chrnalogar. This particular book addresses many of the abusive teachings and tactics of NAR churches.

Join a Support Group

You will likely find it helpful to process with a friend who has had past experiences of spiritual abuse, but if you don't know anyone like that, consider joining an online support group for people who have exited NAR (including Facebook groups, such as the "NAR Recovery Group—Non-Denominational"). Many people have told us about the encouragement they receive in such groups.

At the beginning of this chapter, we shared the story of a couple that was wounded by spiritual abuse in a NAR church. Sheila told us that seven months after leaving that church she was still struggling. Recovery wasn't easy. But she also expressed hope that there is light at the end of the tunnel.

"It's been hard. I often cry—and then cry because I'm crying because I should be happy I am free. It's a process, I am told."

CHAPTER 6

Counterfeit Revival

"Your miracle is here or right around the corner," "God's about to do something big," "Get ready, it's gonna happen in your life," "It's happening," "Revival."
—Former participants in NAR,
"Paul" and "Morgan"[1]

Everyone wants revival. But what is it?

Today's "apostles" and "prophets" claim that we are about to experience the greatest revival the world has ever seen. They believe they and their followers will work stunning miracles, including healing the sick and disabled and raising the dead. These miracles will be performed in large venues—football stadiums, ballparks, and colosseums will be filled to overflowing, and the major news networks will televise the miracles worldwide. A billion people will be saved.[2]

This "billion-soul harvest" will occur in the days right before Christ's return, allowing the global church—under the leadership of the apostles—to take control of the earth and to set up God's physical kingdom or, in NAR lingo, "bring heaven to earth."

This version of events is what NAR leaders mean when they speak of revival. It's behind many of their songs and it drives many of the large prayer-and-fasting rallies held in stadiums around the world.[3] But are crowds, miracles, and the establishment of God's physical kingdom the true hallmarks of revival?

Most people probably associate revival with preachers proclaiming the gospel, altar calls, and countless conversions to Christianity and renewed commitments to Christ. They may think of America's historic revivals led by Jonathan Edwards, George Whitefield, Charley Finney, Dwight L. Moody, and other powerful preachers. Or they might recall their own church's tent revival meetings and the Billy Graham crusades. Most would say that such revivals—and any today that are modeled after them—are gifts from God. Many pray that Christian revival will have positive spillover effects on our cities and nations—stronger families, healthier communities, righteous laws. But these revivals do not focus on flashy miracles or apostolic rulership over society. Proclamation of the Word of God and confession of sin are the dominant features. These are the hallmarks of the great revivals found in Scripture, including the hugely dramatic revivals led by King Josiah and Ezra (2 Chron. 34–35; Neh. 8–10).

Thirteen Signs of Counterfeit Revival

With all the talk of revival today, how can you know if church leaders are referring to true, biblical revival or the NAR counterfeit? How can you tell if a revival event advertised in your community is NAR-influenced? How can you be sure that you don't find yourself, unknowingly, partnering in unbiblical and misguided efforts to bring about NAR revival? If you don't want to get roped into the NAR revival, keep reading. We will identify thirteen clues that show that a song, sermon, or event is promoting NAR revival.

1. *"Ministry Time" and "Activation"*

Some come to NAR revival events seeking healing from a sickness, but many others come for a personal word from God about their destiny, or to feel His closeness and presence. This may come in the form of "holy laughter," being slain in the Spirit (knocked to the ground by the power of the Holy Spirit), or seeing a glory cloud. People crave a "touch from God" in some fashion or other. They want to be noticed by Him and feel special. That's why the highlight of NAR revival is not the message, based on the Word of God, like it is during other revivals (think of Jonathan Edwards's famous sermon, "Sinners in the Hands of an Angry God").

At a NAR event, everyone eagerly anticipates the climactic "ministry time" near the end of a service, when a "prophet" or an "apostle" on stage announces that God is healing people in the audience, or they begin to give prophetic words to specific people in the room. It's an especially thrilling event if the apostle or prophet "lays their hands" on people—so that they can "activate" miraculous gifts in those people. At Bethel Church (and many churches patterned after Bethel), the ministry time includes an often chaotic event called the "fire tunnel." Leaders form two lines, facing each other, and encourage people to walk through the "fire tunnel"—where individuals are believed to have "deep encounters" with the Holy Spirit (seen by their spastic jerking movements and falling to the ground).[4]

It's no coincidence that the tunnels are called "fire" tunnels, as NAR revivals make heavy use of the word "fire" as a symbol for the Holy Spirit. Many revival conferences are titled "Fire Conferences," and NAR organizations are given fire-themed names like "Burn 24-7." Prophets often shout the word "fire" from the stage, to indicate that they are releasing the power of the Holy Spirit over a crowd. In NAR revival, the Holy Spirit is often viewed as a force, or power that can be manipulated, more than as a Person, and that perception often shows up most clearly during the ministry time.

2. Revelation of Divine Strategies for Building God's Kingdom

With NAR revival, there will be lots of talk about "building God's kingdom," "advancing God's kingdom," and "bringing God's kingdom to earth." That language is also sometimes used outside NAR to refer to the expansion of God's kingdom through evangelism, but in NAR it is usually used together with references to "divine strategies" that God has allegedly revealed to modern-day "apostles" and "prophets."[5] One main strategy is known as the "Seven Mountain Mandate"—described as a strategy to "take over the world."[6] According to the Seven Mountain Mandate, believers must "infiltrate" and "occupy" the highest positions in the seven major societal institutions (which they call "mountains"): government, media, family, business, education, church, and the arts.[7] Conquering these "spheres of society" is seen as key to taking dominion of the nations so that God's kingdom can be established.[8] And NAR leaders make it clear that the key to controlling those institutions is the work of "apostles." The apostle Ché Ahn writes, "We must also recognize that apostles have the authority to govern on all seven mountains of culture."[9]

It is astonishing that the "apostles" claim this mandate gives them authority to govern not only the church, but also society. Naturally, this has raised concerns that the NAR movement is seeking to establish a national or global theocracy. In addition to the "seven mountain mandate," listen for references to the "seven mountains of influence" and the "seven mountains of culture."

3. A Distorted Gospel

The gospel, according to Scripture, is the good news that Christ's death and resurrection has made the way for forgiveness of sin, reconciliation with God, and eternal life (John 3:16; 1 Cor. 15:1–8). These benefits are available to all who place their faith in Christ. But NAR leaders claim that this is an incomplete gospel. They claim the *full* gospel includes the message that Christ's death and resurrection has also made way for His followers to take dominion of the earth. They call it the "gospel of the kingdom," and this understanding of the gospel is a critical component of NAR revival.[10] The way the gospel of the kingdom is confirmed is by miraculous signs and wonders.[11] In fact, Bill Johnson teaches that "a gospel without power is not the gospel Jesus preached."[12] Do you want to know which version of the gospel is being promoted at a revival? Then do the "airtime" test: see how many minutes are devoted to talking about forgiveness of sin, salvation, and growth in holiness versus miracles, prophetic words, and Christians "ruling and reigning."

4. Promises that God Will Fulfill Your Dreams and Make You Prosperous

Why did Jesus leave the riches of heaven, come to earth as a humble baby, suffer, and die? So that He could make us wealthy, healthy, and successful in every area of our lives. The "prophet" Kris Vallotton has said, "I want to point out again that Jesus became poor for a reason. His celestial mission was to make us wealthy."[13]

The teaching that God wants all believers to enjoy good health and wealth is known as the prosperity gospel.[14] It's associated with televangelists like Benny Hinn, Joyce Meyer, and Kenneth Copeland, who live in mansions, drive luxury cars, and own private jets. But NAR leaders also teach the prosperity gospel, though they've given it a special NAR spin. They teach that the prosperity gospel is a long-forgotten truth that has been restored by present-day "apostles" and "prophets."[15] Prosperity teachings are essential to NAR because, along with the billion-soul harvest, God plans to fulfill another NAR prophecy called the "end-time transfer of wealth."[16] This second prophecy reveals that God intends to transfer the wealth of the wicked to the righteous so that the apostles have the funds needed to build God's kingdom. So NAR followers are taught to make declarations such as "Lord, release the wealth of the wicked into my hands."[17] And, of course, no prosperity teaching is complete without flattery. NAR leaders boost their followers' egos by saying that the coming revival depends on them: "You are a game-changer," "God is waiting on you," "You are the signs and wonders generation who will finally succeed in bringing heaven to earth."

5. A Novel View of the End Time ("Victorious Eschatology")

Christians have different views about how the last days on earth before Christ's return will unfold. But two of the three main positions (premillennialism and amillennialism) agree that the world will not get better and better. In these views, evil will continue and even increase, and many believe that the church-at-large will experience an "apostasy" where many professing believers will fall away from the faith and follow false prophets.[18] Despite many differences among end-time views, nearly all believers trust that Christians will face some degree of unavoidable persecution until Christ returns victorious for His church, and that obedience to Christ and faithfulness to our calling in the meantime is itself a victory (Rom. 8:28–39; Eph. 6:10–20; James 1:2–4; 1 Pet. 1:6–9; Rev. 3:21; 17:14). Neither premillennialists nor amillennialists expect the church to establish God's kingdom on earth prior to Christ's return. And together, these two groups make up the majority of Christians. (Postmillennialists do seek the expansion of God's kingdom across the earth prior to Christ's return, but, historically, they have sought to do this through gospel proclamation and trust in the Holy Spirit's ability to regenerate human hearts. They have not relied on strategies like those revealed by present-day "apostles" and "prophets.")

NAR teachers have a radically different view. They call the dominant Christian views of the end-time pessimistic, fear-motivated, and escapist. And they believe these teachings are holding back the church's ability to bring God's kingdom to earth.[19] In their "Victorious Eschatology" (also called "apostolic eschatology"), Christians under the leadership of apostles and prophets in the last days will experience great victory by performing signs and wonders that will cause a worldwide revival. Entire nations will convert to Christ.[20] Some even hold that Christians will take vengeance on their persecutors by making prayer declarations that will "loose" the judgments of God described in the book of Revelation (plagues that include hail, falling stars, and an army riding fire-breathing horses).[21] So, rather than undergoing the Tribulation in the last days, Christians will actually *cause* the Tribulation (the future time period referred to by many Christians as the Great Tribulation). NAR leader Mike Bickle (of the International House of Prayer in Kansas City) has said: "A lot of people are waiting to be taken up [or raptured]. They want to go up so they can escape the Tribulation." But he says, "the Lord is waiting for us to grow up to loose the Tribulation through the prayers of faith."[22] These very different teachings about the end time provide one sure sign of NAR revival efforts.

6. Declaration "Prayer"

When NAR revival is afoot, the way believers pray is noticeably different. They do not humbly ask God for such things as healing, financial provision, and the end of societal evils like abortion. Rather they "decree" and "declare" that those things will happen.

Making petitions (or requests) of God is viewed as an inferior form of prayer. To pray powerfully, a believer must assert the authority that they believe God has given them to make "prayer declarations," thereby forcefully speaking things into existence (similar to the way God spoke in Genesis when He created the world).[23]

Indeed, making declarations is a critical practice for the church because God has limited Himself to acting only in response to declarations. Johnson writes: "Nothing happens in the Kingdom until first there is a declaration."[24] He teaches that before Christ came to earth at the Incarnation believers were making prayer declarations. And He cannot return until the church makes a declaration. "Even the return of the Lord will be preceded by the declaration of the bride: 'The Spirit and the bride say, "Come."' If these things were going to happen anyway, what would be the purpose of prayer?"[25] So, Christ's first and second comings are dependent on prayer declarations made by human beings.

But the Bible does not support the notion of prayer declarations. Nowhere does it teach believers to make declarations, and we cannot find a single example of believers making them. When King Jehoshaphat and the people of Judah faced invasion by foreign enemies, they did not decree and declare victory for their vulnerable nation. Rather, they assembled at the temple and Jehoshaphat humbly and reverently pleaded with the Lord for their deliverance, saying,

"O Lord, God of our fathers, are you not God in heaven? You rule over all the kingdoms of the nations. In your hand are power and might, so that none is able to withstand you. Did you not, our God, drive out the inhabitants of this land before your people Israel, and give it forever to the descendants of Abraham your friend? And they have lived in it and have built for you in it a sanctuary for your name, saying, 'If disaster comes upon us, the sword, judgment, or pestilence, or famine, we will stand before this house and before you—for your name is in this house—and cry out to you in our affliction, and you will hear and save.' And now behold, the men of Ammon and Moab and Mount Seir, whom you would not let Israel invade when they came from the land of Egypt, and whom they avoided and did not destroy—behold, they reward us by coming to drive us out of your possession, which you have given us to inherit. O our God, will you not execute judgment on them? For we are powerless against this great horde that is coming against us. We do not know what to do, but our eyes are on you." (2 Chron. 20:6–12)

When faced with a great threat, God's people declared their powerlessness and uncertainty of how to proceed, yet expressed their confident hope in God's power, knowledge, and goodness to act on their behalf. There was no prideful presumption in their prayers. And what about King David, a man after God's heart (1 Sam. 13:14; Acts 13:22)? He pleaded with God for his child's life to be spared; he did not command it (2 Sam. 12:16 NIV). Or

Jesus! Jesus asked for the cup of suffering He was about to endure
to pass and it did not happen. Did He not have enough faith?
Was He wrong not to "declare"? What we see in Hebrews 5:7 is
that Jesus "offered up prayers and petitions" ("pleadings" in some
translations)—"and he was heard because of his reverent submission" (NIV), not for any bold declarations he made. If Jesus, equal
with God and having all power, did not pray in declarations, who
are we to think we have that kind of authority? God the Son does
not demand of God the Father, though He does ask. What a
thought to consider as we seek to be like Him![26]

Given all this, it should come as no surprise that making declarations has not gone well for people in NAR; Bethel's futile effort
to raise baby Olive is only one highly visible example.[27] In 2018,
the declarations of Bethel Church leaders and attenders could not
stop the Carr Fire from burning more than 1,000 homes (including at least forty belonging to members of the Bethel Church community) and killing eight people.[28] Nor could their declarations
prevent a large outbreak of Covid-19 at the church.[29] Still, determined as ever, they remain convinced that making declarations
is the way to pray. In chapter 8, we give examples of how these
declarations show up in NAR music. If you pay close attention
during revival events, you will notice them.

7. 24/7 Prayer Rooms

The presence of a 24/7 prayer room at a church is a good indicator that the church promotes NAR revival. Many churches have
started special 24/7 prayer rooms where people sign up for shifts
engaging in round-the-clock prayer. And many of these prayer
rooms are modeled after the prayer room at the International House
of Prayer in Kansas City, where "prophetic singers" and musicians
have led non-stop, night-and-day worship and prayer since 1999
(with plans to continue until Christ returns). IHOPKC's prayer

room began after the controversial NAR "prophet" Bob Jones (see more on Jones below) gave Mike Bickle a prophecy that he would start a 24/7 prayer and worship ministry, led by young adults, that would lead to worldwide revival.[30] Bickle teaches that these prayer rooms—where declarations are made for revival—will play a central role in bringing about the billion-soul harvest. He also teaches that, through their declarations, end-time Christians will "release" in unison the judgments of God that will kill millions of people and wipe out entire cities.[31] Thus, prayer rooms, multiplied strategically throughout the world, will serve as NAR command centers for a heavenly assault against the Antichrist's global empire.[32] Not all 24/7 prayer rooms promote NAR teachings about revival, and a desire to pray non-stop certainly is not a bad thing—but this typically is a good indicator that a church is influenced by NAR.

8. Revival Hot Spots

If you hear church leaders referencing Toronto, Brownsville, or Lakeland, you know they are promoting the NAR counterfeit revival. Just about every committed NAR person who could traveled to experience the "revivals" occurring at churches in those cities: the "Toronto Blessing" of 1994 (at Toronto Airport Vineyard Church in Toronto, Canada), the "Brownsville Revival" of 1995 (at Brownsville Assembly of God in Pensacola, Florida), and the "Lakeland Revival" of 2008 (at Ignited Church in Lakeland, Florida). The Lakeland Revival, led by the "prophet" Todd Bentley, ended in infamy after disclosures about Bentley's lifestyle came to light, to the chagrin of many high-profile NAR leaders who promoted him.[33]

During these purported revivals, word spread about miracles and strange manifestations of God's presence, including people miraculously receiving gold fillings in their teeth, making animal noises (barking like dogs and roaring like lions), and "getting drunk in the Spirit." Today's popular revival hot spot is Bethel

Church in Redding. But for many people, visiting Bethel isn't enough. They decide to move there permanently so that they can continue to experience the ongoing revival. All the buzz about Bethel Church is further evidence of NAR revival aspirations.

9. Shady Prophets

When attending a NAR revival, you may hear the names Bob Jones, Paul Cain, and William Branham. All are deceased, but they are among the most revered prophets in NAR memory—despite their engagement in sexual misconduct and their heretical teachings. This is NAR's dirty little secret: the pivotal role of immoral and dubious prophets in the movement.

For example, Bob Jones (1930–2014) confessed that he had abused his prophetic office by encouraging women to undress in his office so they could stand "naked before the Lord" in order to receive prophetic words from him.[34] (He was the "prophet" who gave the well-known NAR prophecies about the billion-soul harvest.[35]) Paul Cain (1929–2019) confessed to being an alcoholic and a long-term practicing homosexual.[36] (He gave the highly heralded prophecies about stadiums being filled because of miracles.[37]) William Branham (1905–1965)—the most esteemed NAR prophet of all—taught that Eve had sex with the serpent in the garden of Eden and that God gave His Word in three forms: the Bible, the zodiac, and the Egyptian pyramids. He also denied the doctrine of the Trinity.[38] NAR leaders know about all these things, yet they still regard these men as genuine prophets. Bill Johnson has said that believers are required by God to "honor" modern-day prophets—even those who "ended poorly" and "even when you find out later that the person was living in a secret sin."[39] Remember the words of the apostle Peter: false prophets and false teachers "secretly bring in destructive heresies," they are characterized by "sensuality," and "because of them the way of truth will be blasphemed" (2 Pet. 2:1–2).

10. Fresh Revelation

One of the clearest marks of NAR revival is the label "fresh revelation" for leaders' teachings. The "prophets" and "apostles" claim their offices give them the authority to give new revelation that they have received directly from God. NAR prophets can announce "Thus saith the Lord" and expect their words to be taken seriously.[40]

In addition to giving revelation that guides individuals and local churches, they also give revelation to entire nations and the global church. Kris Vallotton claims that Jesus spoke to him directly about the "new revelation" God is about to give to the global church through apostles: "The Lord also told me, *I am about to open up the vaults of heaven and reveal depths of My glory that have never before been seen or understood by any living creature.*"[41] They present the global church with new teachings and practices, which are called "present-day truths" and "strategies" (such as the Seven Mountain Mandate). One means of receiving this revelation is "prophetic illumination" into specific verses of Scripture, when God shows them the hidden meaning of those verses.[42] For example, they see the Seven Mountain Mandate concealed in the reference to "mountains" in Isaiah 2:2. (We urge you to read the verse and see if you can detect any evidence of a Seven Mountain Mandate there. We sure don't see it.) Bill Johnson speaks of this critical new revelation, given through prophetic illumination, when he says, "No one in their right mind would claim to understand all that is contained in the Bible for us today. Yet to suggest that more is coming causes many to fear. Get over it, so you don't miss it!"[43]

The NAR focus on new revelation is very different from the trend in non-NAR churches, where people gather to hear the Bible preached—responsibly and accurately interpreted in its context—rather than to hear up-to-the-minute fresh prophecies and learn the secret messages contained in Scripture. NAR preaching undermines the teaching authority of the Bible. What value does it have if it hasn't first been sifted by the enlightened NAR prophet, who is alone in being able to reveal its full meaning?

11. Vigorous Spiritual Warfare

NAR leaders teach that, for revival to occur, their followers must engage in peculiar spiritual warfare practices that are not identified in Scripture, such as casting out high-ranking demons (called "territorial spirits") who are believed to rule over cities.

During a NAR-style prayer walk (not all prayer walks are NAR), a group of people will walk through a neighborhood or section of a city (such as a red-light district or skid row) and command territorial spirits to leave that region—a practice known as "warfare prayer." They also will engage in "prophetic acts," which are actions believed to bring "spiritual breakthrough" to a region and release God's power. Common prophetic acts include driving wooden stakes into the four corners of a city or anointing the perimeters of a building (such as a city hall) with oil.[44] A very bizarre prophetic act occurred during a revival event organized by the apostle Lou Engle at the National Mall in Washington, D.C., on October 9, 2017, called Rise Up. Thousands of women got on their knees in a "birthing" position and began to wail for the salvation of their children—a symbol of giving birth to a move of the Holy Spirit, a new "Jesus Movement" (like the "Jesus People" revival that began in California in the late 1960s). Prayer walks and prophetic acts are NAR revival tells.[45]

12. A Diminished Jesus

One of the most controversial NAR teachings is that, when Jesus came to earth, He gave up the use of His divine powers and worked all His miracles as a mere man, through the power of the Holy Spirit. So, contrary to what Christians have believed through the centuries, His miracles were not evidence of His deity.

To be clear: NAR leaders do not teach that Jesus ever stopped *being* divine—even though Bill Johnson (who has popularized this teaching) has made statements over the years that have left people thinking that is what he taught.[46] If he did teach that, it would be overt heresy and should be strongly condemned. But his teachings (though not necessarily heretical) are rather subtle, which compounds their dangerous effect. Johnson and other NAR leaders have asserted that they believe Jesus, while remaining divine, chose not to use His divine powers to perform miracles. Johnson writes:

> Let's face it, if Jesus did all His miracles as God, I'm still impressed. But that is an impossible example for me to follow. . . . When I see that He did what He did as a man following His Father, then I am compelled to do whatever I need to do to follow that example.[47]

But those teachings are based on a serious misrepresentation of Scripture, including Philippians 2:7. This verse says that Jesus "emptied himself, by taking the form of a servant, being born in the likeness of men." But it does not teach that Jesus emptied Himself of His divine powers. The significance of Jesus's self-emptying is explained in the very next verse: "And being found in human form, he humbled himself by becoming obedient to the point of death, even death on a cross." Jesus's Incarnation is a manifestation of divine humility. But by making Jesus out to be a model miracle worker, and looking for a way to justify this claim in Scripture, NAR teachings lower Jesus's status and mislead people into thinking they can perform the same miracles He did. This teaching is another clear sign of NAR revival.[48]

13. Encounters with Angels

At NAR revivals, the prophets and apostles regale their audiences with stories about the visits they have received from angels. That's because, in NAR teaching, "partnering with angels" is the "missing link" for revival.[49] God is currently releasing angels to bring in the end-time harvest of souls.[50]

Pretty much every well-known NAR leader has had his or her own angel encounters, and they claim that you, too, can buddy up with the celestial beings. So be on the lookout for the promotion of books, courses, and conferences that teach people how to meet up with angels—such as the book *Angelic Encounters* by James Goll, the online course "Seeing into the Angelic Realm" taught by Jennifer LeClaire, and the 2018 conference "Angels, Atmospheres, and Assignments: Learning to Navigate the Spiritual Realm." Beware, however, that "angels" who show up for revival may not all be God's own ministering angels, for the apostle Paul warns that "even Satan disguises himself as an angel of light" (2 Cor. 11:14).

True Biblical Revival

NAR revival is more carnival than revival. Dominion, prosperity, thrills, and chills—things that stroke egos and promise earthly pleasure—are what Romans 8:1–13 refers to as "our flesh." And that should send up a red flag. In the Bible, we see that the apostle Paul warned the young pastor, Timothy, about the danger of teachings that cater to people's desires.

> For the time is coming when people will not endure sound teaching, but having itching ears they will accumulate for themselves teachers to suit their own passions, and will turn away from listening to the truth and wander off into myths. (2 Tim. 4:3–4)

The message of NAR revival is that you must seek continual manifestations of God's presence. It's a wild roller coaster of "the feels." But people under pressure to "feel the fire" of revival and continually "burn" for God will inevitably burn out. Many in thrall to Bethel, to Bill Johnson, and to other NAR leaders are in bondage, and do not realize it. A kind of mania takes over. An insatiable addiction to the sensational becomes pervasive. It's oppressive to the soul.

> **NAR revival is more carnival than revival.**

The expectation of one novel revelation or miracle after another is unsustainable. It is an escape from reality into a chamber of paralyzing exuberance. Leaving the NAR movement is akin to leaping from a merry-go-round spinning at top speed—producing a noxious discombobulation. With the relentless flexing of spiritual muscle, a spiritual hypertrophy sets in, and normal spiritual function is ruined. Hyper-spiritualization degenerates into spiritual incapacitation.

What happens when a prophetic word does not come to pass or the supernatural experience someone yearned for doesn't come? People who have come out of NAR have answered that question. For example, Christian YouTubers Paul and Morgan—a married couple—share how significant emotional pain was caused in their lives due to prophetic words they received that did not come to pass (including a prophecy that Morgan would become pregnant). And Morgan says that when she didn't "feel the fire" of personal revival on a daily basis—the times she wasn't experiencing positive, exciting things happening in her life (as the prophets promised), but instead was facing trials and difficulties—she questioned her own salvation. She also says that when she went to a meeting and saw other people getting prophetic words from the speaker (while she was not), she would be resentful. "I was always just like, *Oh Lord, please let them have a word for me,*" she recalls.[51] Others have shared similar reports with us, saying they would be jealous when others, and not themselves, were slain in the Spirit or experienced holy laughter. They'd wonder what they had done wrong, whether they had sinned, or if God was mad at them.

The revival mania that Morgan, Paul, and countless others have found themselves ensnared in stems from a wrong view of the end time (also called "eschatology"). NAR anticipates a "victorious" church that will put on a signs-and-wonders show and trounce God's enemies. But that is a very different picture than the one Jesus painted of the days leading up to His return.

> As he sat on the Mount of Olives, the disciples came to him privately, saying, "Tell us, when will these things be, and what will be the sign of your coming and of the end of the age?" And Jesus answered them, "See that no one leads you astray. For many will come in my name, saying, 'I am the Christ,' and they will lead many astray. And you will hear of wars and rumors of wars. See that you are not alarmed, for this must take place, but the end is not yet. For nation will rise against nation, and kingdom against kingdom, and there will be famines and earthquakes in

various places. All these are but the beginning of
the birth pains.

"Then they will deliver you up to tribulation
and put you to death, and you will be hated by
all nations for my name's sake. And then many
will fall away and betray one another and hate
one another. And many false prophets will arise
and lead many astray. And because lawlessness
will be increased, the love of many will grow
cold. But the one who endures to the end will
be saved. And this gospel of the kingdom will
be proclaimed throughout the whole world as a
testimony to all nations, and then the end will
come." (Matt. 24:3–14)

Jesus is speaking of conditions at the end of the age. He first
describes a series of bad things that will unfold as the end draws
near. These events will cause alarm, although Jesus urges the disciples not to be alarmed. He prophesies tribulation, persecution, and
death. There will be great apostasy. There will be false prophets.
"But the one who endures to the end will be saved."

Between now and the end of the age, it's an endurance race.
Meanwhile, "this gospel of the kingdom will be proclaimed
throughout the whole world." Then what? "Then the end will
come."

The new apostles and prophets have it all wrong. It is true
that Jesus brought His kingdom when He came to earth. But
for now, that kingdom is spiritual, realized chiefly in the fruit of
obedience in the lives of believers and in the churches. The physical kingdom will not be established until Christ's return (1 Cor.
15:24–27). Theologians refer to these present and future aspects

of the kingdom as "already, not yet": the kingdom is already here, but not yet fully realized.

Professor Michael S. Horton, of Westminster Seminary California, challenges the idea that Christians are supposed to "build the kingdom." He says:

> According to the prophets, John the Baptist, and Jesus, the arrival of the kingdom is not an era of gradual human improvement of the world's conditions, but the radical inbreaking of God himself into our history, in judgment and grace. . . . Blessing is not to be taken for granted by those who think they're entitled to it. . . . But in this time between Christ's two advents, it is an opportunity to proclaim the gospel and welcome people "of every nation, tribe, and tongue" to the feast of the Lamb (Rev. 5:9).[52]

Well said. And the gospel we are to proclaim is not confirmed by present-day miracles; it has already been confirmed, once-for-all, by Christ's resurrection (1 Cor. 15:1–8). What modern-day miracle could possibly improve upon that?

True spiritual power is not shown by prophesying or healing. Jesus warned that those who do those things, but fail to live in true obedience and knowledge of Him, will not enter the kingdom:

> "Not everyone who says to me, 'Lord, Lord,' will enter the kingdom of heaven, but the one who does the will of my Father who is in heaven. On that day many will say to me, 'Lord, Lord, did we not prophesy in your name, and cast out demons in your name, and do many mighty works in your name?' And then will I declare to them, 'I

never knew you; depart from me, you workers of lawlessness.'" (Matt. 7:21–23)

Similarly, the Corinthian Christians had miraculous gifts aplenty, but they were short on love, a condition that caused their considerable giftedness to be judged comparatively worthless (1 Cor. 13:1–13). Real spiritual power is displayed by overcoming sin and displaying the fruit of the Holy Spirit: love, joy, peace, patience, kindness, goodness, faithfulness, gentleness, self-control (Gal. 5:16–24). The Spirit seeks to work "moral miracles" in our lives each day. He accomplishes this mighty work through the sanctifying power of the truth revealed in Scripture (John 17:17; 2 Tim. 3:16–17; Heb. 4:12; Ps. 119). This miraculous work of personal moral revival is realized in experience, as relationships are healed, anger is moderated by mercy and forgiveness, suffering is endured with patience, anxiety is replaced by peace, addictions are brought under control, and hope is restored. This is kingdom living.

In short, biblical revival is measured in terms of obedience and holiness. Anything short of that is a counterfeit.

CHAPTER 7

The Passionately Wrong "Bible"

Jesus Christ came into my room. He breathed
on me. And he commissioned me. . . . And
he spoke to me and said, "I'm commissioning
you to translate the Bible into the translation
project that I'm giving you to do."
—The "apostle" Brian Simmons, author of
The Passion Translation of the Bible[1]

Of all the bizarre things NAR apostles and prophets claim to have happened to them, one of the most bizarre stories comes from the apostle Brian Simmons. On a 2015 television program, Simmons claimed that in 2009 Jesus Christ visited him in his room, breathed on him, and commissioned him to write a new translation of the Bible.[2]

Simmons claims that, by blowing on him, Jesus gave him "the spirit of revelation" and would give him "secrets of the Hebrew language." He says, "I felt downloads coming, instantly. . . . It was like, I got a chip put inside of me. I got a connection inside of me to hear Him better, to understand the Scriptures better, and hopefully to translate."

The result of this heavenly visitation is Simmons's Passion Translation of the Bible. He claims that it "unlocks the passion of God's heart and expresses his fiery love" for people in a way that no other Bible translation does.[3] But not everyone agrees with his glowing description of his new translation. Critics say it distorts Scripture and is spiritually dangerous and deceptive. It has so many hazards that one highly respected scholar suggested that it should come with a surgeon general's warning.[4]

Despite warnings against its use, The Passion Translation has become a bestseller. Popular pastors have praised it—including Bill Johnson, Bobbie Houston (who, until recently, was the co-global senior pastor of Hillsong Church in Australia), and Banning Liebscher (founder and pastor of Jesus Culture). Johnson, who sometimes preaches from The Passion Translation, gushes that it's "one of the greatest things to happen with Bible translation" in his lifetime.[5] Bethel Church even has its own 2020 Bethel Edition of the translation with a special foreword contributed by the celebrated pastor.

Apart from an unusual story about its origins, what's wrong with Simmons's so-called "Bible"? Here are three reasons you should steer clear of The Passion Translation.

Reason No. 1: Simmons's Lack of Qualifications

Simmons is not qualified to produce a reliable translation of the Bible. Why do we say this?

First, every major translation of the Bible—such as the New International Version, the New King James Version, the English Standard Version, or the Christian Standard Bible—begins with a team of seasoned scholars assembled for the task. It is never made by one man flying solo, as Simmons has.

Why is this important? Because translation scholars work in teams, it is unlikely that the pet theology of one person will find its way into a translation. Collaboration among scholars from diverse backgrounds reduces the odds that biases and blunders will creep in. It's a matter of deliberate accountability and the pooling of refined expertise. Although Simmons claims that respected scholars and editors evaluate all of his translation work, for years he scrupulously avoided naming those individuals.[6] So he wanted all to believe that his translation had passed inspection by recognized experts in Bible translation, but he didn't want anyone to know who the experts were. After Simmons faced criticism for refusing to reveal the identify of his editors, in 2018 his publisher, BroadStreet, finally did hire several translation consultants to review his work. But the value of the consultants' role remains an open question. Two of those consultants have stated that they merely provided comments and feedback to Simmons, that they had no say in whether or not he adopted their suggestions, and that, in the end, the translation is Simmons's work. And despite the hiring of consultants, The Passion Translation remains rife with problems, as we'll show below. So it appears that the (very late) decision to bring in consultants was more about the optics. The Passion Translation continues to be, essentially, a one-man translation.[7]

Second, legitimate Bible translators have proven expertise in the biblical languages (Hebrew, Greek, and Aramaic). Simmons, however, has no such expertise. He acknowledges this.[8] So what are his credentials?

He uses the title "Dr." before his name, but his diploma was not awarded by an accredited academic institution. Simmons received his title from the non-accredited Wagner University—a NAR organization that offers courses in subjects like spiritual warfare, healing, and dream interpretation, but nothing in the biblical languages and Bible translation.

Simmons did work with New Tribes Mission in the jungles of Central America.[9] He claims that he assisted with New Tribes's translation of the Paya-Kuna New Testament. He has said that his work as a translator with New Tribes qualifies him to make The Passion Translation. But multiple people working with that organization during the same time period dispute his claims. They say he worked as a church planter, not as a Bible translator, and that no one in New Tribes ever approved him to work as a translator. And they report that the Paya-Kuna translation was not completed while he was working with the organization. This conflicts with his assertions made in early interviews promoting The Passion Translation. His version of events is at odds with his colleagues', who say they do not consider his Passion Translation to be a true translation and they caution people away from it.[10]

Heavenly Qualifications

Simmons's lack of traditional credentials does not concern him. His "qualifications" are not academic, they're supernatural. As already noted, he claims he was visited personally by Jesus, who commissioned him to make this new Bible. In addition, he says that an angel named "Passion" accompanies him in his ministry and empowers his work. (His translation is named after this ministry partner.[11])

If you know anything about the history of the Church of Jesus Christ of Latter-day Saints (formerly known as Mormons), you may be picking up on something familiar: Simmons's claims sound eerily similar to those of Joseph Smith, that cult's founder. Smith claimed that he translated the Book of Mormon from golden plates inscribed with so-called "Reformed Egyptian" hieroglyphics (scholars note that no such language as Reformed Egyptian ever existed). Enabling Smith to translate the plates were special stones shown to him by an angel named Moroni. Simmons's fanciful tales are no more credible than Joseph Smith's.

If his heavenly "qualifications" are for real, you would think that Bible scholars examining Simmons's work would be impressed by his incredible insights into the biblical languages. Yet they're far from impressed. A number of reputable Bible scholars have found many problems with Simmons's "Bible" and have sounded the alarm. Among them are Tremper Longman, Nijay Gupta, Douglas Moo, Darrell Bock, Brad Bitner, Alex Hewitson, and Craig Blomberg—a team that pastor and YouTuber Mike Winger commissioned to evaluate Simmons's "translation." What they found did not wow them; it disturbed them.

Mythical Manuscripts

Simmons claims that he has produced his Bible using original Aramaic manuscripts.[12] But scholars know of no such manuscripts. There simply are no *original Aramaic manuscripts*! Except for a few brief Aramaic sections, the Old Testament was written in Hebrew, and the New Testament (apart from a handful of expressions quoting Jesus in the Gospels) was written in Greek.

Simmons is undeterred. When speaking before a live audience, he asserted that scholars had recently made a stunning discovery: virtually all the New Testament was originally written in Aramaic, not in Greek. According to him, "it's been proven that the Greek manuscripts are second-gen copies of the original Aramaic New Testament." This purported discovery has caused all the scholars "to freak out and go back to the trash can, into the dusty corners of their libraries, and pull out all the Aramaic manuscripts and realize that they had thrown away the originals," says Simmons.[13]

Let us pause for a moment and consider. If this discovery were for real, it certainly would be earth-shaking. If the New Testament originally was written in Aramaic, not Greek, then a new translation of the New Testament, based on the original Aramaic manuscripts, absolutely would be called for. Who knows what revolutionary discoveries might emerge, how many translation improvements might be made?

There's just one problem. Contrary to Simmons's claim, no original Aramaic New Testament has been uncovered. Scholars are frankly baffled by Simmons's blunder. Craig Blomberg—a professor of New Testament at Denver Seminary—finds it "astonishing." He says, "There are no Aramaic originals for anybody to consult, anywhere, from the ancient centuries." Blomberg participates in multiple professional conferences each year—including meetings of the Society of Biblical Literature, the Society of New Testament Studies, and the Evangelical Theological Society. These are gatherings of the top several thousand biblical scholars in the world. Despite their widely varying perspectives and theological backgrounds, he says, these scholars "would rise up as one person and say, 'This simply is not true. This is made up. No one has discovered ancient Aramaic New Testaments.'"[14]

Such befuddlement leads us to ask: What Aramaic source did Simmons use to translate The Passion Translation if no original Aramaic manuscripts are known to exist? Some of Simmons's critics have guessed that the Aramaic source he has consulted is the Peshitta, which was written in Syriac, a dialect that is similar to ancient Aramaic. And they have guessed right: though they apparently were not aware of it, Simmons states on The Passion Translation website that the Syriac Peshitta is his Aramaic source![15] But the Peshitta is nothing close to an original Aramaic New

Testament. It was not composed until the third or fourth century—hundreds of years after the time of Christ and the composition of the New Testament in Greek—*and* it is known to have been translated from Greek manuscripts.

This is a big problem for Simmons's translation. Responsible Bible translation demands exacting use of the best manuscripts available. Since the original documents themselves have perished, translations must be made from the best copies we have. These copies should be as close in time as possible to the original documents of the Bible, and in the same language as the original documents. Aramaic was not the original language of the New Testament. The Peshitta is itself a translation, and an inferior one at that. And it dates three centuries later than the original manuscripts. Translating from the Aramaic is not the exciting new key to state-of-the-art Bible translation that Simmons would have you believe; on the contrary, his dependence on the Aramaic is rightly denoted by one highly regarded scholar as The Passion Translation's "fatal flaw."[16]

Brian Simmons's claim is a flat-out deception. There are no such manuscripts as the ones he says used in translation. He implies that his Passion Translation more purely conveys God's Word than other Bible translations, but the notion that his creation conveys God's Word more accurately than other translations is far from the truth, as we'll now show.

Reason No. 2: Adding to God's Word

The Passion Translation is supposed to be exactly that—a translation. Simmons is adamant that his Bible is not a mere paraphrase, like The Message. Rather, it is a bona fide translation, like the New International Version or the New King James Version. He states on The Passion Translation website that it "is an excellent translation you can use as your primary text to seriously study God's Word."[17] Not so.

It is not truly a translation because it does not faithfully preserve the message of the Bible's authors. Throughout his "translation," Simmons has freely sprinkled words, phrases, sentences, and concepts that are not found in the Hebrew and Greek manuscripts.[18] Sometimes words are omitted. All of these changes make the Bible say what he wants it to say, not what it does say. It has become the Word of Simmons, not the Word of God.

Here are two examples.[19] In these examples, we show how three of the major Bible translations have translated a verse and then we show how Simmons has translated that same verse. See if you can spot which one is from The Passion Translation.

Ephesians 3:20

- "Now to him who is able to do immeasurably more than all we ask or imagine, according to his power that is at work within us."
- "Now to him who is able to do far more abundantly than all that we ask or think, according to the power at work within us."
- "Now to Him who is able to do exceedingly abundantly above all that we ask or think, according to the power that works in us."
- "*Never doubt* God's mighty power to work in you and accomplish all this. He will achieve infinitely more than your greatest request, your most unbelievable dream, and exceed your wildest imagination! He will outdo them all, for his miraculous power constantly energizes you."

Could you spot The Passion Translation? Pretty easy, huh? The first translation is the New International Version (NIV), then the English Standard Version (ESV), then the New King James Version (NKJV); the fourth is The Passion Translation.

One thing you probably noticed is that Simmons's rendering adds a lot of new content. His additions don't come close to accurately reflecting what the apostle Paul wrote to the Christians at Ephesus. Instead of its essential focus on God and His greatness, on His worthiness of our worship, it's all about us. The passage, in truth, alludes to what God is able to do (not what He promises to do for just anyone who happens to read the letter). New Testament scholar Darrell Bock corrects Simmons's faulty rendering, saying, "This [verse] is not about our dreams and expectations, but about what God is capable of in relationship to his will through us."[20] Simmons has crafted a Bible that would gladden the heart of a narcissist, while slighting the sovereign exercise of God's will through us.

Notice how Simmons insinuates with this verse that God intends to empower us to work miracles. As Bock points out, Paul's main point here is not about miracles at all. It is about God's power that enables us to walk in His will, as the next three chapters of Ephesians explain.[21]

Romans 8:14

- "The mature children of God are those who are moved by the impulses of the Holy Spirit."
- "For those who are led by the Spirit of God are the children of God."
- "For all who are led by the Spirit of God are sons of God."

- "For as many as are led by the Spirit of God, these are sons of God.

This time, The Passion Translation comes first, followed by the NIV, the ESV, and the NKJV. What's the difference? Simmons has added the adjective "mature" before the phrase "children of God" or "sons of God." And this single word changes the verse's entire meaning.

The original verse teaches that *all* who are led by God's Spirit are children of God. It's a wonderful promise assuring all believers that they are a part of the family of God and have eternal life. But Simmons's decision to insert "mature" has turned this promise given to all believers into a promise for an elite few who have attained a certain level of spiritual development. New Testament scholar Douglas Moo strongly objects to Simmons's rendering. "Paul's promise is for every Christian, however mature they might be."[22]

The idea that certain Christians—specifically, those who follow present-day "apostles" and "prophets"—are more enlightened than other Christians is an implication of NAR teaching. So it is not surprising that such a notion would make its way into Simmons's Bible. He is, after all, a NAR apostle.

In addition, notice that where the other translations say "led by the Spirit," The Passion Translation interprets this as "impulses of the Holy Spirit," implying a specific view of the Spirit's guidance that is not obviously taught.

As we'll show next, several other NAR notions have been smuggled into The Passion Translation.

Reason No. 3: A Hidden (NAR) Agenda

Throughout his translation, Simmons has made changes that misleadingly make it appear that the Bible supports NAR teachings and practices. We note that when he has been caught smuggling in these teachings, he has simply released updated editions of his translation and quietly removed many of them—as if he had never tried to sneak them in. Here are three examples of verses where he has attempted to slip in NAR teachings.

Matthew 10:2

- "These are the names of the twelve apostles: first, Simon (who is called Peter) and his brother Andrew; James son of Zebedee, and his brother John."
- "The names of the twelve apostles are these: first, Simon, who is called Peter, and Andrew his brother; James the son of Zebedee, and John his brother."
- "Now the names of the twelve apostles are these: first, Simon, who is called Peter, and Andrew his brother; James the son of Zebedee, and John his brother."
- "Now, these are the names of the first twelve apostles: first, Simon, who is nicknamed Peter, and Andrew, his brother. And then Jacob and John, sons of Zebedee."

Here The Passion Translation comes last again. Take note of how Simmons has added the word "first" before the word "twelve," even though "first" does not appear in the Greek manuscripts. Why do this? Clearly this move implies that there is biblical authority for claiming that there are other apostles. In fact, he and any other present-day apostle could, on the basis of this verse, declare that the class of authoritative apostles is not limited to those whom Jesus selected when He walked the earth. And Simmons certainly has motive: since he claims to be an authoritative apostle, he wants people to believe that there are, indeed, authoritative apostles who are alive today.

Once critics pointed out that he had added "first," Simmons removed that word, without drawing attention to this change or explaining why he made it. That verse, in his updated 2020 edition of The Passion Translation, now reads similarly to the other major translations. But the damage remains since many people bought The Passion Translation prior to his updated version and, thus, still read this verse as he originally rendered it. In addition, this is a revision of a translation that is supposed to be more reliable. No reputable translation has to be repeatedly revised.

1 Corinthians 12:7

- "Now to each one the manifestation of the Spirit is given for the common good."
- "Each believer is given continuous revelation by the Holy Spirit to benefit not just himself but all."
- "To each is given the manifestation of the Spirit for the common good."
- "But the manifestation of the Spirit is given to each one for the profit of all."

This time, The Passion Translation comes second. Did you spot the difference? It's obvious, right? This verse teaches that the Holy Spirit empowers believers with different spiritual gifts to serve the church. But you can see that Simmons—by willy-nilly changing the word "manifestation" to "continuous revelation"—twists what the verse is about and makes it promote a NAR teaching: that the Holy Spirit is giving new revelation to every Christian and, moreover, that He is doing this continually. Yet this verse says no such thing!

Professor Craig Blomberg points out multiple problems created by Simmons's mistranslation of this verse. For example, he notes that "instead of the Spirit distributing his gifts to believers as he sees fit"—which the verse teaches—"The Passion Translation insists that 'each believer is given continuous revelation.'"[23] He also states that—even if the verse does refer to some type of "spiritual illumination" or prophetic gift—"it still does not provide a promise of anything constant." And he adds that many gifts of the Spirit—such as giving, helping, administration, and faith—"really don't have anything to do with revelation at all."

John 14:12

- "'Very truly I tell you, whoever believes in me will do the works I have been doing, and they will do even greater things than these, because I am going to the Father.'"
- "'Truly, truly, I say to you, whoever believes in me will also do the works that I do; and greater works than these will he do, because I am going to the Father.'"
- "'Most assuredly, I say to you, he who believes in Me, the works that I do he will do also; and greater works than these he will do, because I go to My Father.'"
- "'I tell you this timeless truth: The person who follows me in faith, believing in me, will do the same mighty miracles that I do—even greater miracles than these because I go to be with my Father!'"

In this verse—again, fourth in the list—Simmons sneaks in the NAR teaching that all Jesus's followers can work the same miracles that Jesus did—and even more amazing miracles than Jesus did. This astonishing teaching is promoted by today's "apostles," such as Bill Johnson, who teach that Jesus's words in John 14:12 are a promise of miracle-working power for the followers of today's apostles and prophets. How convenient now to have a "translation" that actually says this in no uncertain terms!

Yet most Bible scholars do not believe that Jesus's promise is primarily about miracles.[24] That's because the Greek word Jesus used in this verse is *erga*, meaning "works," not "miracles." Jesus made this promise during His last supper with His disciples (it is part of the "Upper Room Discourse"). When He promised that they would do "greater works" than He did, He was not promising that they would work more spectacular miracles than He did. That understanding of His promise makes little sense, since no miracle could possibly be more spectacular than calming storms, giving sight to the blind, and raising the dead.

No, Jesus was promising them that their works—which may include miracles but would most certainly encompass evangelism and acts of service—would be greater in that they occur after Jesus's death and resurrection and bear unprecedented fruit, both in type and quantity. That explains the import of Jesus's words "because I am going to the Father." In other words, their works would communicate the message of the gospel in a fuller way than would have been possible before Jesus died on the cross, rose from the grave, and ascended into heaven. As New Testament scholar D. A. Carson says, "Both Jesus's words and his deeds were somewhat veiled during the days of his flesh; even his closest followers . . . grasped only part of what he was saying." But that was about to change, since very soon his followers would "know and make known all that Jesus is and does."[25]

Their immense work is seen in the foundation of the church of Jesus Christ, beginning with the work that Peter did on the Day of Pentecost in drawing many thousands to resurrection faith (Acts 2). With Christ Jesus Himself as the cornerstone, the apostles and biblical prophets laid the foundation upon which Christ has built His church (see Eph. 2:19–22). Their work was a literal extension of the work of Jesus their Master (see John 17 for details).

Simmons replaces the accurate English word "works" with "miracles." He also inserts the word "mighty" (though it cannot be found in the Greek manuscripts). In this way, he misleads his readers and insinuates that they can perform mightier miracles than Jesus did—thereby performing a mighty service to teachers at the Bethel School of Supernatural Ministry who use The Passion Translation.

New, But Definitely Not Improved

Brian Simmons presents his translation as a serious translation for serious study of the Bible. But it's clear that The Passion Translation is not a "translation" at all. Nor is it even a satisfactory paraphrase, since so many of the changes Simmons has made radically alter the meaning of Scripture and support his own interpretations and NAR beliefs. Altering Scripture to suit ourselves is dangerous business. Scripture contains stern warnings about adding to, or tampering with, God's Word (Deut. 4:2; Prov. 30:6; Rev. 22:18–19).

Simmons wants us to believe that all other Bible translations are inferior to his. But we are blessed today to have many trustworthy translations of the Bible produced by teams of qualified translators.[26] Thus, we have no need for a new "translation" of the Bible produced by a lone man with fantastical stories and mythical manuscripts.

CHAPTER 8

Toxic Worship Music

*Music bypasses all of the intellectual barriers,
and when the anointing of God is on a
song, people will begin to believe things
they wouldn't believe through teaching.*
—The "apostle" Bill Johnson

One main way that NAR has gained entrance into churches is through its music. Turn on any Christian radio station or open a popular playlist, and you will almost surely hear songs by Bethel Music, Jesus Culture, Hillsong Music, Forerunner Music, or Gateway Worship. These wildly popular music labels all hail from large and influential churches that are either overtly NAR or exhibit significant NAR influence.[1] In addition, other music labels created by non-NAR churches, such as Elevation Worship, also show signs of NAR influence. These groups' music is among the most used in worship services throughout the world, but especially in America and Australia.

Music is a means of worship. Music reinforces beliefs. And music prepares us for action. Lyrics, rhythm, and beat all contribute to the effect that music has in our lives. Heartfelt song expresses our outlook on life, the things we believe, our expectations and emotions. Music inclines us to be receptive or unreceptive to certain messages. Our experience of God is conditioned by the songs we sing.

The songs Christians sing, especially in church services, are powerful. They aren't just words on your lips, they express beliefs that penetrate your heart. Many people go home after a service and keep singing the songs long after they've forgotten the pastor's message. Like it or not, belief is woven into hearts through music. Contemporary Christian music is the catechism of today's evangelical church. So we must always ask what message is being conveyed by a song's lyrics.

> Contemporary Christian music is the catechism of today's evangelical church.

Striking a Chord

We believe NAR music is a trojan horse for the NAR movement. We will demonstrate some of the dangers of this music, and alert you especially to the presence of harmful teachings in popular worship songs. And we will suggest ways you can respond to its growing and destructive influence.

Bethel Music's Popularity

Many of the songs sung in American churches are produced by Bethel Music, songs like "Reckless Love," "Raise a Hallelujah," and "We Will Not Be Shaken." And at home and in their cars, many Christians are singing and humming along to Bethel tunes. According to Bethel Church's 2019–2020 annual report, Bethel songs were streamed on Spotify more than 249 million times that year.[2] These songs frequently top the Christian music charts. Given their popularity, it's no surprise that Bethel Music has racked up several awards and nominations. Clearly, its music is resonating with people. But why?

"I Wanna Feel Something"

One of the most common things fans say about Bethel Music is that it makes them feel closer to God. It moves them emotionally in a way that other Christian music simply doesn't.

One Amazon reviewer of the album *Be Lifted High* writes: "When I started playing it, the presence of God was so strong in my little studio that I broke down into tears." Another, regarding *You Make Me Brave*, raves: "This album has been rockin' my world for the last three weeks. . . . Such depth to the lyrics, I can't describe."

Other reviews of NAR-influenced songs and records include such phrases as, "I was in a lot of darkness and this song pulled that away and brought in life," "Amazing music for those who are looking for something deeper," and "If you want to know the sound of Love, of Heaven, and Jesus, you'll need to listen to this album!" When is the last time you heard such gushing descriptions about the non-NAR songs and hymns sung in churches? Not lately, huh?

The music from Bethel and other NAR churches is seen as coming straight from "the throne room" of heaven.[3] Many of those who listen to it believe the lyrics are "prophetic," that they communicate new revelation from God that the global church needs in that moment. Marketing the music as prophetic helps sales too, since listeners do not want to miss out on the latest revelation.

Captivating Young Adults

Young adults are especially drawn to NAR music. Bethel Music concerts are packed out with youthful fans in their twenties and thirties—mirroring the ages of the Bethel singers on stage. And many parents and church leaders are more than happy to fan these flames, because they've seen far too many Christian young people turn away from the faith. According to a 2014 Barna poll, "Fifty-nine percent of Millennials who grew up in the church have dropped out at some point." And a 2018 poll revealed that "the percentage of Gen Z that identifies as atheist is *double* that of the U.S. adult population."[4] These statistics have parents and pastors running scared and feeling desperate. So when young people are drawn to Christian music of any kind—as long as it is not outright heretical—it's a relief. They're naturally pleased as punch to have Bethel Music used in their churches.

The Dangers of Bethel/NAR Music

NAR music may seem harmless. But there are some real dangers. Here are three.

Danger No. 1: Their Music Smuggles in NAR Theology

Sketchy NAR teachings have been smuggled into many popular worship songs. Here we sample several, highlighting key phrases for analysis. Because this is copyrighted material, we do not provide the full lyrics for these songs. Most of these songs appear in full in various places online, and we encourage you to consult those for the full context.

Our first example is from the Bethel Music song "Be Lifted High." It speaks of our generation as the one that will be "calling down the reign of Heaven." What's the NAR teaching promoted here? At first glance, you may not notice anything wrong with the lyrics. Aren't we supposed to long for God's kingdom to come to earth? Isn't that what Jesus taught His disciples to pray for when He taught them the Lord's Prayer (Matt. 6:9–13; Luke 11:2–4)?

Yes, but also, no. Yes, Jesus did teach His disciples to pray for God's kingdom to come. But, no, He did not teach that Christians will bring God's physical kingdom to earth prior to His return.

And the choice of the words "calling down" is not coincidental. They are buzzwords—or words used by NAR insiders—to allude to another specific NAR teaching. That is the teaching that God has given believers the authority to miraculously bring things into existence (that is, "call [them] down"). They do this through their spoken words or "prayer declarations."

Once you recognize these NAR teachings about bringing God's kingdom to earth through prayer declarations, you will start noticing them in more songs. In fact, Bethel Music and other NAR songs are viewed by their producers as "prayer declarations," and they are explicitly described as being declarations in Bethel Music's advertisements.[5] So the very act of singing these songs is seen as making prayer declarations that bring new realities into existence. But the view that singing a song is making a prayer declaration is very different from the standard Christian view of worship. Do you realize, if you sing along with Bethel Music, that Bethel Church sees you as partnering with them to alter reality by adding your voice to their declarations?

In the Bethel Music song, "Champion," we see the teaching that Christians have been given the authority to work miracles by making prayer declarations. Just open your mouth and "miracles start breaking out." What you have here is a specific view of God's kingdom manifest on earth. It will allegedly be marked by a far greater number of supernatural events or miracles. It will be brought about through the spoken words of believers. It will happen during this generation. And you can be a player in the action, if you recognize your authority and act on it. Consider what you're supposed to believe, how it makes you feel, and what you should be prepared to do and expect as you sing these words together with those surrounding you.

Another song, "One Thirst," written by former Bethel Music leader Jeremy Riddle and featured on the Bethel Music album *Be Lifted High*, prays that God would "Anoint us for the greater things." What's the NAR teaching promoted in this song? Notice the definite article: "*the* greater things." Something very specific is being referred to. "Greater things" is another NAR buzzphrase. This one references the NAR teaching that all Christians can work greater miracles than Jesus did. Yet how many Christians, when singing this song, realize they are asking God to give them the ability to work more amazing miracles than Jesus did? Would they be so quick to sing along if they knew what they were saying? As you're being seated after singing this song, you might try asking your neighbor, "What are some of the greater miracles you hope to do with your anointing now?" Listen hard for something greater than the miracles that Jesus did.

What NAR teaching is promoted in the Bethel song "Too Good Not to Believe"? In this case, it's not so much an overt teaching as it is an unbalanced emphasis on miracles. This song makes it seem as if miracles—such as healings from cancer, resurrections of the dead, and the disappearance of metal plates that hold broken bones together—occur regularly and should be expected as routine. What's more, these healings are presented as evidence of God's love for someone. And not expecting a miracle is presented as a lack of faith that is worthy of a rebuke: "Don't you tell me He can't do it."

In response, we heartily affirm that God can perform miracles whenever He chooses. But even in Scripture (including the book of Acts), miracles are remarkable for being infrequent, and they never seem to be within the ability of every true believer to perform. Nor are they ever guaranteed. God could love someone and decide, in His own wisdom and for His own reasons, not to heal them of a sickness or disease. But you would not get that idea from this song.

Worship songs should instill a deep faith in God even when He decides not to work a miracle. You may feel closer to God if you think you have His anointing to work miracles, but experiencing the power of God's love in the midst of unrelieved pain and suffering is of far greater value.

Again, the song "This Is a Move," co-written by Bethel musician Brandon Lake, suggests that miracles are happening all the time, including, shockingly, the raising of people from the dead. You may wonder, *Where are all these alleged resurrections occurring?* The song doesn't say. But if you pay attention to many of today's worship songs, you will find that modern-day resurrections are a common theme. This is not to say that witnessing the resurrection of someone today would not be faith-building; but many now depend on an endless stream of contemporary miracles for vibrant faith and hope. In making these alleged modern-day resurrections the focus, the songs direct our focus away from the historical resurrection of Christ, which should be the basis for our faith and hope, regardless of the disappointments we face (see 1 Corinthians 15).[6]

Another NAR buzzphrase that is found in many songs is "open heaven." In NAR, the concept of being "under an open heaven" refers to a moment in time when God is supposedly making His presence tangible in a church, city, or nation. He makes His presence known by speaking to people in dreams and visions and giving them new revelations. An open heaven can also result in visitations from angels, healings, and other miraculous signs and wonders (such as the so-called "glory cloud" that appeared at Bethel).[7] We see this expressed in Hillsong's "Open Heaven (River Wild)." Other songs that reference an "open heaven" include Bethel's "Deep Cries Out" and Jesus Culture's "Revival."

The lyrics of Forerunner Music's "You Won't Relent," coauthored by Misty Edwards, are taken from Song of Solomon 8:6–7. This song characterizes the relationship between Jesus and individual Christians as romantic and sensuous, based on a bizarre interpretation of the Song of Solomon. The idea that the Song of Solomon—a poetic book in the Bible that is about the love between a husband and his wife—is actually an allegory about Jesus's relationship with the individual Christian is taught by many NAR leaders—including Mike Bickle (of the International House of Prayer in Kansas City, home to the Forerunner Music label). In fact, Bickle claims that in 1988 God spoke audibly to the "prophet" Bob Jones and told him to instruct Bickle to make the message of those two verses the focus of his entire life ministry.[8] And Bickle believes the Lord is giving that same message of Jesus's "fiery love" for believers as a message for the global church.[9] His promotion of this teaching led him to help organize the enactment of a massive "wedding" ceremony. In 2002, 20,000 mostly young people gathered in the Kansas City Convention Center on New Year's Eve for an event titled The Call. "From noon until midnight they danced and sang, fasted and prayed, and got ready to get married to Jesus," according to a news report.[10] It is true that Christ loves us, but it is inaccurate to describe Him as our lover. Viewing His love for us as romantic in nature can result in some very odd notions and a fickle faith that relies too heavily on emotions and experience.[11]

The fact that music contains NAR theology is not accidental. It's by design. Bill Johnson says that he has instructed the musicians at his church to think about what they'd like the church to look like in five years—what beliefs they want Christians to hold—and then write songs incorporating that specific theology so that people could "sing [their] way into it."[12]

Danger No. 2: Their Music Draws People to NAR

Many people may hear a song by Bethel Music and experience emotions they have not experienced while listening to other Christian music. When they discover that Bethel is behind the music, they're drawn to Bethel Church. Before long, they're following Bethel on Instagram, buying books written by Bill Johnson, and signing up to attend a Bethel conference in Redding. In this way, Bethel Music is a "gateway drug" to the New Apostolic Reformation. People experience the Bethel "high" and must have more.

Keep in mind that the music makes it seem that miracles are happening all the time. Yet few Christians have actually witnessed miracles on such a scale. Since the reality of what is described in the music is not matched by their own experience, it is natural for them to seek out a place where they believe revelations are received and miracles are frequent. If they look around and none of the churches they know of are experiencing miracles, why wouldn't they consider making the trek to Bethel where the action is?

Consider the words of one woman, who identified herself online as "Katiejoy." The church's music got its hooks so deeply into her that it caused her to pack up her entire life and relocate. She reported: "Bethel Music drew me to Bethel. In fact, I moved to Redding, mesmerized by the passion and beauty of its music."[13] Another woman, "RachelleL," wrote a review on Amazon, urging people to buy a specific Bethel Music album (*Be Lifted High*) and telling them, if they liked what they hear, to be sure to get connected with a Bethel-type church.

> Get this and then tell everyone you know to do
> the same. If you want more, visit ibethel.org or
> . . . ibethel.tv to watch their services and music
> live. Then find a place where you can connect
> with the same spirit of God. If you don't live
> in Redding, CA check out some of their other
> churches in Global Legacy [Bethel's network].[14]

No one should be surprised that Bethel Music attracts people to Bethel Church. Bethel's own leaders state openly that they view their music as a tool to "plant" Bethel Church's teachings and practices in other churches throughout the world. Bill Johnson's own words reveal that this is their goal:

> We're exporters, I don't ever want to change
> that. . . . Let's get a model that can be duplicated
> anywhere in the world. . . . And let's take it some-
> where. And let's plant it. Let's plant it through
> Jesus Culture, let's plant it through the music we
> write. Let's plant it through the conferences that
> we do.[15]

Both Jesus Culture (which was founded at Bethel Church in 1999) and Bethel Music are a deliberate means to an end—spreading their NAR teachings.[16]

Johnson's statement undermines one of the most common defenses made by pastors and worship leaders who allow Bethel Music to be used in their churches. They say they are fine using the music from NAR churches (even though they may disagree with those churches' theology) as a long as the lyrics are sound. In other words, they believe the source of the music doesn't matter. They point out that no church or songwriter has perfect theology (which is true, but there is a big difference between expecting a church to have *perfect* theology vs. expecting them not to promote harmful and dangerous teachings). Ironically, those same pastors would probably never allow their churches to use music from a controversial church like Westboro Baptist Church in Topeka, Kansas. They (rightfully) would not want to look like they are promoting the hateful rhetoric spouted by that church. So, though they say the source of a song doesn't matter, it's doubtful that they truly believe that.

When churches that are otherwise sound use NAR music, the leaders are giving an implied pass to the churches that produce that music. Whether intentionally or not, they are communicating that Bethel or Jesus Culture or the International House of Prayer are okay churches, even good and admirable churches. Their song selection legitimizes those churches in the eyes of their people, putting them at risk of getting caught in spiritual bondage to NAR apostles and prophets. And support for Bethel Music undercuts any meaningful effort to cross-examine the theology and practices of Bethel Church and its leaders. Even songs that are innocent in themselves can be dangerous when an agenda lies behind them.[17]

Danger No. 3: Their Music Divorces the Heart from the Head

Carefully crafted music is emotionally powerful, and it can therefore be quite seductive. It has a way of bypassing a person's head and going straight to their heart.

Maybe you're like us and you've caught yourself singing along to a song with lyrics you don't agree with—and with content you find morally objectionable—because the tune is catchy, the singer's voice exudes passion, and you aren't paying much attention. You've just been "feeling the music." It can be a bit jarring, even embarrassing, to realize that you've been heedlessly paying tribute to some pagan sentiment or lustful impulse. To paraphrase an actual song, "How can it be so wrong when it feels so right?"

Likewise, many love the way NAR music makes them *feel*. Emotions are forefront. The focus is on experiencing and encountering God apart from rational thought. And music is an ideal vehicle for subverting thoughtful engagement with a message. Bill Johnson believes that this capacity of music, when used in worship songs, should be exploited, saying, "Music bypasses all of the intellectual barriers, and when the anointing of God is on a song, people will begin to believe things they wouldn't believe through teaching."[18]

His words give insight into how he views Bethel Music: as a mechanism for getting people to accept teachings they would not normally be inclined to accept. But he reverses the proper order of things. Truth should come first, with emotions following. Johnson puts the cars ahead of the engine, and that can only lead to a train wreck.

It is risky business singing along mindlessly to Bethel songs, or any other worship songs, simply because we find the music tantalizing or emotionally and spiritually moving. When our emotions are running wild and our mental barriers are down, all kinds of half-baked or dead wrong ideas can sneak by and lodge themselves in our minds. Divorcing the heart from the mind is dangerous. It leads to a feeble faith and makes us vulnerable to deception. NAR buzzwords may have a nice ring to them, especially when accompanied by snazzy melodies. But the doctrines they stand for are poison in the bloodstream of church life. You can be sure that if the message of a lyric is false, it does not have the anointing of

You can't test the truth of the message with your feelings.

God on it. And you can't test the truth of the message with your feelings.

We are not knocking heartfelt worship, but Jesus said that God is to be worshipped "in spirit and *truth*" (John 4:23–24).[19] And what does *truth* have to do with worship? At the very least it means that the song must express the truth, and the feelings it draws out must be anchored in the truth. In addition, when you sing along, you "confess" that the words you are singing are true. That means the things you sing as a worshipper of God must be things you actually believe. It is not true worship if you are singing a message you don't agree with. The intellect must be working in concert with the heart.

To ensure that your worship is as true as it is heart-felt, we offer three suggestions. These suggestions will help you evaluate *all* worship music, not just the music produced by NAR churches.

1. Ask yourself these questions about the lyrics of a song: *Do I believe that what they are saying is true? What are my reasons for believing they are true? Are they consistent with Scripture? Or do I believe they're true simply because everyone singing around me, in a worship service, seems to believe they are true? And what are the lyrics telling me about how I should live my life or act? Are they encouraging me to live in a manner consistent with or contrary to the teachings of Scripture?*

2. If the lyrics seem true enough, you should ask some additional questions: *Are they profound? Do they express truths of special importance, or are they theologically weak, vague, and overly repetitive? Taken together, do the songs we sing*

highlight various aspects of God and Christian belief, or harp on the same few subjects over and over (such as miracles, miracles, and more miracles)? To help you answer these questions, compare the words of a popular NAR tune with a theologically rich and long-treasured hymn that has stood the test of time. Or read the Bible's songbook, the Book of Psalms (most of which was composed by King David). The paltry lyrics of so many of today's songs reflect the paltry theology of the songwriters.

3. Pay attention to how the lyrics are "packaged" by the beat, the melody, the fog machines, the singers and the way they dress (and otherwise present themselves) on stage, and so forth. It is important to pay attention to the non-lyrical aspects because you may find that you're responding emotionally to a song because of how it is packaged, not because of the truth of the actual lyrics. One way to determine whether the lyrics have merit on their own, apart from the external trappings, is to read them online without listening to the music. When you look closely at the lyrics of a song you like the sound of, you may find that they are theological fluff and that you're disappointed by their lack of doctrinal depth. In fact, you may discover that they have very little rational content— that they actually don't say much of anything. They may be merely expressive of the songwriter's feelings. As you investigate the

repertoire of "Christian music," you might be pleasantly surprised to discover much that is substantive and in alignment with the truth of Scripture. You shouldn't have to sacrifice production quality for the sake of truth in music, but production quality shouldn't be your first consideration.

Responding to NAR Music

Maybe you already had concerns about today's popular music. Knowing what you know now, how should you respond if the songs your church is using are questionable?

If you're wondering, you're not alone. Some of the most frequent questions we receive, during interviews and in e-mails from our readers, are *Is it okay for my church to use Bethel Music? What should I do if my church is using Bethel Music? How do I share my concerns about the music with my pastor?* Here are our answers to those questions along with some additional advice.

Is It Okay for Churches to Use NAR Music?

We advise churches to avoid using NAR music as a matter of practical wisdom and discernment. And they should be alert to the potential for NAR influence on any song, whether or not it is produced by a known NAR church. They should not allow anything in a worship service that will prime people to be more receptive to NAR teachings and will advance the NAR agenda.

When churches choose to use NAR songs, they reflect a basic principle of economics called "opportunity cost." This principle acknowledges the fact that making choices always comes at the cost of ruling out, or eliminating, other choices. Applied to churches, this means that, in those moments when a church is using theologically suspect and impoverished songs—or otherwise sound songs that might introduce people to a theologically suspect movement—they're not using other songs that would serve to build up their churches in solid, sound theology and in mature experience of God. And churches that use this music have, knowingly or not, approved of the songwriters as theologians for their churches.

Leaders should understand that NAR music may be a stumbling block to those who have come out of NAR churches and will feel drawn back in by the music (Mark 9:42) or be confused by the uncertain message of a church that denies NAR teaching but incorporates NAR music. And they should also keep in mind that some people in their churches will have embraced NAR beliefs, and that use of the music affirms them in those beliefs.

Additionally, leaders have an obligation to steward their church finances. Churches pay to use worship music. Those royalties—in the millions of dollars for labels such as Bethel Music—fund and fuel the spread of NAR teachings. The use of NAR music also creates an appetite for it among church members and attenders, leading to increased sales of albums and ticket sales for music events. Payment for worship music subsidizes the composers and producers and the organizations they work for. It promotes the complete package of teachings and practices associated with the label.

What Should I Do If My Church Is Using NAR Music?

Never feel obliged to sing along with a song in a church service or other group gathering, without first having a chance to determine if you agree with the song. You may feel less holy if you don't instantly join in with the crowd, but you're honoring God by being careful to ensure the truth of what you're singing. Don't make the mistake of assuming that because your church is using a song, it is necessarily biblically sound. The worship leaders who choose the songs are often young and a little short on theological training. You have the freedom not to sing at all if you are uncertain about the lyrics of a song or you disagree with them.

How Do I Share My Concerns about the Music with My Pastor?

We commend your desire to share your concerns with your church leadership. Of course, always do so respectfully. Most pastors are extremely busy, and it is difficult for them to keep up with every new group or movement that promotes poor theology. Many do not know what Bethel or other NAR churches teach, and they need to be educated about the dangers. Pastors will not be attuned to the use of NAR buzzwords in songs if they aren't familiar with the loaded messages conferred on those buzzwords by NAR doctrine. Be prepared to explain the NAR background to the phrases embedded in the music.

If you take your concerns to your worship leader, and you feel that he or she is dismissive of those concerns, you may want to consider sharing your concerns with the senior pastor or other theological stakeholders in the church, such as the elder board if your church has one. Perhaps others in your church will want to share their concerns, as well. The more people in your church who say something, the more those in leadership will know that this is a substantial concern.

If a church that is otherwise biblically sound uses a Bethel song or two, that is probably not cause for serious alarm and immediate departure from your church. But make a mental note and keep your eyes (and ears!) open for other developments. Music has proven to be a convenient foot in the door for NAR influence, so use of the music in your church should put you on alert for signs of additional influence.

Outside of the church, give attention to the music you listen to on a regular basis. Especially if you have children, expose them to some of the classic hymns and contemporary music with theologically strong lyrics. While there is no guarantee that a hymn's theology is completely sound, the hymns, in general, have a much more robust theology than so much of today's popular music. They have stood the test of time. And some of today's music groups do give careful attention to the theology of their songs. Expand your family's awareness of, and taste for, music besides the same songs played repeatedly on the radio or at the top of the charts.

You can also seek out music that puts Scripture to song. It has become popular today for some Christians to talk about "praying the Scriptures," by which they mean that Scripture serves as a model to guide their prayers. They do this so that their prayers align more with how God would want them to pray so that they do not focus on their own desires. Wouldn't it be wonderful if the idea of "singing the Scriptures" caught on?

Tuning Out NAR Music

Though NAR music has taken churches by storm, there have been some encouraging signs of pushback. A growing number of Christian leaders, aware of the dangers of Bethel/NAR music, have publicly spoken out against its use by churches. One pastor's sermon warning about Bethel Music was posted to YouTube and received several million views.[20] Recording artist and worship leader Mackenzie Morgan—of Refine Church in Lascassas, Tennessee—posted on Facebook about why she felt convicted to end her use of music from bands she believed to be theologically compromised. Her post went viral, receiving more than 10,000 shares, and her story was picked up by Christian news outlets, including the *Christian Post*.[21] People are waking up.

We pray this trend continues. When it comes to music, may churches become more discerning. May they recognize the dangers of NAR music, refuse its use, and replace it with biblically sound music!

CHAPTER 9

Is It Always God's Will to Heal?

And many followed him [Jesus],
and he healed them all.
—Matthew 12:15

The apostle Matthew wrote that, as Jesus traveled through the cities of Israel preaching and teaching, many followed Him, "and he healed them *all*."[1] How would you understand that statement if you were in NAR? You would understand it the same way Bill Johnson does, that "Jesus healed all who came to Him, no exceptions."[2] And, like Johnson, you'd take it a step further: the same Jesus who healed all who came to Him during His earthly life desires to do the same today—except now He does so through us.[3]

One of NAR's most controversial teachings is that it is *always* God's will to heal a person of sickness or disease. The goodness of God requires that it is always His will to heal. (This is one of the revelations God has supposedly given the church through today's "apostles" and "prophets.") Believing that to be true, thousands of people desperate for healing have made the trek to Redding, California, or to other "revival" hot spots. But they've returned home—sadly, as sick and suffering as ever.

The NAR teaching that it is God's will to heal everyone does vastly more harm than good.

Take the tragic case of Nabeel Qureshi. Nabeel had been a devout Muslim, but—after discovering evidence for Christ's resurrection and Jesus's claims to be God—he converted to Christianity. He wrote a book describing his dramatic transformation, the *New York Times* bestseller *Seeking Allah, Finding Jesus*. But in 2016, when he was just thirty-three years old, he was diagnosed with advanced stomach cancer. A devoted husband and father to a young daughter, he wanted desperately to live. So, at the urging of friends, he traveled to Bethel Church seeking healing. We know this because he talked about his visit to Bethel—and his hopes that he would find healing there—during a series of vlogs he uploaded to YouTube documenting his battle with cancer.[4]

During his visit to Bethel, about 1,700 people made "prayer declarations" for his healing at a service. "We thank you that he is even now being healed," declared a leader from the stage.[5] But sadly, less than a year later, Nabeel died of the devastating disease.

The failure for Nabeel to be healed at Bethel was damaging for the reputation of the church—though Bethel leaders never acknowledged this publicly and they still claim that people are being healed at the church all the time. You would think that if anybody were truly going to be healed at Bethel it certainly would have been Nabeel. Because of his status as a well-known author, people throughout the world were watching his YouTube updates, including many Muslims. If God healed Nabeel of cancer and extended his life, it would prove to his Muslim viewers the truth of Christianity—at least that was what some of his Christian friends thought. It would allow him to continue his powerful apologetics ministry. And it would prove the truth of NAR teachings about healing to those who are skeptical.

The reason so many know about Bethel's failure to heal Nabeel is that his battle with cancer played out in a very public way. But he is only one of many who expected a miracle through the Bethel healing ministry and were disappointed.

Jessica Miller was introduced to NAR teachings about healing during a vulnerable time in her life—when she was suffering from infertility. When she wasn't healed, she began to blame herself. Since it is always God's will to heal, she reasoned, she must be doing something wrong. "My emotions were a roller coaster as I sought to 'believe for a miracle' and was devastated month after month when my prayers went unanswered. God wanted to heal me, I was told. If the problem wasn't with him, perhaps it was with me? What was I doing wrong?"[6]

But Jessica didn't do anything wrong. Neither did Nabeel, or any other person who sought healing, believed for healing, was given hope for healing . . . and returned home without the expected miracle. What is wrong—what has caused so much discouragement and despair in the lives of people like Jessica—are the NAR teachings that it is always God's will to heal and that every believer can heal sick people, just as Jesus did.

But that's the thing: Jesus didn't always heal. Consider the townspeople of Capernaum in Luke 4. He healed scores of them, including Simon Peter's own mother-in-law, but eventually at daybreak He withdrew to a solitary place. The townspeople followed Him and begged Him to stay—to continue what He had been doing the day before. They tried to keep Him from leaving. He declined. "'I must preach the good news of the kingdom of God to the other towns as well; for I was sent for this purpose.' And he was preaching in the synagogues of Judea." Jesus was healing, yes—but then He stopped, withdrew, and declined the invitation to stay and continue healing. He had a gospel to preach, and He needed to move on to the next town. The sick people left in Capernaum who didn't get their healing the day before were most certainly disappointed. But that's how Jesus chose to handle the situation. He didn't remain and heal everyone in that town. And more than once, when He did heal someone, He commanded that person to keep the healing a secret, such as the leper whom He told, "See that you say nothing to anyone" (Mark 1:44). He did not want the word to get out about His miracles because the news would draw crowds clamoring for their own healing, hindering His ability to preach the gospel. And that's exactly what happened. In the leper's excitement, he could not keep quiet about what Jesus had done for him, "but he went out and began to talk freely about it, and to spread the news, so that Jesus could no longer openly enter a town, but was out in desolate places, and people were coming to him from every quarter" (Mark 1:45). He was swarmed by people seeking more healings—the very thing He had sought to avoid.

It is clear that Jesus did not always heal when greater purposes were at stake. Consider His own apostles. Most of them are believed to have died a martyr's death! Jesus did not supernaturally intervene, shield them from their enemies, or miraculously heal their wounds as their oppressors afflicted them. He not only permitted their death, He also did not raise them afterward as He did Lazarus. And Paul, also an apostle called by Jesus on the road to Damascus, asked for relief from his "thorn" (which many scholars believe was a physical ailment). Three times he prayed in faith. And yet the answer from heaven was no. The answer was "my grace is sufficient" (2 Cor. 12:9). The answer was that the thorn was there to keep him from becoming conceited. That thorn had a divine purpose, and God wasn't going to relieve Paul of it.

Likewise, the apostles did not heal every sick person they encountered. What do we see Paul instructing Timothy to do for his ongoing stomach ailment? Make prayer declarations? Engage in exercises to activate a gift of healing in himself? Seek greater and deeper "kingdom breakthrough"? No. Paul instructs Timothy to simply drink a common remedy used for gastrointestinal issues at that time—wine (1 Tim. 5:23). Paul, who had healed others (Acts 20:9–10; 28:8-9), did not heal Timothy.

NAR leaders conveniently overlook the biblical evidence that contradicts their teachings about healing.

Peculiar Healing Practices

Those NAR teachings have led to the profusion of several peculiar practices popping up in churches: healing rooms, "treasure hunts," Dead Raising Teams, and Sozo. In this chapter, you will learn about each of these practices. We will also show how Scripture and life experience—including Bill Johnson's life experience—contradict NAR teachings about healing. And we'll identify some problems and dangers associated with NAR teachings about healing. In conclusion, we'll contrast NAR "faith" in healing with a picture of true biblical faith.

Healing Rooms

In small towns and large cities, people who follow NAR apostles and prophets have opened "healing rooms" operating out of store fronts and churches. People with all manner of physical illness and psychological disturbance, desperate for healing, come to these rooms to be restored. Many of the healing rooms are affiliated with Healing Rooms Ministries, based in Spokane, Washington. The "apostle" Cal Pierce founded this organization following a divine encounter that happened while he served on the leadership of Bethel Church.[7] Today, hundreds of healing rooms in sixty-eight nations are affiliated with Healing Rooms Ministries. There very likely is one near where you live.

In these rooms, it is reported, people are miraculously healed from cancer, brain damage, depression, alcoholism, and many other infirmities. Their testimonies are shared on the Healing Rooms Ministries website. Here are two. The first was reported by Healing Rooms SW England:

> A young boy's first teeth turned black and fell out due to meningitis. His second teeth were also black, and his dentist wanted to remove them, but his mother said no, and she brought him into Healing Rooms. His dentist checked him over later, and to his amazement, discovered a perfect third row of teeth growing.[8]

And this report came from Healing Rooms of Green Bay, Wisconsin:

> I was a smoker since I was eighteen years old. I'm forty-seven now. I smoked for twenty-nine years! I had tried quitting so many times I can't even remember. I never succeeded. I recently went to my doctor, and she said that I should really try harder to quit smoking due to health reasons. This was it. I had enough! I had to quit! . . . I made up my mind to go to the healing rooms to be prayed over. . . . I believe as I was being prayed over that a [demonic] spirit of nicotine came out of me. . . . As I was being prayed over I kept coughing and spitting up this mucus stuff and

making weird sounds, kind of gross I know, but
lo and behold I never smoked again.[9]

Certainly, many people believe they have been healed in these
rooms, though, as we'll explain later in this chapter, much more
evidence is required to show that a miracle of healing has actually occurred than what is given in those testimonies. And there
is another major concern when it comes to healing rooms: They
are based on NAR beliefs, including the idea that everyone can
be healed and that every Christian can learn to heal people. In
addition, this healing ministry promotes the practice of making
"prayer declarations." Healing Room members claim to receive
"revelations" from God about why people are sick (for example,
demonic spirits may be causing the illness, or some specific sin
may be the reason for the person's malady) and they make "prayer
declarations" commanding the sicknesses to leave—commands
like "Let new organs appear" and "You shall not die but live." If
workers in these healing rooms were merely asking God for His
healing of these people, and humbly submitting to the outworking
of His will in the matter, there would be no concern. But clearly
there is more going on here.

Treasure Hunts

In this new type of evangelistic outreach, team members
approach complete strangers and declare that God is healing
them, in that very moment, of their illness. This practice was
popularized by the Bethel School of Supernatural Ministry and
has been picked up by well-known evangelistic groups such as
YWAM.[10] (Treasure hunting is also sometimes referred to as
"prophetic evangelism" or "supernatural evangelism.") During a
typical treasure hunt, a team of three to five people will ask God
to give them "clues"—through prophetic words—that will lead

them to "treasures" (specific people) in their community who need healing or some other "divine encounter" showing God's love for them. These clues may include locations where they will find such people (for example, a park or a shopping mall) and descriptions of what the individuals look like (such as the color of their clothing or whether they have any tattoos). Team members will record the clues on a "treasure map" and set off on the hunt.

The method is illustrated by what happened during one treasure hunt at a park, where a team spotted a young man carrying a skateboard and wearing a white T-shirt and black pants. One team member had prophetically received the clues "white T-shirt" and "black shorts," so the group felt like they had the right guy. They approached the young man (named Frank) and told him about the treasure hunt, and that God had led them to him because of his white T-shirt. Then they showed him the other clues on the map they had crafted and asked him if he had any of the physical conditions listed there. He said his knee was injured, so they asked if they could place a hand on his knee. With his permission, they made a "prayer declaration" for his healing: "We just command all the pain to leave right now." Afterward, Frank said he experienced no pain.[11]

Though treasure hunters believe they are helping people like Frank, and some of their targets may even appreciate their efforts, their unusual practice is not always welcomed. Understandably, Redding residents have felt harassed and hounded by BSSM students canvassing the city seeking sick people to heal. An article that appeared in *BuzzFeed* reported about the locals' vexation over the practice:

> There's a story about Bethel students swarming an elderly woman in a wheelchair in a parking lot and encouraging her to walk; massages, dental

appointments, and shopping trips interrupted by Bethel students' "treasure hunts." The biggest local tourist attraction, the Sundial Bridge, was briefly "ruined," residents complained, by students looking to practice their prophecy on the banks of the Sacramento River. (They are no longer allowed to prophesy to tourists around the bridge.)[12]

We, too, have heard stories from people who live in the Redding area, complaining about Bethel students' treasure hunting activities.

Dead Raising Teams

NAR leaders train people to heal the sick, but they have even greater aspirations. They also train them to raise the dead.

For example, the Dead Raising Team was founded in 2006 by a graduate of the Bethel School of Supernatural Ministry, a fellow named Tyler Johnson (no relation to Bill Johnson). This team is invited to churches to train other teams (more than sixty worldwide, to date) to go to the scenes of accidents, hospitals, and morgues and to pray for resurrections. They claim to have produced fifteen resurrections to date.[13] Bill Johnson publicly praised this team during a message he gave at Bethel Church and claimed that it had received support from local government agencies and businesses:

> They actually have been given badges so that their ministry people can go behind police lines if there's an accident and a fatality. . . . The county lists their services. . . . Amazing. And so the mortuary has their business cards: "If you have a loved one you'd like to get back, we provide this

service: We have a Dead Raising Team." . . . That
is too cool.[14]

Johnson, somewhat jokingly, suggested that the people at
Bethel Church need their own Dead Raising Team badges.

Johnson's public praise for the Dead Raising Team shows that
the church's attempt to raise Olive, which we described in chapter 1, was not an isolated incident. Dead raising is encouraged at
Bethel; as a result, the practice is spreading to other churches.

Another attempt occurred in a church of more than 200
people in central Oregon. A couple at the church lost their son,
a promising college student, in a drowning accident. So church
members—some of whom had traveled to Bethel Church and
returned to spread Bethel teachings—sought to raise him. This
is the sad story as it was told to us by Mark and Shelley, former
members of that church:

> The family planned a "dead raising ceremony"
> at the church, and the mother invited only those
> women who would stand and believe with her
> for the resurrection of her son, whose body
> was in the coffin in the sanctuary. The teenage
> sister of the deceased had painted a big ban-
> ner with the words, "Welcome Back!" with her
> brother's name on it. It was going to be a grand
> celebration. There were several hours of prayer
> and worship over the young man's dead body,
> with no success, and the "dead-raising" event
> did not end as planned. The entire community
> mourned. The memorial service filled the entire
> high school gymnasium, while the mother still
> looked expectantly at the coffin for its lid to
> raise. The son was subsequently buried in a

family-only ceremony. In subsequent years, the
devastated parents divorced. Their other children
grew into depressed, defeated young adults. A
once tight-knit, Christ-worshipping family was
splintered, and their faith was deeply shaken. As
far as we know, none have recovered from chronic
depression.

This encouragement to attempt to raise the dead, in full
expectation that it is certain to happen, is an alarming form of
pastoral malpractice. Pastors should not foster misplaced hope.
Rather, they should encourage grieving families with true hope:
the promise of God's presence and comfort as they walk through
"the valley of the shadow of death," and the guarantee that the
Savior will raise their loved ones and reunite them at His return
(Ps. 23:4; 1 Thess. 4:13–18).

Sozo

Another healing practice, popularized by Bethel and now
found in many other churches, is called "Sozo." This practice,
rather than seeking physical healing, focuses on emotional and
spiritual healing. Do you struggle with anxiety, depression, memories of past traumatic experiences, feelings that God doesn't love
you, or habitual sin? Then you need to be "Sozoed." Sozo is advertised as a "powerful tool" for inner healing and demonic deliverance that helps people "uncover and address root issues that hinder
[their] personal growth and relationship with God and others."[15]
Root issues may include the activity of demonic spirits that need
to be exorcised and family curses that must be broken.

People book an appointment for a Sozo session with one to
three trained "Sozo ministers." These ministers—who claim to
be prophetically gifted—lead the Sozoee in "prayer," asking the

Holy Spirit to reveal the source of their struggles. One of the ministers takes notes. During the session—which can last up to a few hours—the Holy Spirit may reveal lies the person has accepted, emotional wounds that need healing, people they need to forgive, unhealthy relational (or generational) ties, and sins to renounce.[16] Sozo ministers have six tools for prompting Sozoees: Father Ladder, Four Doors, Presenting Jesus, The Wall, Trigger Mechanism, and Divine Editing. Using these tools, the Sozo minister will often ask the Holy Spirit to bring forth memories. But attempting to conjure up memories in this manner is viewed by most expert psychologists as a dangerous practice—a form of "recovered memory therapy"—that should not be attempted.[17] It often results in false memories.

In chapter 10, we share stories about young people who, having participated in Sozo sessions, accused their parents of abuse. Another former participant in Sozo shares that they told the Sozo minister they had been in an abusive marriage. The minister asked what came to mind after the minister prayed for them to have a memory. They said they had a mental image of their mother looking angry. This is what happened next, according to the Sozo participant:

> I was then led, via suggestion and further "revelations" (supposedly from God), to accept that my spouse was, in fact, *not* abusive in the ways I'd described. In fact, I was led to believe that I was projecting my mother's abuse that I experienced in my childhood onto my spouse; and had unfairly filtered my spouse's words and behavior towards me through this lens. I was subsequently led through a series of prayers of forgiveness towards my mother and repentance

for believing "lies" about my spouse. I was left
with "memories" of my mother being abusive and
a renewed attitude of acceptance and submission
to the ever-increasing abuse from my spouse. The
truth, however, was the polar opposite of what
was "revealed" in this Sozo session! My mother
was and remains an amazing, loving, patient,
generous woman who was *never* abusive to me or
any of my siblings. I thank God that I quickly
realized that the scandalous accusations levelled
against her by the Sozo practitioners were utterly
false.[18]

This person was able to discern that the Sozo practitioners had
themselves made "scandalous accusations," and, in effect, sinned
against this person and her mother.

Critics have also raised concerns about Sozo ministers who
delve into very serious and traumatic issues in people's lives
(including mental health issues and abuse), when they do not have
the psychological or other relevant training for this responsibility.
A person can leave a Sozo session falsely believing they are cured
of depression, an addiction, or marriage problems. The source
of their problems likely will be misdiagnosed (for example, they
might be led to believe a demon is the cause of their problems
when there are other—and sometimes multiple—complex causes,
such as behaviors, thought patterns, medical conditions, and
genetics). The Sozoee may then become fixated on demons and
overlook other contributing factors. Sometimes they might incor-
rectly conclude that a loved one, such as a parent, is the cause of
their troubles. In these ways, a Sozo session may cause serious psychological and interpersonal harm, violating the doctor's motto,
"First, do no harm." Yet more than 100 Sozo ministries, which

are formally affiliated with Bethel Sozo, have been established in the United States, and they are spreading to other nations of the world, including Iceland, Kazakhstan, Mexico, Netherlands, Nicaragua, New Zealand, Norway, Russia, Singapore, South Africa, and Taiwan.[19]

No Biblical Support

These peculiar healing practices, hyped by NAR leaders and organizations, spring from the belief that it is always God's will to heal every sick or emotionally suffering person. They say they know this is His will because Jesus healed every sick and demonized person He encountered (though we've shown that is not true).[20] And, as Bill Johnson says, "Jesus Christ is perfect theology."[21] In other words, Jesus fully illustrates God's will to heal every sick person. And Jesus commissioned us to do the same when He said, "As the Father sent me, I send you" (John 20:21).[22] That is what so-called "normal Christianity" should look like—believers healing sick people regularly, as a part of their normal daily lives.[23]

Another reason they give for knowing that it is God's will to heal is that there is no sickness in heaven. And they believe that the Lord's Prayer—which states, "your will be done, on earth as it is in heaven"—indicates that God's will is for the earth to look exactly like heaven, including the total absence of sickness, disease, and depression.[24]

Of course, most Christians believe that God can and does heal people today. That is not unique to NAR. But most do not believe it is *always* God's will to heal *in this life*. They do not see any support for that teaching in Scripture. The fact that Jesus had an extraordinary healing ministry does not mean that His followers—who are not the divine Messiah—can or should have the same ministry. The Bible shows that believers, like all people, experience sickness, aging, and death (2 Cor. 5:1–4; Rom. 8:18–23). Pentecostal and charismatic Christians, who believe that some Christians today have been given the spiritual gift of healing people, do not all believe that every Christian can have that gift or that it is obtained through "activation exercises."[25] They don't believe that Christians can bring God's physical kingdom to earth prior to Christ's return. So—though they do believe in divine healing—they do not have the same expectations as people in NAR about the degree or manner of healing that can be experienced in this life. Outside NAR, Christians agree that God—in His sovereignty, for His own reasons—does not always choose to heal.

Unlivable Theology

Scripture does not support Johnson's teaching that all believers can be healed. And neither do believers' life experiences—including Johnson's own. Johnson wears eyeglasses to correct his poor vision. His father, M. Earl Johnson (a previous pastor of Bethel Church), died from pancreatic cancer, and his wife, Beni, is undergoing chemotherapy for breast cancer as we write this book. To be clear, we don't mention these cases of personal physical suffering in order to be cruel—we have great sympathy for the Johnsons, just as we have great sympathy for the parents and family of little Olive. Rather, we point out these truths to show the inconsistency and contradictions between what Bethel leaders say and the reality they live.

Cancer has visited Johnson's family with disconcerting vigor, despite Bethel leaders' prayer declarations for Bethel to be a "cancer-free zone."[26] Bill Johnson's son, Eric—who was a senior pastor at Bethel from 2011 to 2021—suffers from deafness despite receiving many prophecies and prayer declarations over the years that he would be healed. He took part in Sozo to see if he could uncover a spiritual cause for his deafness, yet still he is not healed.[27] If Johnson's teachings about healing were true, we might expect freedom (if not immunity) from such illness in his own family.

Problems and Dangers

NAR healing practices pose many problems and dangers. It is highly presumptuous to expect God to provide healing on demand—whether in a healing room, on a treasure hunt, or during a Sozo session. These teachings presume to know the will of God for all who suffer infirmities. And the practices themselves border on manipulation of God. Some have likened such practices to expecting God to play parlor games. But He is sovereign. We shouldn't venture to tell Him how He must work.

Moreover, approaching a person and declaring that God intends to heal them is a misrepresentation of God if He hasn't actually spoken. In that event, the "healer" is guilty of speaking falsely for God, which is a serious offense according to Scripture (Deut. 18:20–22). A person may reject a form of Christianity that is based on false promises. And even if the "healer" is sincere, it is cruel to tell people that God is healing them when He clearly is not.

This cruelty is compounded when, consistent with NAR teachings, either the sick person or the healer is blamed for a failed attempt to heal. The lesson, whether explicit or implied, is that they did not have enough faith. NAR leaders sometimes downplay this implication. For example, Bill Johnson says Christians should never tell a sick person they were not healed because of a weak faith. But that is the inevitable conclusion of their teachings.[28] What else are we to think, when Bill Johnson makes frequent statements like these:

- "The reality of Jesus's success in ministry doesn't change because not everyone I pray for gets healed. He is the standard, not me. He is the leader, and I'm learning to follow. Any discrepancies are on my end, not His."[29]
- "For many, it's just become easier to blame God by calling it the 'mysterious will of God' [when someone is not healed] than it is to accept the fact that we've not arrived yet and get alone with God."[30]
- "We owe them [the world] our best attempt at representing Him [the Lord] well [by working a miracle of healing], making sure that, when there's breakthrough, He gets the credit, not us. And when it doesn't work, I take the responsibility."[31]

How can Johnson say, on the one hand, that people must take responsibility when they try to heal someone and fail, and, on the other hand, say they should never blame a lack of healing on a weak faith? His teachings are confusing, inconsistent, and add further insult to injury.

What is the relationship between faith and healing? NAR teaching fosters the fear that the humble acknowledgment that God may not will to heal a particular sickness is a lack of faith. This lack of faith, they think, jinxes the possibility of a healing miracle. This is magical or superstitious thinking. God isn't any less likely to heal when we acknowledge that His will may be different than what we desire. A person is not at greater risk when we trust the sovereign wisdom of God to heal them. Here is an example of a way we may pray in faith for divine healing:

Dear heavenly Father, we do not know what You know. We do not know what is best, all things considered, as You do. But we deeply desire the healing of this dear one, and we know that You can heal him/her. So we affirm our trust in You, in Your goodness, Your power, and Your wisdom, while we ask for healing. And we rest in this knowledge, that all things do work together for good to those who love You. Your Spirit intercedes for us according to Your will. Our hearts are strengthened by the knowledge that our present sufferings will be overcome with future glory. And we anxiously await the day when creation will be set free from its bondage to corruption and our bodies will be redeemed. This is our hope. This is our joy. This is our confidence in You. And how awesome will that victory over sin and sickness and death be when we all are finally raised to newness of life, as guaranteed by the resurrection of Your Son and our Savior, through faith in Jesus Christ. Amen.[32]

This is truly a prayer of faith.[33] We want God to answer our prayers in accord with His will. We want to be able to say that we do not wish to live one moment longer than God in His good and infinite wisdom intends. And we want to embrace whatever suffering God does not relieve as part of His calling in our lives to bring Him utmost glory. All affliction in this life is "momentary" and "light" in comparison with what awaits us hereafter (see 2 Cor. 4:16–5:9; 1 Cor. 15:19–20, 51–58).

NAR teachings about healing also create an unhealthy dependency on the "apostles" and "prophets." What happens when their followers fail to heal someone, as they inevitably will? The message that is tacitly suggested by the "apostles" and "prophets" is, *Oh, you're not able to heal people? Well, I have a better track record than you, so you'd better hang out with me.* People will naturally turn to those who are more "advanced" in healing, those who have greater, more effective faith.

The perception that NAR leaders are regularly working miracles is an illusion. Some NAR leaders have been exposed for demonstrably faking their healings. Todd White, the well-known healing evangelist, practices a form of supernatural evangelism by going to the streets and "praying" for people's healing. Many of his "healings" are posted on YouTube. In a number of instances, White tells people that they are experiencing pain because they have one leg that is longer than another. He then claims to cause their shorter leg to grow so that their legs become even. But investigators have shown that he does not really lengthen legs; he only appears to do so by employing a common trick used by phony healing evangelists—moving his hands to shift people's feet in a way that gives the illusion that their "shorter" leg has grown.[34] The mentalist Derren Brown—who shows his television audiences how fake healers use psychological techniques to manipulate people—says this leg-lengthening trick is "the mark of the charlatan."[35]

Here are some ways to judge when miracles are genuine, not cheap knockoffs:

- First, know the definition of a miracle. God sometimes exercises His unique prerogative to do something that would not happen in the ordinary course of things, as determined by the natural laws that He ordained "in the beginning" when He "created the heavens and the earth" (Gen. 1:1). This is what we mean by *miracle*. It is a special act of God to produce an effect that would not happen otherwise. (See a fuller explanation in the Special Appendix.)

- Know the marks of a genuine miracle. The Gospels report that when Jesus worked His awesome miracles, people immediately and spontaneously responded in awe and glorified God (Mark 2:12), or with a mixture of fear and conviction that He was a prophet of God (Luke 7:11–17), and that He certainly was no ordinary man (Matt. 8:23–27). That God was at work doing something unusual was undeniable. So, if NAR miracles are to match the greatness of Jesus's own miracles (or exceed their greatness, as NAR leaders claim with their "greater works" teaching), then their miracles should likewise be easy to recognize, and they should get as much press as Jesus's miracles did.

- Save the term *miracles* for real miracles. In Christian circles, when someone receives an answer to prayer, they commonly say, "It was a miracle!" We should always rejoice over answered prayers, but not all good things that happen in our lives are miracles by any proper definition. For example, healing that occurs because of medical treatment is a blessing from God, but not a miracle. Words matter. Overuse of the word "miracle" cheapens it and leads to careless claims that many things are miracles that are not. When everything is called a miracle, nothing is a miracle.

- Be careful about repeating stories of miracles that you have heard secondhand but have no evidence for. Ask questions. Who experienced the miracle? When did it happen, and where? Who observed the miracle firsthand? Who "performed" the miracle? Christians often speak of miracles that have occurred in faraway places, among remote people groups, and yet they offer few specific details. For that matter, they don't even know the details. They confidently repeat stories they've heard from an "apostle," a "prophet," or some other trusted Christian leader. Rumors of miracles evolve and are passed around. This fosters the impression that miracles are occurring all the time, which plays into the NAR agenda.[36] We should not be gullible, and we should never feel pressured to believe that a miracle has occurred when we have not been presented with reasonable evidence. *It is not a lack of faith to ask for evidence.*

To be clear: We believe God can and does do miracles whenever He pleases. But Christians should have a healthy dose of skepticism when it comes to claims that miracles have occurred. Miracle claims are a dime a dozen; genuine miracles are relatively infrequent. And we definitely do not look for miracles to prove God's goodness or the truth of the gospel message, both

It is not a lack of faith to ask for evidence.

of which were already adequately demonstrated in Christ's sacrificial death and resurrection.

True Biblical Faith

NAR teaching perpetuates the double deception that *our faith multiplies the occurrence of miracles* and *our faith depends on the occurrence of miracles*. There is no doubt that God is good. But His goodness does not require that it is always His will to heal, this side of eternity. True faith is not the belief that God will heal because He is good; rather, it is trust that He is good no matter what He decides.

We see such faith described in Hebrews 11, which lists heroes of the faith who exhibited trust in God's promises even though they did not see complete fulfillment during their earthly lives. Those heroes include Abel (an innocent man who was murdered by his own brother), Abraham and Sarah (who lived as nomads, in a foreign land), Isaac and Jacob (who never saw the great nation that was promised to their descendants), and Joseph (who never saw the Exodus or the Promised Land). These all showed trust in God, though their hardships were not eliminated, and their life paths weren't smooth and paved with rose petals. Their experiences are recalled for our instruction, as examples of what it means for us to have faith here and now.

We see such faith expressed by believers today, people like author and radio host Joni Eareckson Tada. Since the time of her diving accident as a teenager, Joni has faithfully encouraged many others by her example of finding great hope in God after being paralyzed from the shoulders down. And her organization Joni and Friends has brought the gospel—along with wheelchairs and other practical help—to people with disabilities around the world. Her life is a picture of true faith, and it is has clearly resonated with others, as can be seen in the response to her autobiography, which has sold more than five million copies and been translated into dozens of languages.[37]

Faith is also seen in the loving self-sacrifice made by Robertson McQuilken. He was a successful president of a Christian college, Columbia Bible College and Seminary (now Columbia International University). But Robertson resigned his post, at the peak of his career, to care full-time for his ailing wife, Muriel. She had Alzheimer's disease and was terrified to be without him.

At first, he arranged for a companion to care for her so he could keep going to work. But as soon as he left, she would follow him. She would make the mile round trip up to ten times in a day. When Robertson helped her undress at night, he sometimes found bloody feet.[38] But he rejected the advice of some friends who encouraged him to put her in an institution, and he was so glad he did. He told *Christianity Today*:

> When the time came, the decision was firm. It took no great calculation. It was a matter of integrity. Had I not promised, forty-two years before, "in sickness and in health . . . till death do us part"?
>
> This was no grim duty to which I stoically resigned, however. It was only fair. She had, after all, cared for me for almost four decades with marvelous devotion; now it was my turn. And such a partner she was! If I took care of her for forty years, I would never be out of her debt.[39]

Robertson's resignation speech, given at Columbia, was listened to by thousands of people around the world, and he wrote a book called *A Promise Kept*, sharing their struggles and the lessons they learned through them.[40]

Robertson McQuilken, Joni Eareckson Tada, and many others whose names are known only by God, walked paths of suffering and experienced blessings. They found firsthand the truth in the Bible's promise "that for those who love God all things work together for good," including sickness (Rom. 8:28).

CHAPTER 10

Deception-Proofing Your Children

My only prayer is that I will get to
see my child again before I die.
—A heartbroken mother

NAR's music, ministries, and marketing magnetically attract young adults. How can parents protect their children from NAR—a movement that aggressively targets them?

Educate Yourself about NAR

You must approach this challenge in much the way you would when protecting them from any danger—first, by educating yourself about it. So there's homework involved. And you'll need some practice communicating what you have learned with your children and equipping them to respond to NAR when they encounter it—which they inevitably will. We'll expand on each of these guidelines in this chapter.

Stories of the Danger

First, parents must recognize that NAR poses a serious threat to the spiritual vitality of their children. Many moms and dads, unaware of NAR's existence, are blindsided when their children fall prey to the movement. We've interacted with many parents about this problem. Most of them have approached us first, with heartbreaking stories of relational loss and uncertainty.

One parent we've heard from is "Steven." His young adult daughter, Kimberly, grew up attending a biblically faithful church with the rest of her family. But after going away to college, she became involved with NAR-influenced churches and ministries.

At first, her parents were supportive. They were happy that she was active in church. But they noticed her vocabulary began to change. She talked about seeing angels and having visions. She acted irresponsibly and out of character. She broke off close relationships with those who gently and lovingly voiced concerns about her behavior. And she refused to accept counsel from anyone who was not a "prophet."

Steven and his wife, "Janice," did not know what had happened to their sweet-natured daughter until they discovered she had traveled out of state to Bethel Church in Redding, California. That's when they did some research and discovered NAR. Looking back, they can see that she had been drawn into NAR teachings over a period of time while attending various church meetings. Steven explained to us that he was well-versed in Scripture and had always taken his daughter's spiritual life seriously. Yet, having never heard of NAR, he was unprepared for what unfolded.

Another pair of distressed parents told radio host Jan Markell that they had "lost" their daughter to Bethel Church.[1] A married couple who attended Bethel had persuaded the young woman to move to Redding and to enroll in the Bethel School of Supernatural Ministry (BSSM). This couple told her she had a special musical ability that was needed at Bethel. They also prophesied a threat: if she would not go to BSSM, then a past sickness—a serious illness that she believed had been healed by God—would return. In addition, bad things would happen to her family if she didn't obey God.

Under the influence of this couple and Bethel Church, she underwent a complete change in personality. Somehow, she even came to believe that her parents had abused her, so she cut off all contact with them. Her parents suspect that she "recovered" false memories while taking part in Sozo sessions at Bethel.

One couple we've talked with said they've heard from dozens of parents with the same heartache. They all claim that their children cut them off after arriving at Bethel. Many of them report that their children also have made allegations of parental abuse.[2]

These children have all come to view their own families as enemies. Shattered parents have told us they weren't even invited to their children's high school graduations or weddings. One mother, through tears, said, "My only prayer is that I will get to see my child again before I die."

Besides dividing families, NAR stunts young people's spiritual growth. It does this by exalting supernatural experience over sound theology so that they come to view miracles as more important than the gospel. Let us give you an example.

Many Christians were disturbed by a video uploaded to YouTube of a group of students from Bethel Church in Redding.[3] The video shows them interacting with a Christian street preacher named James Bynum. The interaction took place in front of a Benny Hinn "Miracle Service" in San Jose, California. James was warning passersby that Hinn is a false teacher. The young people apparently took issue with his warnings and a dialogue ensued.

Throughout the exchange, one of the students, who identifies herself as Allison, appears to be under the influence of a chemical, though she says it's the Holy Spirit. Allison jumps around in circles, makes jerking movements, and falls to the ground—all the while, a large smile is plastered to her face. She never stops laughing. Actually, it's more like a grating giggle. It seems that her extended outburst of laughter was an exhibition of the NAR phenomenon of "laughing in the Spirit."

But what's more concerning than Allison's strange actions are her words. In an effort to dissuade James from criticizing Hinn, she tells him, "We don't have to worry about theology. Let's just be in His presence. Let's just be in His presence—of God."

Allison's glib dismissal of theology obviously concerns James. He presses her to clarify her views. "So, doctrine doesn't matter?" he says, and then asks, "Every person goes to heaven?"

Allison replies, "I don't know. I can't claim to know what happens after we die." (To which we say, really? The Bible is clear that many people will not go to heaven. So how can she say she doesn't know whether every person will go there?)

Wishing to determine whether she understands the supreme importance of the gospel, Bynum questions Allison about what she would tell a person who had been lethally injured by a knife, had merely five minutes to live, and expressed concern about what would happen to them after they died. What would she say to such a person? Before Allison can answer, a young man steps forward and answers for her: "She would pull the knife out of your back and heal it, right now." The young man then laughs at his own response. Allison, also laughing hysterically, agrees: "I would say, 'God, heal him right now!' And the sword would fall off, and they'd be fine, and then we'd hug."

That, of course, was not the answer Bynum was hoping for. He wanted to know if she would tell the man that he could be forgiven from his sins and made right with God because of Jesus's death on the cross and resurrection, and that he only needed to receive, by faith, God's offer of salvation. Then he could have assurance that he would go to heaven when he died. But the students said no such thing. Rather than presenting the vital truth of the gospel in a man's dying moments, they talked, lightheartedly, of healing him.

Though the scenario was hypothetical, one thing is crystal clear: the Bethel students didn't see theology as important (they said so themselves). As a result, their own theology was muddled and confused to the point that they didn't even seem to have clarity about the basic message of the Christian gospel (1 Cor. 15:1–8).[4]

Bizarre beliefs and an inability to articulate the gospel make young people ripe for spiritual deception. And that is no laughing matter.

Learn How to Detect the Danger

The danger to children is real. How can you, as a parent, know NAR when you see it? How can you spot it? What should you look for?

To begin with, you must have a clear understanding of what NAR teaches. One primary goal for this book is to explain NAR teachings. So reading it is a good start.

To summarize, the core teaching is this: apostles and prophets *must* govern churches. Churches must submit to the authority of apostles and prophets, who can then bring critical new revelation that Christians need for developing miraculous powers, setting up God's kingdom on earth, and paving the way for Christ's return. There are many different revelations, coming from different apostles and prophets, but they all boil down to one thing: they are strategies equipping the global church to rise up as an end-time army of miracle-working Christians.

In addition to knowing the NAR teachings, you should also be tuned into other signs of NAR influence on a church or Christian organization. This includes knowing the influential NAR players, practices, and buzzwords.

- Prominent NAR leaders and churches: Bill Johnson; Kris Vallotton; Mike Bickle; Heidi Baker; Bethel Church in Redding, California; Jesus Culture in Sacramento, California; and, the International House of Prayer in Kansas City, Missouri

- NAR-influenced music groups: Bethel Music, Gateway Worship, Hillsong Music, Forerunner Music, Elevation Worship, and Jesus Culture

- NAR practices: Sozo, fire tunnels, prophetic evangelism (known, at Bethel, as "treasure hunting" evangelism), prophetic activation exercises, classes teaching people to prophesy or work miracles, "impartation" of miraculous gifts through the laying on of hands, 24/7 prayer rooms, healing rooms, prayer walking, warfare prayer, "soaking prayer" (or "soaking worship"), and making "prayer declarations"[5]

- NAR buzzwords: Apostles and prophets (also "apostolic" and "prophetic"), spiritual covering, alignment, spiritual fathers and mothers, fivefold ministry, Seven Mountain

Mandate, bringing heaven to earth, "Normal Christianity," glory realms, spiritual atmosphere, open heavens, spiritual breakthrough, anointing, activating, awakening, birthing, the "greater works" (or "greater things"), "decree and declare," "bind and loose," billion-soul harvest, and end-time transfer of wealth[6]

These are representative teachings, practices, and terminology associated with NAR. There are others. But knowing these will give you a big head start in detecting the presence of NAR in your surroundings.

Monitor Your Kids' Intake

It's crucial that you know who, exactly, has spiritual influence on your children. Don't make the mistake of presuming your kids are automatically safe at your church. Many church leaders have—whether knowingly or not—embraced NAR beliefs and seek to teach those beliefs to others, including children.

In the case of Kimberly (whose story we shared at the start of this chapter), her exposure to NAR came through NAR-influenced churches. (Her parents didn't know, at the time, that those churches had been influenced by NAR. They thought they were simply churches that had a charismatic bent.) But other parents have told us that their children were introduced to NAR in biblically conservative churches where the parents had presumed they were safe. In some instances, the youth were taught NAR teachings and practices by their youth pastors who had an agenda that was hidden from the parents.

There are many ways and places that youth, and even very young children, can come into contact with NAR—some that you may never suspect. NAR music—which is used in many main-stream churches—is one of the most subtle and significant means of introducing unsuspecting worshippers to NAR.

- Sunday school classes: We mentioned in the first chapter that children in Bethel classes are taught to raise the dead. Bethel Church's leaders have also produced teaching materials that are purchased and used by other churches. For example, the "Revival Kids" curriculum is aimed at children ages five to twelve and introduces them to extreme NAR teachings and practices, including "advanced activation in the prophetic" (that is, teaching children to prophesy) and the teaching that "God wants perfect health zones" (or zones where no one experiences sickness or other health problems).[7]

- Children's books: Bill Johnson is coauthor of a book for children called *Here Comes Heaven: A Kids Guide to God's Supernatural Power*. Shockingly, this book teaches children that, when Jesus came to earth, He "could not heal the sick" and "He could not help people who were bothered by the devil, either" because "He did not bring any special powers with Him when He came to earth." Even though He was fully God, "He chose to live on earth as a regular person just like you." Why would He do that? According to the book, when Jesus healed the sick and raised the dead, He did so as a man (and not as God) to show the children that "you can too!"[8] We spoke with a Sunday school teacher named Jessika Wilson whose senior pastor instructed her to read this book to her Sunday school class. She was handed the book just moments before she was expected to read it. She started to read it aloud—with all the children seated in front of her, eagerly listening—but she couldn't continue. She was appalled by its teachings and misuse of Scripture. "I could only read three pages before I had to put down the book," she said. "There was no way I was going to read it to the kids."[9] Not all children are fortunate to have teachers who are so discerning and bold!

- Vacation Bible schools: NAR teachings have also snuck into vacation Bible schools through teaching materials such as the "Supernatural Kids VBS: Bringing Heaven to Earth" (also sold by Bethel Church). To illustrate, Day 2 of the Supernatural Kids VBS curriculum includes a skit teaching the children to make NAR "prayer declarations" (or words spoken aloud that are believed to alter reality and create miracles).

- Church clubs: PowerClubs—founded by Becky Fischer of Kids in Ministry International— are the NAR counterpart to Bible clubs like Awana. But rather than Scripture memorization and theology, a major focus in PowerClubs is teaching kids to operate in "signs, wonders, and miracles."[10]

- Summer Camps: In 2006, an Oscar-nominated documentary titled *Jesus Camp* was released featuring the NAR summer camp "Kids on Fire School of Ministry" (located just outside Devils Lake, North Dakota, and operated by Kids in Ministry International). The controversial film shows kids in military fatigues taking part in a choreographed musical performance that depicts them prophesying and assuming their role in God's end-time, kingdom-building army. Due to the negative publicity, the camp no longer operates, but other NAR camps include the "Signs and Wonders Camps" run by the International House of Prayer in Kansas City. Needless to say (given the title of the camp), the campers are not merely sitting around the campfire and singing "Jesus Loves Me."

- Christian schools: Many NAR churches have started K–12 Christian schools. Bethel Christian School, run by Bethel Church in Redding, is a notable example. But NAR schools can be found in many other communities. Parents who are not NAR—and know nothing about this movement—eagerly enroll their children in those schools, unaware of their connections to a dangerous movement.

- Youth conferences and worship concerts: Watch out for conferences and music festivals designed for middle school-age and high school students. Many of these events feature NAR speakers and musicians.

- Missions trips and organizations: We've heard stories of youth being drawn into NAR while taking part in their church mission trips. Even though their churches weren't NAR, the organizations hosting the trips, and other churches taking part, had NAR influence. Also, high school students, deciding to take a gap year between high school graduation and college, should be alert to missions organizations that have significant NAR influence, including Youth with a Mission (YWAM).[11]

It's not surprising when NAR churches take their youth to a Bethel Music concert or when they host a camp teaching NAR doctrine. But parents are caught off guard when their children are exposed to NAR in a mainstream church. Questions they should ask of churches include:

- Do you know what curriculum your church uses in its classes and special programs? Do you know which publisher or church produced the curriculum? Is that publisher or church known to be biblically sound? Did any reputable Bible scholars contribute to it or endorse it? To find out the answers, ask your church leaders to see the curriculum, or at least get the name of it so you can research it online. Churches should welcome questions about curriculum. If they don't, that is not a good sign.
- Have you had personal conversations with your child's Sunday school teacher or youth

pastor during which you could get a gauge on
their theological views?

- Do you know who will be speaking or leading worship at any camps, conferences, or
worship events your child attends and who
the sponsoring organization and partnering
organizations are?

The bottom line: don't just drop your kids off at a church
class or youth group and trust they will be taught well. Be vigilant.
Ask questions and do research. You have the right—actually, the
moral duty—to protect your kids and know what your children
are being taught.

Educate Your Children About NAR

Educating yourself about NAR is crucial. But don't neglect to
inform your kids about it too.

Warn Your Children

Many Christian parents believe it is important to prepare their
children before they come across non-Christian worldviews, such
as atheism and Islam, or cults of Christianity like the Jehovah's
Witnesses. But what about NAR?

Since you can't be everywhere all the time, educate your children about NAR. Put it on their radar. Just saying something as
simple as, "Hey, did you know there are people in the church who
believe there are apostles and prophets today (much like the New
Testament apostles and Old Testament prophets in the Bible)?
They could be anywhere, and this is what they teach." Then
briefly explain some of their teachings and practices.

Alert Your Children to NAR Tactics

Give your children a heads-up about the tactics commonly used by NAR leaders to draw them in. Here are five specific tactics:

1. "Love bombing": Love bombing is the practice of flattering individuals or showering them with affection to draw them into a group, community, or organization. Lindsay Davis, a former BSSM student who now warns people about the dangers of the school, said many people there gave her prophetic words, saying, "You're amazing," "Oh my gosh, I love you so much," and "You have such a calling on your life." The fact that she had recently experienced a life crisis (she had disentangled herself from an end-time cult-like group) made her especially vulnerable to the love bombing technique.[12]

2. Equivocating on terms: NAR leaders use many of the same words used by other Christians, but they use these words with very different meanings. Take "prayer," for example. In NAR, this word typically does not refer to the practice of prayer as it is taught in the Bible and as it has been understood through history—such as making requests of God. It generally refers to the practice of making "prayer declarations," words spoken in "faith" that are believed to create or alter reality. Another example of a word that is often used differently by

those in NAR is "faith." True biblical faith
is shown by having a confident trust in
God despite difficult circumstances (Heb.
11). Yet, NAR "faith" gives one an "ability
to see into the spiritual realm" (i.e., "God's
kingdom" or "heaven")—where there is no
sickness or poverty. With such "faith," a
person can make prayer declarations that
produce miracles (such as miracles of healing).[13] This NAR type of "faith" is akin
to the New Age view of faith: that we can
control reality with our thoughts.[14] By redefining key Christian words, NAR leaders are
quite literally redefining the Christian faith.
But unsuspecting young people—unaware
of this doublespeak—get drawn into NAR
churches, thinking they are biblically sound.

3. Exploiting a fear of missing out: NAR leaders
    often portray non-NAR churches as spiritu-
    ally dead, powerless, ineffective churches that
    don't have a fully caffeinated, fully amped
    Christianity—a robustly "supernatural"
    Christianity that includes signs, wonders, and
    miracles. They, in one fashion or another, tell
    young people, "You don't really want to go
    to your mom's boring Baptist church, hang
    out with pew-sitting Presbyterians, or join
    the masses of non-miraculous megachurch-
    goers, do you?" Thus, they imply that NAR
    churches are the only ones where authentic
    Christianity can be found. Caricaturing non-
    NAR churches is an especially effective way

NAR leaders hook young people, who are at a stage in their lives when they crave excitement and significance.

4. Misrepresenting other Christians: NAR leaders frequently (and falsely) claim that all churches that do not accept the authority of modern-day "apostles" and "prophets" also deny modern miraculous gifts (such as speaking in tongues and prophesying). And they suggest that they are the only churches that "truly" believe that God still works miracles or "really" take seriously the reality of angels and demons. In other words, they accuse non-NAR churches of ignoring the supernatural parts of the Bible that are uncomfortable for them. Of course, those depictions are not true. This tactic employs a logical fallacy known as a "straw man." The truth is that all Bible-believing Christians believe in angels and demons. And even those who do not believe that God still gives miraculous gifts (as He did in the early church) and do not believe there are modern-day miracle-workers, still do believe that God can and does work miracles whenever He so chooses. They just do not believe in NAR's extreme emphasis on miracles or its teachings that miraculous powers can be "activated" in any believer who desires them. And they do not believe in chasing miracles and supernatural experiences as a deliberate

means of "feeling close to God," "building His kingdom," or "growing in faith."

5. Saying, "That's not us": Ironically, many NAR leaders deny that the New Apostolic Reformation exists. Or, if they do acknowledge its existence, they deny that it is a major movement or that they have any involvement with it. This should not be surprising since devotees of other controversial religious movements also resist labels that expose them and that distinguish them from mainstream Christians.[15] They do not want to be associated with anything fringe and extremist. They just want to be seen as Christians (but the purest kind). Therefore, it is important for young people to realize that asking a leader if their church is NAR is not good enough. They must go beyond the pat answers and determine what that church or leader actually believes and teaches.

Use Teaching Opportunities

When you see manifestations of NAR, use those times to teach your children about it and clue them in. Maximize teachable moments. Don't let those moments pass without seizing the opportunities they provide. Talk about wrong teachings, why they're wrong, and how they lead people astray.

And if you're driving by a NAR church in your city, or you see an advertisement for a book written by a NAR leader pop up on your Facebook feed, point those things out to your children. Debrief them by asking questions to see if they understand what NAR teaches, where those teachings depart from Scripture, and why they are harmful. Once their antennae are raised, they will be able to detect NAR influence themselves and won't be totally dependent on you to do so. You are raising them to exercise discernment based on knowledge.

Equip Your Children to Think Biblically and Critically

Warning children about the dangers of NAR is very important. But play offense, too, by making sure your children are equipped to evaluate *all* teachings they encounter on the basis of Scripture.

This requires not only that they read Scripture, but also that they learn to read it as the original writers intended for it to be read—in its literary context and in light of its historical and cultural background. Once taught how to properly read the Bible, they will see through the manipulative Scripture twisting that is so common in NAR. One good book for parents and young adults, that teaches the proper skills for understanding Scripture, is *How to Read the Bible for All Its Worth*, by Gordon D. Fee and Douglas Stuart (Zondervan).

Young people should also be taught basic Christian theology. A text such as *Introducing Christian Doctrine*, by Millard J. Erickson, provides a broad sweep of the major areas of theology, including revelation, God, creation, providence, humanity, sin, Jesus Christ, atonement and salvation, the church, and eschatology (end times). Be sure to include a study of the Holy Spirit (known as "pneumatology") since this is one area of theology where NAR teachings are especially off. And young people should be introduced to apologetics—the field of theology that teaches Christians how to defend their faith intellectually. When youth are given solid evidence for the truth of Christianity—including historical, scientific, and philosophical evidence—they will discover that their faith is reasonable and be better prepared to respond to all attacks on their faith—whether they come from atheists, non-Christian religions, or even aberrant theological movements such as NAR. They will see that, unlike the picture of Christianity presented by NAR leaders, our faith is not based on emotions, subjective experiences, and dubious miracle claims, but on a sure and stable foundation.[16]

Consider setting aside a time each evening when you read the Bible together. When your children are young, simple Bible stories will do. But as they grow older, focus on reading through the whole Bible (including the warnings about false prophets and false teachers). What a great goal it would be to have read the entire Bible as a family prior to launching them into the world of adult responsibility. This would be a natural time to incorporate discussions about theology and principles for properly reading Scripture and applying it to daily life.

Also, talk about the persecution Christians have experienced throughout church history and still do in many parts of the world. And share stories about Christians who, despite experiencing tremendous suffering and sickness, have served God faithfully and joyfully. Such sober discussions will protect against the intrusion of giddy NAR notions that believers can "decree and declare" their own health, wealth, and success.

And this is key: teach your children to think critically. Today, in our anything goes, you-be-you culture, the idea of being critical about anyone's beliefs is frowned upon. Sadly, this thinking has been adopted by many Christians who sometimes equate thinking critically with being judgmental and unloving. But to think *critically* is to think clearly and rationally. Sloppy thinking does not honor God. Rather, we are called to love Him with all our heart, soul, and *mind* (Mark 12:30). Children should be encouraged to think critically about any message they hear—whether from a book, a movie, a song, or a sermon. Ask your children what they thought about them and ask if they agree. Encourage them to support their evaluations with Scripture and solid evidence. They should also be taught to detect logical fallacies, including the straw man fallacy used so much by NAR leaders (that we mentioned earlier). Training your children to think critically will inoculate them against NAR. One resource that can assist you with this task is *The Fallacy Detective: Thirty-Eight Lessons on How to Recognize Bad Reasoning* (designed for ages twelve through adult).[17]

Finally, be sure to feed your own enthusiasm for God and His Word. "Passion" is a big draw to NAR. Youth are drawn to NAR leaders because they are zealous and appear confident in their faith. But if your kids see you get excited about Bible reading, church, and serving others, your vibrant spiritual walk will break any illusion of a "dead" faith. When NAR leaders tell them that they have not experienced a full Christianity, they will know that's a mischaracterization of the Christianity they saw and lived in their home while growing up.

What to Do If Your Son or Daughter Becomes Ensnared in NAR

If you do all this, your kids will be safe, right? While we wish we could say yes, there are no guarantees. So, what should you do if your child has already been hooked on NAR?

Our advice to parents is to gently challenge their children to support their newfound beliefs with Scripture and solid evidence. But that is difficult to do if they have cut you off completely or they are not communicating with you. Maybe your child hasn't cut you off, but your relationship is strained, and it is difficult to talk with them. Broaching these issues with sensitivity, and the right timing, is essential.

If either of us had a child who was communicating with us only briefly and not talking much about their NAR beliefs with us, we'd probably focus, at that point, on nurturing the relationship and letting them know how much we love and care about them and that we're always there for them. Sometimes a child may not be ready to hear a parent's concerns about their beliefs until those beliefs (or the leaders teaching them those beliefs) let them down. You could also use this time to hone your understanding of what Bethel and other NAR churches teach and where those teachings err, so you are prepared to discuss your concerns with them when they are ready.

When the time is right, asking questions is a powerful strategy for helping someone think critically about *any* beliefs they have adopted—whether political, ethical, or religious.[18] We want to get them thinking. If they regard a certain church leader as an apostle, you might ask them why they believe that person is an apostle. What has that person done to demonstrate this? What does Scripture teach about apostles and the requirements for being one?

Or if they believe that a certain prophet works miracles, you can ask how they know. Have they seen the miracles themselves? What evidence do they have for believing genuine miracles have occurred? Is that evidence sufficient? Are there any other explanations for the alleged miracles? What does the Bible have to say, or show us, about miracles and miracle-workers?

Always bring the conversation back to the Bible. This is effective because those in NAR claim to have a high regard for Scripture, so they shouldn't shy away from attempting to support their beliefs with Scripture. And when they do point to a chapter or verse in support of their NAR beliefs, ask them if they have considered other ways of understanding that passage of Scripture, or if they have ever consulted any Bible commentaries to learn the views of those who have spent their lives studying those particular passages.

And, of course, pray for your children's eyes to be opened to the deception they have embraced. You can pray even when your child isn't communicating with you. And we know from Scripture that prayer is a critical component of our spiritual warfare (Eph. 6:18). One mother wrote us:

> For now, prayer is my weapon in fighting for my daughter. The Holy Spirit helps me with self-control when she is visiting as she is often judgmental and condescending toward me. I continue to offer her my love and support in prayer and availability. That's all that I am being called to do at this point. I often pray for her own discernment in the Holy Spirit and/or someone to come into her life to whom she will listen.

That's brilliant!

The Takeaway

Christians parents, understandably, are thrilled when their teenage and young adult children show spiritual interest as they head off into the world on their own. But don't be naïve. Don't get so excited when your kid shows any spiritual interest if it means supporting involvement with NAR. Family division and an unbalanced, unhealthy, unfruitful spiritual life are very real and dangerous consequences of this movement.

CONCLUSION

Joining the Resistance

*"I know your works, your toil and your
patient endurance, and how you cannot
bear with those who are evil, but have
tested those who call themselves apostles and
are not, and found them to be false."*
—Jesus, commending the first-century
church in Ephesus (Rev. 2:2)

Now what?

You've peered behind the curtain of the New Apostolic
Reformation—a global movement of so-called apostles and prophets who have infiltrated churches, perhaps even your own. We've
shown you what those "apostles" and "prophets" teach—that they
are supposed to have tremendous authority in the global church.
Their authority extends beyond churches to societal institutions.
It reaches to angels who must fulfill their "prayer declarations."
Rank-and-file Christians depend on these apostles and prophets to
bring critical new revelations. Without their new revelations, the

rest of us cannot develop the miraculous powers that are required if we are to take dominion of the earth and establish God's physical kingdom. And to help accomplish this mission, they've introduced unusual practices—including what are essentially New Age and occult practices disguised as Christian practices.

We've explained that some of NAR's most controversial teachings are not taught openly but are hidden behind Christian terminology and loaded lingo. We've also shared accounts of Christians who have experienced spiritual abuse and other harm under the rule of NAR apostles and prophets. And we've shown how NAR is dividing churches and families—turning children against their own parents in many cases. This movement has also divided marriages. (Many people have shared with us about strained marriages and divorces where conflict over NAR involvement was a major contributing factor.) We've also shared about people who have grown disillusioned with their Christian faith because they couldn't separate the craziness promoted by NAR from the gospel. Regrettably, this movement continues to spread like wildfire. It stands as one of the top competitors with historic Christianity today, alongside progressive Christianity.[1]

As you've read this book, we hope you have noticed something else, something positive—the rise of a countermovement. Former members of NAR churches, pastors, and worship leaders have begun taking a public stand by warning people about NAR's dangerous deceptions. And a countermovement—a resistance—is exactly the response that is needed. It will take nothing less than a vigorous movement to turn back NAR. You may be wondering what you can do to help stem the tide. Here are five ways you can join the resistance:

1. *Continue to educate yourself about NAR.* You've begun that process already by reading this book. Keep learning by reading

other books and becoming acquainted with the excellent resources others have produced on podcasts and YouTube.[2]

2. Educate your children about NAR. Take pains to teach them how to read the Bible properly so they can detect when NAR leaders are misusing it.

3. Stay alert for signs of NAR encroachment in your own church. Don't let it be taken over by "apostles" or become "Bethelized." Watch out for NAR music, use of The Passion Translation of the Bible, or references from church leaders to notable NAR figures, like Bill Johnson. Warn others of what you have learned about NAR. If you have any type of leadership position, use your influence to keep NAR from wriggling its way in. Closely monitor all teaching materials that are used and any outside people who are brought in. If you are on your church mission committee, agree to support missionaries only if they are not promoting NAR teachings and practices on their fields abroad. Don't let your church funds be used to spread a distorted NAR gospel, and don't assume your church is automatically safe if it is governed by a board of elders. In churches where the pastor is viewed as an apostle, he or she typically calls the shots—even when those churches have an elder board.

4. If you are a pastor or elder in a church, be diligent to prevent mission drift. Consider adopting a position paper for your church that makes clear where your church stands on NAR teachings.[3] Determine not to use music produced by overtly NAR churches and organizations, and screen all potential hires for signs of NAR influence. This includes finding out where they received their education, taking a close look at prior churches and ministries where they have been involved (did any have NAR influence?), and asking them specific questions. Here are some examples: "Have you heard of Bethel Church in Redding? If so, what are your views about their teachings and practices?" "Do you believe there are modern-day apostles and prophets? If there are prophets, what is your understanding of them—are they people with a spiritual gift of prophecy or are they more authoritative church leaders?" "What is your view of revival—are miracles an essential feature of any true revival?" "Can every believer be trained to prophesy and work miracles?" "Is it always God's will to heal?" You could generate similar types of questions based on each chapter of this book.

5. *If you are the head of a Christian organization, be alert to NAR leaders seeking to hijack the organization for their cause.* We've heard from the leaders of pro-life ministries and homeless shelters who recognized, to their dismay, that NAR leaders had been moving in, right under their noses. We've seen NAR teachings spread through homeschool co-ops (unbeknownst to parents). And we've heard of Christian politicians being cozied up to by "apostles" intent on using them to enact the NAR Seven Mountain Mandate.

When you join the resistance, be prepared for pushback. That very well may come—and sometimes from people you wouldn't expect. Perhaps even your pastor will frown on your efforts. You may be discredited and marked as divisive, like Mark and Shelley, whose story we shared in chapter 9. This couple says:

> We alerted our then pastor of unbiblical teachings emanating from the NAR and infiltrating the body, and warned of the subversive (and spiritually seductive) nature of what was happening in the women's ministry [where NAR teachings were being introduced]. We spoke the truth in love; but he censored us as small group leaders, requesting that we cease and desist from sharing "discernment research," and so we of course resigned. Then he went as far as to forbid us from inviting church friends to our home.

And then there is Teasi:

> I have paid a high personal price for trying to
> bring awareness to this deceptive and destructive
> movement. I served a church I loved for twenty-
> three years (nearly half of my life) when a NAR
> prophet named Lou Engle was invited to come
> speak. I had been studying the dangers of this
> movement for several years and tried to bring
> a loving warning that he would bring a differ-
> ent spirit into our church. Lou Engle's presence
> ushered in such a spirit of confusion followed by
> massive division. I was labeled a heresy hunter
> and even linked to the "Jezebel spirit" for try-
> ing to warn the people I loved. After only a few
> months of trying to navigate the utter confu-
> sion left in the wake of this NAR prophet, my
> husband and I were shown the door. It is hard
> to put into words the devastation we have had
> to navigate for the past several years. We have
> had to completely rebuild our lives. The ripple
> effects have wounded my entire family including
> extended family. It is insidious![4]

Like these individuals, you may be accused of creating division. But don't allow yourself to be silenced or discouraged by
manipulative demands to preserve the unity.[5] Rest assured, if you
approach your church leadership respectfully, out of genuine love
and concern, you are not the one creating division. The leadership will be responsible for breaking the unity of fellowship by
introducing false and divisive teachings that separate A-Class
Christians (those who follow the "apostles" and prophets") and
B-Class Christians (who will allegedly miss much of what God

intends for them). If the cost of preserving unity is to subvert the truth, that price is too high.

Like Teasi, you may be called a "heresy hunter," a "Jezebel" or even a "critic of revival." Who wants to be called any of those things? But remember, if they merely call you names, then those people have not responded to your actual concerns. So don't let them dissuade you or keep you from speaking up. It may cost you, but it is worth any cost to please Jesus, who praised the church folk in Ephesus for standing their ground against false apostles. He warned that believers would be canceled for standing up for Him long before cancellation was cool (Matt. 10:22)!

Also, don't doubt your resolve just because your church leaders tell you the names of well-known Christians who defend NAR leaders. We know of a few Christian authors who have used their influence to defend NAR leaders. But the fact that someone you respect defends NAR is no guarantee that the movement is sound or safe. Many off-key movements during the course of church history have had influential defenders.[6] Thoughtful Christians must defend the historic Christian faith from assaults during each generation (Jude 3).

When you join the resistance, expect to hear certain predictable responses—we hear them all the time. For example, if you question the authority of today's apostles and prophets, you may be called a cessationist (one who does not believe that God still performs miracles through spiritually gifted believers, like He did in the first century). Whether you are a cessationist or not, don't let this response throw you. It is a distraction tactic and it is irrelevant to the concerns we have raised about NAR. Many Pentecostals and charismatics (who are not cessationists) are also very concerned about the teachings of today's "apostles" and "prophets." Moreover, sometimes cessationists are falsely accused of denying the ongoing work of the Holy Spirit.

Another response you will likely hear is that the apostles and prophets do not really claim to have extraordinary authority and they certainly don't believe their words have the same authority as Scripture. But when you hear these things, remind your critic not only to listen to what NAR leaders say, but also to scrutinize what they do. They may say their prophetic words should never be treated like Scripture. That is well and good. But this does not cancel their expectation that you take their words very seriously. Some claim to give revelations that apply to the global church— revelations all Christians must accept if they are going to bring God's kingdom to earth (such as the Seven Mountain Mandate and that God's goodness requires that He always intends to heal every sick person). By claiming to give revelation to the global church, they are claiming authority over the global church, *and* they are challenging the unique authority of Scripture (which is the only revelation that has authority over all Christians). Scripture is sufficient. It contains all the instruction we need to please God and fulfill His purposes. The apostle Paul told Timothy, "All Scripture is breathed out by God and profitable for teaching, for reproof, for correction, and for training in righteousness, that the man of God may be complete, equipped for every good work" (2 Tim. 3:16–17). Simply put, Scripture has the power to make us complete. We don't need additional revelations to please our Lord or live according to His will for our lives.

You will also likely hear denials that certain "apostles" and "prophets" are part of NAR. As we explained in chapter 10, many NAR leaders deny that they are part of NAR (though not all). But if someone promotes the NAR theological framework that we have described in this book (and summarized at the start of this chapter) they are part of NAR—whether or not they believe it themselves or are willing to acknowledge it.

The leaders of Bethel Church may respond to this book by saying they have already released a series of videos on YouTube addressing many of the criticisms we raise. We're referring to their six-part Rediscover Bethel series. Yes, we know about those videos, and we have watched them in their entirety. We, along with many other viewers, believe the moderator (Bethel lead pastor Dann Farrelly) generally does not press Bill Johnson and Kris Vallotton with appropriately hard-hitting questions, and Johnson and Vallotton dodge many important issues and respond with pat answers. The video series raises more questions than it answers. It is telling, we think, that Bethel Church leaders felt the need to produce the videos. What other church has faced so many accusations of bizarre and unbiblical practices? They know that skepticism is mounting among a growing number of observers. We believe the production of these damage-control videos shows that the countermovement is having an effect.

We are often asked, do we believe the NAR apostles and prophets are intentionally lying to their followers, or do they really believe what they teach? We are reluctant to assign motives to church leaders, as only God knows their hearts. The truth is, the damage is the same whether a leader misleads someone intentionally or does so sincerely. So in a certain sense, it does not really matter what their motives are for teaching the things they do.

That being said, both psychologies may be at work. When he was warning the young pastor Timothy about false teachers in the church, the apostle Paul said, "Indeed, all who desire to live a godly life in Christ Jesus will be persecuted, while evil people and impostors will go on from bad to worse, deceiving and being deceived" (2 Tim. 3:12–13). Notice that the false teachers are both "deceiving" others and simultaneously "being deceived." Sometimes it's both/and.

You may think that today's "apostles" and "prophets" cannot possibly be intent on deceiving others. But even if that is so, this does not exonerate them. Ministers of the Lord are duty-bound to expound the Scriptures with accuracy, and to caution believers to submit their minds, their wills, and their emotions to the authority of Scripture. Even if they believe every word they say and have the best of intentions, these teachers have not heeded the warnings of others. And they have explicitly discouraged their followers from rational evaluation of their teachings. All of this makes them responsible.

But their guilt does not exempt the rest of us from responsibility. We must be discerning. We must take responsibility for our beliefs. Manipulative teachers target the naïve, and they exploit their emotional vulnerabilities by appealing to their pride. Paul warned the Christians in Rome about this very thing:

> I appeal to you, brothers, to watch out for those who cause divisions and create obstacles contrary to the doctrine that you have been taught; avoid them. For such persons do not serve our Lord Christ, but their own appetites, and by smooth talk and flattery they deceive the hearts of the naive. (Rom. 16:17–18)

Indeed, many people who have contacted us over the years have acknowledged that they were not merely victims of the "apostles" and "prophets," but they allowed themselves to be drawn in because these teachers flattered their egos and told them exactly what they wanted to hear. They express marked humility and sincere repentance for their lack of discernment and failure to test all teachings by Scripture.

So, the best thing believers can do to protect themselves from false teachings is to grow in their knowledge of Scripture and to take responsibility for their own spiritual growth, so that they are not easy to deceive—regardless of the motives of NAR leaders.

We want to be clear: people in NAR are not our enemies. So many are lovely, good-hearted, genuine believers who have gotten caught up with faulty beliefs. We do not doubt the sincerity or the salvation of those people. But this sincerity needs to be coupled with increasing wisdom and discernment. People flock to Bethel Church, Jesus Culture, IHOPKC, and other NAR churches because they believe they are places where "God is moving" and where "real Christianity" is happening. They believe they will witness miracles—the raising of the dead and the driving out of demons—things that Jesus did and that any true follower of Jesus may do also (they say). They see an expectation of God to work powerfully and supernaturally today. But what they miss out on is sound biblical teaching, sound theology, and spiritual growth. On close examination, as you've seen, NAR theology and practice do not hold up biblically or logically. It is perilous to fall into the grip of a spiritual movement that is headed in the wrong direction. Armed with this knowledge, you are prepared to join the resistance.

On Miracles and NAR

by R. Douglas Geivett

The universe itself is a marvel. And the laws of nature would not be what they are if God had not organized the natural world in the way that He did. The laws of nature are themselves evidence of God's existence, attesting as they do to the wisdom and power of God to design a world of patterned regularity (Ps. 19; Rom. 1). We take the ordinary course of things (described by what we call the "laws of nature") as a point of reference for making sense of those special divine acts that we call "miracles."

God sometimes exercises His unique prerogative to do something that would not happen in the ordinary course of things, as determined by the natural laws that He ordained "in the beginning" when He "created the heavens and the earth" (Gen. 1:1). This is what we mean by *miracle*. It is a special act of God to produce an effect that would not happen otherwise. As such, it is intentional and purposeful. If God wills for something to happen, that would not happen through His usual providential government of the universe via the routine of natural law, He can "intervene" to bring it about. Such an event is not "natural" but "supernatural."

We again witness the wisdom and power of God, now manifest differently, when He acts in some way that departs from the usual run of things. Thus, these supernatural marvels or wonders often act as "signs." And "signs and wonders" is the language customarily used in the Bible to speak of divine acts that we call miracles (see, for example, Exod. 4:1–8; 7:3; 11:9; Ps. 135:9; Acts 2:22, 43; 4:31; 5:12; 6:8).[1] Under this description, they are generally meant to capture our attention and deliver or confirm a message from God. Often they serve to authenticate the human agent's function as a prophet sent by God, since, in the case of a genuine miracle, God acts through that person as His representative.

Signs and wonders are important to the NAR vision of the end times. The idea is that there will be an abundance of high-magnitude miracles, equal to the miracles performed by Jesus Himself, indeed, greater than the miracles He did. This is their understanding of Jesus's message to His disciples in John 14:12. It is helpful to keep this in mind when we consider the problem of knowing when a miracle has occurred. Miracles may happen that we will never be able to recognize as such. Or it may be difficult at times to be sure that what happened was a miracle. But NAR emphasizes high-profile miracles that should be fairly easy to identify as special divine acts. Examples abound in the pages of Scripture.[2] The Gospels report that when Jesus worked His awesome miracles, people immediately and spontaneously responded in awe and glorified God (Mark 2:12), or with a mixture of fear and conviction that He was a prophet of God (Luke 7:11–17), and that He certainly was no ordinary man (Matt. 8:23–27). That God was at work doing something unusual was undeniable. Identifying that work as a miracle wasn't much of a problem.

If NAR miracles are to equal or exceed the greatness of Jesus's own miracles, then they should likewise be easy to recognize, and they should likewise elicit well-publicized acclamations that God is at work. The infirm and the demon-possessed crowded around Jesus because they knew that He could heal or deliver them, as He did quite consistently (Matt. 8:16). If countless individuals really have been "activated" to perform the kinds of miracles projected by NAR teachers, the world would surely know. For the time being, they have not lived up to their billing.[3]

Notes

Chapter 1: Wake Up, Olive

1. Andy Peck, "Bethel Church: Heaven on Earth?" *Premier Christianity*, December 15, 2015, accessed February 22, 2022, https://www.premierchristianity.com/home/bethel-church-heaven-on-earth/1366.article.

2. These three comments, made by separate individuals, were posted along with more than 2,000 other comments to the request made by Bethel Church (on Facebook) to join the church in declaring a resurrection for Olive. See Bethel Church, Redding, 2019, "Our God is the God of miracles," Facebook, December 15, 2019, accessed February 13, 2022, https://www.facebook.com/profile/100044385190800/search/?q=declaring%20resurrection%20life%20for%20olive.

3. Kari Jobe (@karijobe), "We're still standing," Instagram, December 17, 2019, accessed August 8, 2021, https://www.instagram.com/p/B6MPihMHtO7.

4. Tanya Chen and Stephanie McNeal, "The Evangelical Parents of a Young Girl Who Died Are Using Social Media to Ask for Her Resurrection," *BuzzFeed*, December 20, 2019, accessed November 1, 2021, https://www.buzzfeednews.com/article/tanyachen/evangelical-parents-of-a-young-girl-who-died-social-media.

5. Kalley Heiligenthal (@kalleyheili), "Day 4 is a really," Instagram, December 17, 2019, accessed February 22, 2022, https://www.instagram.com/p/B6L6hfTloDF/?hl=en.

6. To watch a video of Olive's parents leading Bethel churchgoers in the singing of those lyrics, see "Olive, Come Out of That Grave (Andrew Heiligenthal)," YouTube video, 2:27, uploaded by Priyesh Hiwaley, December 18, 2019, accessed February 22, 2022, https://www.youtube.com/watch?v=tHGPjndU7LU&t=8s.

7. Kalley Heiligenthal (@kalleyheili), Instagram, December 18, 2019, accessed February 22, 2022, https://www.instagram.com/p/B6OzhNWl6WT.

8. Hemant Mehta, "Bethel Church Finally Admits a Dead Child Will Not Be Resurrected," *Patheos*, December 23, 2019, accessed November 1, 2021, https://friendlyatheist.patheos.com/2019/12/23/bethel-church-finally-admits-a-dead-child-will-not-be-resurrected.

9. Suzanne Titkemeyer, "Did Bethel and Bill Johnson Exploit the Death of Olive Heiligenthal?" *Patheos*, July 15, 2020, accessed November 1, 2021, https://www.patheos.com/blogs/nolongerquivering/2020/07/did-bethel-and-bill-johnson-exploit-the-death-of-olive-heiligenthal.

10. Andreas Wiget, "Interview with Jesse, a Former Charismatic and Bethel Grad," *Medium*, May 2, 2022, accessed May 9, 2022, https://medium.com/@andreaswiget/interview-with-jesse-a-former-charismatic-and-bethel-grad-7a5418a23208. In private correspondence with us, Jesse confirmed that he observed Bethel senior leaders, including Beni Johnson, promoting grave soaking.

11. "Bethel Church Soaking Up the 'Anointing' of Dead Men, or Grave-Sucking," YouTube video, 5:45, uploaded by Raideragent, December 9, 2011, accessed November 1, 2021, https://www.youtube.com/watch?time_continue=124&v=LrHPTs8cLls.

12. Beni Johnson made this statement in a private message sent to Bart McCurdy on Facebook and posted publicly, May 19, 2015, on a popular Facebook page operated by McCurdy that is critical of Bethel Church, titled "Bethel Church and Christianity."

13. Beni Johnson, "Wakey, Wakey," *Benij.org* (blog), March 16, 2009, archived at the Wayback Machine February 15, 2020, accessed November 1, 2021, https://web.archive.org/web/20200215173044/http://www.benij.org/blog.php?id=1.

14. Johnson, "Wakey, Wakey."

15. "Black and White—Jenn Johnson—Women's Conference," YouTube video, 12:11, uploaded by Bethel TV, May 21, 2011, accessed November 1, 2021, https://www.youtube.com/watch?v=qdeqtJvkE5w&fbclid=IwAR2dqJzgtorjU1BdUqwW5c-zp-evqun-a7-yA9FH_TN317aYZYdHDhsc5xo.

16. Jenn also has described the Holy Spirit as a "sneaky" blue genie—"like the genie from *Aladdin*." See "Jenn Johnson—Holy Spirit Is like a Sneaky Blue Genie," YouTube video, 1:26, uploaded by Elmoziffle, June 22, 2013, accessed December 21, 2021, https://www.youtube.com/watch?v=-Wu-WqLjoJo&t=3s. Bill Johnson has said he did not approve

of this analogy and spoke with Jenn about using it. See Michael Brown and Bill Johnson, "Dr. Brown Interviews Pastor Bill Johnson," YouTube video, 46:31, uploaded by AskDrBrown, October 12, 2016, accessed December 21, 2021, https://www.youtube.com/watch?v=Af1hswGOjZg (24:00). But the fact that she did use it raises serious questions about her views of the Holy Spirit and her qualifications for being a pastor at Bethel Church.

17. Bill Johnson, Ché Ahn, Ed Silvoso, and Marlyne Barrett, "Gandalf Staff Prophetic Word with Bill Johnson," YouTube video, 5:47, uploaded by Megan Verdugo, September 2, 2020, accessed November 1, 2021, https://www.youtube.com/watch?v=O8b3yumhMNU&t=175s.

18. "Glory Cloud Rises at Bethel Church," YouTube video, 1:55, uploaded by David Thuman, July 3, 2012, accessed December 27, 2021, https://www.youtube.com/watch?v=lQrTjbzbByA.

19. Bill Johnson, "Response to Glory Cloud at Bethel," YouTube video, 14:17, uploaded by Pastorkimo4960, October 22, 2011, accessed February 22, 2022, https://www.youtube.com/watch?v=tcPkOR4Lwj0.

20. Kris Vallotton, "Multi-Generational Vision," podcast audio, 1:30:23, KrisVallotton.com, December 18, 2016, accessed November 1, 2021, https://www.krisvallotton.com/multi-generational-vission/?fbclid=IwAR2GJt6ulUoqLBmsRxzHMtgCBRUn6CvnTdrPY-aXSsyxj4rI3VVbQCSC-jU.

21. See Bob Jones and Bonnie Jones, "Bob Jones 3rd Heaven Activation," YouTube video, 24:54, uploaded by Raideragent, December 25, 2021, accessed December 26, 2021, https://www.youtube.com/watch?v=QfmLK4qxlrA.

22. Deborah Reed, "Bethel Church Children's Director and 'Trips to Heaven,' with Kids," YouTube video, 10:21, uploaded by Raideragent, March 14, 2014, accessed December 22, 2021, https://www.youtube.com/watch?v=gZxijRzkyrA&t=50sC; Hope Flinchbaugh, "Ignite the Fire," *Charisma Magazine*, February 28, 2007, accessed November 1, 2021, https://www.charismamag.com/site-archives/146-covers/cover-story/2172-ignite-the-fire.

23. Todd M. Johnson and Gina A Zurlo, *World Christian Encyclopedia*, 3rd ed. (Edinburgh University Press, 2019), 849–56. Note that the Bethel Church attenders are not included in that number because Bethel Church is classified by the *World Christian Encyclopedia* as an independent nondenominational megachurch that finds its way into their "Other independent churches" category.

Chapter 2: Who Are the New Apostles and Prophets?

1. Bill Johnson, *When Heaven Invades Earth: A Practical Guide to a Life of Miracles* (Shippensburg, PA: Destiny Image, 2003), chapter 10, Kindle.

2. Johnson, *When Heaven Invades Earth*, chapter 10, Kindle.

3. Kris Vallotton, "Prophetic Gifting vs. Calling: How to Know Which One You Carry," KV Ministries, June 4, 2021, accessed August 9, 2021, https://www.krisvallotton.com/prophetic-gifting-vs-calling.

4. Kris Vallotton, *Heavy Rain: How to Flood Your World with God's Transforming Power* (Bloomington, MN: Chosen, 2016), chapter 1, Kindle.

5. You may wonder how someone becomes an apostle or prophet in NAR. They believe God gives them a spiritual gift of apostleship or prophecy that is recognized by others. The office of apostle or prophet is often conferred on them during a public commissioning ceremony. People who aspire to be an apostle or prophet sometimes pay to take an online course and receive a certificate confirming that they are an apostle or prophet. For an example of a former NAR apostle who became an apostle in this way, see Alisa Childers and Dawain Atkinson, "An Ex-NAR Apostle Tells His Story, with Dawain Atkinson," YouTube video, 44:26, uploaded by Alisa Childers, February 28, 2021, accessed December 23, 2021, https://www.youtube.com/watch?v=PwlfBFbh3rk&t=1424s.

6. For example, listen to the audio recordings of the conversation between the prophet Bob Jones and NAR leader Mike Bickle, detailing Bickle's alleged trip to the courtroom of heaven. See Mike Bickle and Bob Jones, "Visions and Revelations: Mike Bickle with Bob Jones 1988," Internet Archive, accessed December 21, 2021, https://archive.org/details/VisionsAndRevelations-MikeBickleWithBobJones1988 (starting with recording No. 3 at 1:21:00 and continuing to recording No. 4).

Chapter 3: Hogwarts for Christians

1. Molly Hensley-Clancy, "Meet the 'Young Saints' of Bethel Who Go to College to Perform Miracles," *BuzzFeed*, October 12, 2017, accessed November 1, 2021, https://www.buzzfeednews.com/article/mollyhensleyclancy/meet-the-young-saints-of-bethel-who-go-to-college-to.

2. Another type of "speaking in tongues," believed by some to be a gift bestowed by the Holy Spirit, supernaturally enables a Christian to

speak in a natural human language, such as Spanish or Japanese, without prior study of the language. This is not the type of tongues-speaking typically practiced at Bethel Church.

3. This is how the teacher interprets 1 Corinthians 14:3. But this interpretation fails to recognize the ways that so-called negative prophecies, such as exposing sin in someone's life or words of correction, may be used for their spiritual edification.

4. This has been called the "golden rule" of cold reading: "Always tell your subject what they want to hear. Try to turn every negative into a resounding positive." (See "How Does Cold Reading Work?" *Vanishing*, accessed October 13, 2021, https://www.vanishingincmagic.com/mentalism/articles/how-does-cold-reading-work.)

5. Psychic powers are not usually called "gifts" by New Agers; they are viewed as natural but latent. And the term "prophets" is not generally used New Agers. No one in the New Age seeks to get a word or message from God. (Thanks to Marcia Montenegro for these insights.)

6. "How Does Cold Reading Work?"

7. Beni Johnson, "Prayer Servant Training," YouTube video, 01:24, uploaded by Bethel Store, March 23, 2012, accessed November 29, 2021, https://www.youtube.com/watch?v=BHxqAdhvPCU. We note that when Beni Johnson uses the word "praying," the type of "praying" she refers to is not traditional prayer, as in making requests of God; rather, it is a form of NAR "prophetic" praying, which involves receiving revelation from God about the person one is praying for and making "prayer declarations." In addition to cold readings there are also "hot readings." In chapter 4, we explain hot readings, and show an example of a NAR prophet who has been accused of engaging in hot readings.

8. In the example we gave above, one part was right, namely, the date. That's called a "hit" in mentalism circles. And practiced mentalists have well-honed strategies for disguising their "misses." Notice that Beni Johnson even uses the word "hit" in her guidance on prophetic praying.

9. The mentalism community frowns upon the pretense of genuine psychic ability. Phony psychics, "Shotgun" statements, "Barnum" statements: these can all be illustrated in the pattern of Bethel prophecy-activation.

10. The following source explores the challenge of characterizing New Age spirituality with any precision: Steven J. Sutcliffe and Ingvild Sælid Gilhus, eds., *New Age Spirituality: Rethinking Religion* (London and New York: Routledge, 2014).

11. For an alternative view of spiritual gifts, see Kenneth Berding, *What Are Spiritual Gifts?: Rethinking the Conventional View* (Grand Rapids, MI: Kregel, 2006).

12. For a basic introduction to several prominent views on this, see Wayne Grudem, ed., *Are Miraculous Gifts for Today? Four Views* (Grand Rapids: Zondervan, 1996).

13. Ellyn Davis, "Extracting the Precious from the Worthless," in *The Physics of Heaven: Exploring God's Mysteries of Sound, Light, Energy, Vibrations, and Quantum Physics*, eds. Judy Franklin and Ellyn Davis (Shippensburg, PA: Destiny Image Publishers, 2012), chapter 2, Kindle.

14. Jonathan Welton, "Authentic vs. Counterfeit," in *The Physics of Heaven*, chapter 5, Kindle.

15. See, for example, these pro-New Age sites that discuss portals: Lisa Mills, "Spirit Portals," *Selffa*, May 3, 2019, accessed October 13, 2021, https://selffa.com/spirit-portals; Nefer Khepri, "How to Locate and Close Spirit Portals," *The Magickal-Musings of Nefer Khepri, PhD* (personal blog), August 11, 2016, accessed October 13, 2021, https://magickalmusings.blog/2016/08/11/how-to-locate-close-spirit-portals; Jade Eden, "How to Open and Close Dimensional Portals," personal blog, November 8, 2012, accessed October 13, 2021, https://jadeedenopeningandclosingportals.blogspot.com. The influential NAR prophet John Paul Jackson (of Streams Ministries International), who taught about the importance of Christians locating and opening portals, acknowledged that many in the New Age movement also practice opening portals. (See John Paul Jackson, "Heavenly Portals," article reposted by "Silvia" of *Garden of Grace* (personal blog), June 20, 2010, accessed October 13, 2021, https://daughterofgrace777.webs.com/apps/blog/show/4074757-heavenly-portals.)

16. In her eye-opening and insightful book, Marcia Montenegro, a former professional astrologer who became a Christian, describes how the Harry Potter series has been responsible for introducing and drawing many children to the occult. See Marcia Montenegro, *Spellbound: The Paranormal Seduction of Today's Kids* (Colorado Springs: David C. Cook, 2013).

17. Banning Liebscher, founder and director of Jesus Culture, acknowledges the occurrence of these antics and shrugs them off as innocent practice and "pressing into the supernatural." See Jessilyn Justice and Taylor Berglund, "Year in Review: Banning Liebscher: Why Bill Johnson Didn't Immediately Shut Down Grave Sucking," *Charisma News*, April 18, 2018, accessed November 1, 2021, https://

www.charismanews.com/us/70619-bethel-pastor-why-bill-johnson
-didn-t-immediately-shut-down-grave-sucking.

18. Justice and Berglund, "Year in Review."

19. This practice is described in a student testimonial featured at the BSSM school planting website. See "Are You More Religious Than Jesus?," BSSM School Planting, accessed October 13, 2021, https://bssm. net/schoolplanting/2017/11/14/are-you-more-religious-than-jesus. At the time of writing, this student planned to return home to Australia to plant a school of supernatural ministry.

20. Our emphasis. For the complete account, see Acts 3:1–4:20.

21. "'Christian' Tarot Cards and Fortune Telling," YouTube video, 28:06, uploaded by Fighting for the Faith, February 19, 2019, accessed October 13, 2021, https://www.youtube.com/ watch?v=kFIS6gPeVUY&feature=emb_logo.

22. See Holly Pivec, "The 'Christian' Tarot Card Controversy at Bethel Redding," HollyPivec.com, December 15, 2017, accessed October 13, 2021, https://www.hollypivec.com/blog/2017/12/the-christian-tarot-card-controversy-at-bethel-church-in-redding-california/7409.

23. A screen capture of a Facebook posting by Christalignnment's founders, Ken and Jenny Hodge, where they shared this testimonial, was preserved by Steven Kozar, "Christalignment Bethel Fortune-Telling New Age Naked with Jesus Extravaganza!," *Pirate Christian Media*, February 19, 2019, accessed February 22, 2022, https:// www.piratechristian.com/museum-of-idolatry/2019/2/christalignment -bethel-fortune-telling-new-age-naked-with-jesus-extravaganza.

24. This testimonial is preserved at "'Christian' Tarot Cards and Fortune Telling," YouTube video, 28:06, uploaded by Fighting for the Faith, February 19, 2019, accessed February 22, 2022, https://www. youtube.com/watch?v=kFIS6gPeVUY (15:00).

25. Kris Vallotton's Facebook page, December 15, 2017, accessed October 13, 2021, https://www.facebook.com/kvministries/posts/ here-is-a-beautiful-letter-i-received-today-amazing-people-trying-to-be-destroye/10155320301218741; Theresa Dedmon, "A Christmas Critique of 'Destiny Cards,'" TheresaDedmon.com, December 19, 2017, accessed October 13, 2021, https://www.theresadedmon.com/blog/a-christmas-critique-of-destiny-cards. (Dedmon has developed her own version of Destiny Cards, also used by BSSM students at the church. She claims that she coined the phrase "destiny cards," "to reflect that we call out the gold in others, and prophesy life and encouragement to them, as 1 Corinthians 14:3 instructs." Her cards are designed to be used in

"creative evangelism." Notice that Dedman assumes that prophecy is to be incorporated into evangelism.) See Theresa Dedmon, "Sharing God's Love Through Destiny Cards," personal blog, December 29, 2017, accessed October 13, 2021, https://www.theresadedmon.com/blogsharing-gods-love-through-destiny-cards.

26. "Bethel Statement Regarding Christalignment," Bethel.com, January 5, 2018, accessed October 13, 2021, https://www.bethel.com/about/christalignment.

27. "Our Cards Lead the Way," Christalignment, archived at the Wayback Machine December 13, 2017, accessed November 1, 2021, https://web.archive.org/web/20171213060600/http://www.christalignment.org/destinyreadingcards.

28. "Seth Dahl: How to Hear Your Child's Spirit Speak Inside Your," video, 6:46, uploaded to Bethel Church and Christianity's Facebook page, December 20, 2017, accessed February 22, 2022, https://www.facebook.com/BethelChurchandChristianity/videos/1503833259653692.

29. "Ben Armstrong—The Next Level," YouTube video, 8:40, uploaded by Snowballsgalore, July 15, 2009, accessed October 13, 2021, https://www.youtube.com/watch?v=LucEsXO5adQ&fbclid=IwAR3tV10CHjQjDiPpbN4hI43WIhvtKngOTq8VaeOyiLd77w7nVNu4V01U4lU.

30. The "cloud of witnesses" in Hebrews 12:1 refers to those Old Testament believers who lived by faith, mentioned in chapter 11. We do not think this verse teaches that dead believers are observing Christians from heaven, but rather that they witness to us through their example of faith. Still, even if it did mean that, that would not give us grounds for trying to communicate with them.

31. Betheltv Facebook page, video, 8:34, November 13, 2015, accessed October 13, 2021, https://www.facebook.com/watch/?v=10153685868930930.

32. Shawn Bolz, "Shawn Bolz Stories: Your Destiny Doesn't End with You," YouTube video, 6:30, January 28, 2017, accessed December 22, 2021, https://www.youtube.com/watch?v=BU-olI6jO0Y.

33. Ben Fitzgerald of Awakening Europe and musician Kim Walker-Smith of Jesus Culture are examples of this.

34. See BSSM School Planting, accessed October 13, 2021, https://bssm.net/schoolplanting.

35. Marcia Montenegro, Doreen Virtue, Melissa Doughtery, and Steven Bancarz are among the former New Agers sounding the alarm about occult practices infiltrating Christian churches. See Virtue,

Deceived No More: How Jesus Led Me Out of the New Age and Into His Word (Nashville: Thomas Nelson, 2020).

Chapter 4: Jesus's Overlooked Warning

1. The first test, the Orthodoxy Test, is given in Deuteronomy 13:1–5. It requires that we make sure that a prophet's words line up with the revelation God has already given us in Scripture. We apply this test throughout this book, showing where NAR teachings do not line up with Scripture. The second test, the Lifestyle Test given by Jesus in Matthew 7:16–23, requires that we test the "fruit" or conduct of prophets' lives. We apply this test in chapter 6, where we identify highly revered NAR prophets who have confessed to significant moral failures.

2. See chapters 5 and 10 for our description of a proper Bible study method and the recommendation of a book that teaches this. We also recommend the following books: J. Scott Duvall and J. Daniel Hays, *Grasping God's Word: A Hands-On Approach to Reading, Interpreting, and Applying the Bible*, 4th ed. (Grand Rapids: Zondervan Academic, 2020); Lindsay Olesberg, *The Bible Study Handbook: A Comprehensive Guide to an Essential Practice* (Downers Grove, IL: InterVarsity Press, 2012); R. C. Sproul, *Knowing Scripture*, expanded edition (Downers Grove, IL: IVP Books, 2016).

3. Is this a negative test or a positive test? In one respect, it is a negative test. A pattern of negligence in teaching already revealed truth disqualifies a person who claims to have special insight into divine truth. However, the larger point is that a prophet must acquit himself as one who handles divine revelation responsibly—and that is a positive test. The prophet of God will have reliable access to new truth only if he is tuned in to God's purpose and character as disclosed in Scripture.

4. The apostle Paul states that the signs of a true apostle included "signs and wonders and miracles" (2 Cor. 12:12).

5. The penalty of death may seem severe. But it surely would have had a deterrent effect. One would tend to enter the domain of the prophetic with extreme caution, knowing the consequences of getting it wrong. While the urgency to discern true from false prophecy remains, and the risks are as great today as they ever have been, the penalty of death no longer applies. As we've written elsewhere, "Christians today, of course, don't customarily stone false prophets, as was lawful in the Old Testament (Deut. 13:5, 6–10; 18:20). This is partly because the church is not a theocratic nation and is not under the Mosaic law." See

R. Douglas Geivett and Holly Pivec, *A New Apostolic Reformation? A Biblical Response to a Worldwide Movement* (Bellingham, WA: Lexham Press, 2014), chapter 14. While the consequences have changed, false prophecy is still a morally serious failure and there are warnings in the New Testament to that effect (Matt. 7:15; 24:11, 24; 1 John 4:1; see also 2 Cor. 11:13–15). However, no precise penalty is specified.

6. Julia Duin, "Charismatics Are at War with Each Other Over Failed Prophecies of Trump Victory," *Religion Unplugged*, January 12, 2021, accessed December 3, 2021, https://religionunplugged.com /news/2021/1/12/charismatics-are-at-war-with-each-other-over-failed -prophecies-of-trump-victory.

7. Kris Vallotton, "Sovereign Providence," podcast audio, 46:27, The Kris Vallotton Podcast, December 27, 2019, accessed May 14, 2022, https://soundcloud.com/krisvallotton/sovereign-providence. (This message was uploaded to Vallotton's podcast after he delivered it at Bethel Church.)

8. Kris Vallotton, Facebook post, video, uploaded to Kris Vallotton's Facebook page, November 7, 2020.

9. Kris Vallotton, "My Apology–U.S. Presidential Election Prophecy 2020," video, 5:24, uploaded to Kris Vallotton's Facebook page, January 8, 2021, accessed December 3, 2021, https://fb.watch/9s-odP6gP7. Notice these three features of Vallotton's "apology." First, he calls his original prediction a "prophecy." Second, he chapter that he got it wrong. Third, he excuses a "credibility gap" as somehow tolerable for a prophet of God.

10. Jeremiah Johnson, "My Public Apology and Process," *Charisma News*, January 7, 2021, accessed December 3, 2021, https://www. charismanews.com/opinion/83947-jeremiah-johnson-my-public- apology-and-process; Shawn Bolz, Facebook post, January 8, 2021, accessed December 3, 2021, https://www.facebook.com/ShawnBolz/ posts/10165166390920657. Some NAR prophets doubled down and continued to believe that God was going to restore Trump to the White House even after his successor, Joe Biden, was inaugurated and took office. See Julia Duin, "The Christian Prophets Who Say Trump Is Coming Again," *Politico*, February 18, 2021, accessed December 3, 2021, https://www.politico.com/news/magazine/2021/02/18/how-chris- tian-prophets-give-credence-to-trumps-election-fantasies-469598.

11. Prophetic Standards Statement, April 29, 2021, accessed December 31, 2021, https://propheticstandards.com. This document was initiated by Joseph Mattera—the convener for the United States

Coalition of Apostolic Leaders (USCAL)—and USCAL member and radio host Michael Brown. See Joseph Mattera, "The Need for Prophetic Standards in the Church," May 4, 2021, accessed February 18, 2022, https://josephmattera.org/need-prophetic-church. We note, with concern, that this document allows that prophets (authoritative "prophetic ministers" and not just believers with a mere gift of prophecy) can make errors while prophesying and still be considered genuine prophets of God. Thus, the drafters of this document (and presumably its signers) believe that the Fulfillment Test does not apply to today's prophets.

12. Duin, "The Christian Prophets Who Say Trump Is Coming Again"; Sam Kestenbaum, "Life after Proclaiming a Trump Re-election as Divinely Ordained," *New York Times*, September 19, 2021, accessed December 3, 2021, https://www.nytimes.com/2021/09/19/business/trump-election-prophecy-charisma-media.html.

13. Hemant Mehta, "Here Are 12 Christian Preachers Who Wrongly Predicted Trump's Re-Election," *Patheos*, November 24, 2020, accessed December 3, 2021, https://friendlyatheist.patheos.com/2020/11/24/here-are-12-christian-preachers-who-wrongly-predicted-trumps-re-election.

14. Those prophets included Chuck Pierce and Tracy Cooke. See Michael Brown, "This Is a Great Time to Test Contemporary Prophetic Words," *The Stream*, March 30, 2020, accessed December 3, 2021, https://stream.org/this-is-a-great-time-to-test-contemporary-prophetic-words.

15. Caleb Parke, "Christian Pastor Shawn Bolz: 'Lord Showed Me the End of the Coronavirus,'" *Fox News*, March 3, 2020, accessed December 3, 2021, https://www.foxnews.com/faith-values/coronavirus-christian-pastor-shawn-bolz.

16. Parke, "Christian Pastor Shawn Bolz."

17. Mike Bickle, *Growing in the Prophetic: A Practical, Biblical Guide to Dreams, Visions, and Spiritual Gifts*, rev. ed. (Lake Mary, FL: Charisma House, 2008), MikeBickle.org, accessed August 14, 2014, http://mikebickle.org/books, 41, PDF e-book.

18. In defense of their position that today's prophets need not be totally accurate, many NAR leaders point to arguments made by the influential Christian theologian Wayne Grudem, who wrote a book claiming that prophets' words in the New Testament, unlike prophets' words in the Old Testament, sometimes contained a mixture of truth and error. See Wayne Grudem, *The Gift of Prophecy in the New Testament and Today*, rev. ed. (Wheaton, IL: Crossway, 2000). For a good treatment of the problems with this view, see Thomas R. Schreiner, *Spiritual*

Gifts: What They Are and Why They Matter (Nashville: B&H Publishing, 2018), chapter 7. Although Schreiner is a cessationist, we do not see why a continuationist could not agree, against Grudem, that all New Testament prophecy is infallible. We commend Schreiner for his able critique of Grudem on this point. We don't mean, in this, to be endorsing his cessationism because we believe a continuationist could, and should, believe that all prophecy is infallible. Robert L. Saucy, who is not a cessationist, also has argued effectively against prophetic fallibilism, in "An Open but Cautious Response to C. Samuel Storms," in *Are Miraculous Gifts for Today? Four Views*, edited by Wayne A. Grudem (Grand Rapids: Zondervan, 1996), 229–32.

19. During a Q-and-A session, Bill Johnson is asked directly how to test prophecy. In his answer, he passed rather glibly over the urgent question, how may we know that a prophetic word truly comes from God? He offers no clear instruction for discerning what is and what is not genuine prophecy. See Bill Johnson and Dann Farrelly, "How a Word from God Is Tested," YouTube video, 6:23, uploaded by Bill Johnson Teaching (Official), July 6, 2020, accessed December 31, 2021, https://www.youtube.com/watch?v=14-58SLUTX4. Also, the only positive test suggested in the Prophetic Standards Statement is that "our own spirit bears witness with it [the prophetic word]." This test is presented in the document as a confirming test, but it is highly subjective and oddly spiritualistic, and, therefore, not useful. Plus, where is this test ever given in Scripture?

20. Bill Johnson, "You Will Recover All (Full Sermon)," YouTube video, 46:09, uploaded by Bill Johnson Teaching (Official), January 7, 2022, uploaded by Bill Johnson Teaching (Official), accessed February 22, 2022, https://www.youtube.com/watch?v=ZGj5KKTwhUY. Doug attended this service in person and Holly watched the livestream.

21. This council was founded by the "apostle" C. Peter Wagner in 1999 and is led by Cindy Jacobs.

22. "ACPE Word of the Lord for 2020," God Encounters Ministries, accessed February 16, 2022, https://godencounters.com/apce-word-of-the-lord-for-2020.

23. "Jonathan" shared a video recording of his prophetic Zoom session with us. To protect his anonymity, we do not include his last name.

24. What kind of training do you need for giving prophecies like this one? Actually, it's a good question. These Zoom handlers are, after all, trained to conduct sessions with guests. It isn't hard to imagine what kind of training they're given. We reckon, however, that trainers must be

careful to maintain the charade that the handlers are actually engaged in giving prophetic words since the handlers probably think that's what they're doing.

25. Brian Carn, "2020 Word of the Lord," Brian Carn Ministries, accessed December 3, 2021, https://briancarn.com/2020wordofthelord.

26. Sophie Dodd, "Remembering the Stars We've Lost in 2020," People.com, December 31, 2020, accessed December 3, 2021, https://people.com/celebrity/stars-who-died-2020.

27. Author emphasis.

28. A video clip of Goll's prophecy is shown and analyzed by Winger while Winger was a guest on Remnant Radio's webcast. See Joshua Lewis, Michael Rowntree, Michael Brown, Craig Keener, Sam Storms, Ken Fish, Jack Deere, Michael Miller, Dawson Jarrell, Joel Richardson, and Mike Winger, "Testing the Prophets: Testing the Prophecies Given in 2020," YouTube video, 8:11:30, uploaded by The Remnant Radio, December 30, 2020, accessed December 3, 2021, https://www.youtube.com/watch?v=GgE85J1mF9s&t=27915shttps://www.youtube.com/watch?v=GgE85J1mF9s&t=3s (6:33:00).

29. See, for example, Brian Schwartz and Tucker Higgins, "With Ruth Bader Ginsburg's Health in the Spotlight, Attention Turns to Abortion Foe Waiting in the Wings," CNBC, August 30, 2019, accessed December 3, 2021, https://www.cnbc.com/2019/08/30/with-rbgs-health-in-the-spotlight-attention-turns-to-judge-barrett.html.

30. Jonathan Swan and Sam Baker, "Scoop: Trump 'Saving' Judge Amy Barrett for Ruth Bader Ginsburg Seat," *Axios*, March 31, 2019, accessed December 3, 2021, https://www.axios.com/supreme-court-trump-judge-amy-barrett-ruth-bader-ginsburg-11d25276-a92e-4094-8958-eb2d197707c8.html; Bradford Betz, "Trump 'Saving' Judge Amy Coney Barrett to Replace Ginsburg: Report," *Fox News*, April 1, 2019, accessed December 3, 2021, https://www.foxnews.com/politics/trump-saving-judge-amy-coney-barret-to-replace-ginsburg-report; Tamar Lapin, "Trump Already Has a Replacement for Ruth Bader Ginsberg's Seat: Report," *New York Post*, April 1, 2019, accessed December 3, 2021, https://nypost.com/2019/04/01/trump-already-has-a-replacement-for-ruth-bader-ginsburgs-seat-report.

31. See "Shawn 'Smart Phone' Bolz: Cold-Reading False Prophet!" YouTube video, 17:05, uploaded by The Messed Up Church, August 27, 2021, accessed October 13, 2021, https://www.youtube.com/watch?v=1a5HSYu1dY8&t=2s.

32. "Watch: Shawn Bolz Receives Confirmation for Incredible Words of Knowledge at The Send," *Charisma Magazine*, February 28, 2019, accessed December 3, 2021, https://www.charismamag.com/1586-media/video/40546-watch-shawn-bolz-receives-confirmation-for-incredible-words-of-knowledge-at-the-send. Bolz also gave "words of knowledge" to two other people at the event. These, too, are featured in the video shared by *Charisma Magazine*. Both of those people, predictably enough, also appeared awed by Bolz's intimate knowledge about details of their lives.

33. Bolz acknowledged, during the Send Conference, that he has been accused of researching information about conference attendees online since he often looks at his phone while prophesying. But he assures his audience that he is only looking at his notes, text messages, or other things online and has not conducted prior research about audience attendees. See Shawn Bolz, "Reactions to Words of Knowledge in a Stadium of 70,000!," YouTube video, 9:51, uploaded by Everyday Prophetic, February 25, 2019, accessed December 3, 2021, https://www.charismamag.com/1586-media/video/40546-watch-shawn-bolz-receives-confirmation-for-incredible-words-of-knowledge-at-the-send (04:00).

34. "Shawn Bolz and Sid Roth: Wifi Scam Artists," YouTube video, 20:41, uploaded by The Messed Up Church, April 8, 2020, accessed December 3, 2021, https://www.youtube.com/watch?v=AcrQJRAyiEU.

35. See John Andrew Collins, *Jim Jones: The Malachi 4 Elijah Prophecy* (Jeffersonville, IN: Dark Mystery Publications, 2017), 161–64. Collins notes that the prayer cards were numbered and people were placed in a "healing line" according to that number. This raises the suspicion that the successful functioning of Branham's prophetic "gift" depended on people remaining in the line's order. For evidence that Branham himself insisted that people line up in the order assigned by their numbered prayer cards before he prophesied to them, see William Branham, "Christ Knocking at the Door," sermon transcript, Voice of God Recordings, accessed December 29, 2021, https://table.branham.org.

Chapter 5: The Apostolic Takeover and Spiritual Abuse

1. Amy Spreeman, "Leaving the NAR Church: Dean's Story," May 10, 2017, *Berean Examiner*, accessed November 19, 2021, https://pirate christian.com/berean-examiner/leaving-the-nar-church-deans-story.

2. The "apostle" Ché Ahn, for example, oversees Harvest International Ministry based in Pasadena, California—an apostolic network encompassing more than 25,000 affiliated churches and organizations in more than 65 nations.

3. Kris Vallotton, "The Power of the Five-Fold Ministry—Sunday AM," video, 43:22, Bethel.TV, February 9, 2020, accessed May 15, 2022, https://www.bethel.tv/details?id=61ae5556e4b04a88409261b9& type=vod.

4. The term *fivefold ministry* is also sometimes used by Pentecostals and charismatics to refer to the spiritual *gifts* of apostle, prophet, evangelist, shepherd, and teacher rather than to the governing *offices*. But if they believe that Ephesians 4:11 describes governmental offices (or authoritative positions) in the church, then they hold to the NAR doctrine of fivefold ministry even if they use the word *gifts* rather than *offices*. Some NAR teachers use "gift" and "office" more or less interchangeably.

5. Interestingly, most churches today, even many NAR churches, do not have formal offices for "evangelists" and "teachers." But NAR leaders seem concerned only about the missing apostles and prophets.

6. "Our Mission," Bethel Redding, accessed December 23, 2021, https://www.bethelredding.com/about/our-mission.

7. See Bill Johnson, *Open Heavens: Position Yourself to Encounter the God of Revival* (Shippensburg, PA: Destiny Image Publishers, 2021), chapter 14, Kindle.

8. The Assemblies of God, the world's largest Pentecostal denomination, does not recognize the present-day offices of apostle and prophet. See "Apostles and Prophets," General Presbytery of the Assemblies of God, August 6, 2001, accessed December 23, 2021, https://ag.org/ Beliefs/Position-Papers/Apostles-and-Prophets.

9. For our in-depth description and documentation of NAR teachings about apostles and prophets bringing critical new revelation to the church, see R. Douglas Geivett and Holly Pivec, *A New Apostolic Reformation? A Biblical Response to a Worldwide Movement* (Bellingham, WA: Lexham Press, 2018), chapters 4, 5, 10, 11.

10. Kris Vallotton, *Heavy Rain: How to Flood Your World with God's Transforming Power* (Bloomington, MN: Chosen, 2016), chapter 5, Kindle.

11. In support of his teaching that apostles have authority over angels, Vallotton observes that, in the book of Revelation, Jesus instructed the apostle John to write letters to seven churches. And each letter was to be addressed to the "angel" of a particular church (see Rev. 2:1, 8, 12, 18; 3:1, 7, 14). Vallotton teaches that specific angels are assigned to serve apostles and their mission through their churches (see Vallotton, *Heavy Rain*, chapter 4, Kindle). However, the Greek word for "angel" used in Revelation 2 and 3 may actually refer to human messengers or human pastors, rather than to angelic beings. And even if the letters to the seven churches are addressed to actual angels, that does not support Vallotton's astounding assertion that apostles have authority over angels.

12. Vallotton, *Heavy Rain*, chapter 4, Kindle.

13. Vallotton, *Heavy Rain*, chapter 4, Kindle.

14. Danny Silk, *Culture of Honor: Sustaining a Supernatural Environment* (Shippensburg, PA: Destiny Image, 2009), chapter 2, Kindle. Silk also speaks of the need for pastors to be "submitted to apostolic leadership" (72). "As I mentioned," he says, "the teacher is generally accepted as the highest anointing level in the American church. But the truth is that it is not the highest anointing, but only the third level of anointing. It is a 'C' in a grade scale, and it is what keeps the Church only average in its effects and influence. Our need and opportunity to upgrade the anointing to an 'A' [apostle] is growing" (67). Silk claims that 1 Corinthians 12:27–28 teaches that apostles have an A-level anointing, prophets have a B-level anointing, and teachers have a C-level anointing.

15. For a detailed explanation of what the Bible teaches about the apostles of Christ, including their callings, criteria for inclusion in their group, and their proper functions, see Geivett and Pivec, *A New Apostolic Reformation?*, chapter 6. In chapter 7, we identify others referred to as "apostles" in the New Testament and argue that those others functioned as missionaries and messengers on behalf of the churches who sent them out, and we note that (in contrast to the apostles of Christ) they probably did not exercise great authority in the early church.

16. The Latter Rain Movement promoted many of today's NAR teachings before NAR came on the scene, though this movement fizzled out after the General Council of the Assemblies of God in the United States passed a resolution denouncing it on September 13, 1949. The

Irvingites of the 1830s and the Apostolic Church of the early 1900s also promoted the restoration of apostles and prophets to church government.

17. https://www.merriam-webster.com/dictionary/euphemism

18. Vallotton, *Heavy Rain*, chapter 3, Kindle.

19. Ché Ahn, *Modern-Day Apostles: Operating in Your Apostolic Office and Anointing* (Shippensburg, PA: Destiny Image Publishers, 2019), chapter 8, Kindle. We note that Bill Johnson supplied the foreword for Ahn's book.

20. We note that apostolic networks open major sources of revenue to the apostles and prophets because church leaders and churches make financial contributions to be part of the networks.

21. See "Apostles and Spiritual Covering," Peace Apostolic Ministries (Rock Hampton, Queensland, Australia), accessed November 19, 2021, https://peace.org.au/apostolic/the-apostolic-revelation/apostles-and-spiritual-covering.html.

22. This phrase may also sometimes be used of the other fivefold ministry leaders, but most typically is used of the apostles and prophets.

23. *Bethel Leaders Network Information Packet*, PDF, Bethel Leaders Network, updated March 12, 2021, accessed November 19, 2021, https://s6avwg5v.pages.infusionsoft.net.

24. Teachings about the importance of believers forming "covenant relationships" with their spiritual leaders were central in the "Shepherding Movement" (also known as the "Discipleship Movement") of the 1970s and 1980s, which began in Ft. Lauderdale, Florida. Many NAR leaders have acknowledged that spiritual abuse occurred in that movement, yet they still promote covenant relationships (minus the pyramid-like leadership structure of the Shepherding Movement).

25. Vallotton, *Heavy Rain*, chapter 4, Kindle.

26. Vallotton, "The Power of the Five-Fold Ministry," (31:00).

27. Silk, *Culture of Honor*, Introduction, Kindle. Silk goes on to identify apostles and prophets specifically in connection with the culture of honor: "Names and titles are important. Mother, father, son, daughter, apostle, prophet, Christian, human being—such names define a person's role and identity and when used correctly, establish God-designed relationships in which specific 'rewards' are given and received to build and strengthen us."

28. "The NAR Debate! Randy Clark Responds to Dr. Doug Geivett and Holly Pivec," YouTube video, 1:41:55, uploaded by The Remnant Radio, April 19, 2022, accessed May 17, 2022, https://www.youtube.com/watch?v=Bz8yCZXjH7I&t=4212s (27:00).

29. For another reference to Bentley and the scandal surrounding the Lakeland Revival, see chapter 6.

30. Bill Johnson, "Eat Meat, Don't Eat the Bones—Love-Joy-Peace-Hope EL007 YouTube," video uploaded by Live Forever BJ, March 30, 2015, accessed November 19, 2021, https://www.youtube.com/watch?v=5igclUvzKKI&t=6s (30:00).

31. Bill Johnson, *When Heaven Invades Earth: A Practical Guide to a Life of Miracles* (Shippensburg, PA: Destiny Image, 2003), chapter 7, Kindle.

32. See chapter 3 for our explanation of these manifestations.

33. Mike Bickle, *Growing in the Prophetic: A Practical, Biblical Guide to Dreams, Visions, and Spiritual Gifts,* rev. ed. (Lake Mary, FL: Charisma House, 2008), MikeBickle.org, accessed August 14, 2014, http://mikebickle.org/books, 113, PDF e-book.

34. Chuck Pierce, Robert Heidler, and Linda Heidler, *A Time to Advance: Understanding the Significance of the Hebrew Tribes and Months* (Corinth, TX: Glory of Zion International, 2011), chapter 1, Kindle.

35. Johnson, *When Heaven Invades Earth*, chapter 8, Kindle.

36. See Tim Challies, "Putting God in a Box—Doctrine," Challies.com, May 19, 2005, accessed December 23, 2021, https://www.challies.com/articles/putting-god-in-a-box-doctrine.

37. Johnson, *When Heaven Invades Earth*, chapter 10, Kindle.

38. For example, Johnson has pinned his critics with negative labels including: "fear-oriented theologians," "soul-driven" and "carnal" Christians, and "self-appointed watchdogs who poison the Church with their own fears" (see Johnson, *When Heaven Invades Earth*, chapters 4, 7, Kindle).

39. Prophetic Standards Statement, April 29, 2021, accessed December 31, 2021, https://propheticstandards.com.

40. Author emphasis.

41. There are lots of plans for reading the Bible through in a year or, for a slower pace, two years. And it can take much less time per day than you might think—as little as 10 to 15 minutes with some plans. For an overview of some of those plans (including their pros and cons), see "Top 11 Best Bible Reading Plans," Bible Study Together, accessed December 11, 2021, biblestudytogether.com/top-best-bible-reading-plans.

42. The Lausanne Covenant is a statement of faith that is highly regarded by evangelicals across many denominations and has been adopted for use by many missions organizations.

Chapter 6: Counterfeit Revival

1. Melissa Doughtery, "Paul" and "Morgan," "Why These Christian YouTubers Left the Hyper-Charismatic Movement," YouTube video, 1:10:22, uploaded by "Melissa Doughtery," November 29, 2021, accessed December 9, 2021, https://www.youtube.com/watch?v=qGNMBamDqmk&t=2090s.

2. For an example of two NAR leaders who promote teachings and prophecies about the billion-soul harvest, see Bill Johnson, *When Heaven Invades Earth: A Practical Guide to a Life of Miracles* (Shippensburg, PA: Destiny Image, 2003), chapter 17, Kindle, and Mike Bickle, *Growing in the Prophetic: A Practical, Biblical Guide to Dreams, Visions, and Spiritual Gifts*, rev. ed. (Lake Mary, FL: Charisma House, 2008), MikeBickle.org, accessed August 14, 2014, http://mikebickle.org/books, 77, 81–82, PDF e-book.

3. These stadium events include those organized by Lou Engle of The Send (formerly The Call).

4. For an example of a fire tunnel, see "Tunnel of Fire at Bethel Church 01/20/2012," YouTube video, 0:59, uploaded by The Outlet Church, January 21, 2012, accessed December 26, 2021, https://www.youtube.com/watch?v=PqGLJ0b5lh4.

5. We avoid the use of this language because we do not want to contribute to the confusion about what is meant by "building" or "advancing" God's kingdom.

6. See Lance Wallnau and Bill Johnson, *Invading Babylon: The Seven Mountain Mandate* (Shippensburg, PA: Destiny Image, 2013), chapters 1, 2, Kindle.

7. Wallnau and Johnson, chapter 2, 3, Kindle.

8. The NAR teaching that the church, under the leadership of apostles and prophets, has been tasked with setting up God's physical kingdom on earth is known as "Kingdom Now"—a version of dominion theology.

9. Ché Ahn, *Modern-Day Apostles: Operating in Your Apostolic Office and Anointing* (Shippensburg, PA: Destiny Image, 2019), chapter 15, Kindle.

10. For example, the NAR "gospel of the kingdom" is taught in multiple books by Bill Johnson, including, *When Heaven Invades Earth*, chapters 2, 17, Kindle; *Open Heavens: Position Yourself to Encounter the God of Revival* (Shippensburg, PA: Destiny Image Publishers, 2021), chapter 11, Kindle; *God Is Good: He's Better Than You Think*

(Shippensburg, PA: Destiny Image, 2016), chapter 3, Kindle. See also Johnny Enlow, *The Seven Mountain Prophecy: Unveiling the Coming Elijah Revolution* (Lake Mary, FL: Creation House, 2008), 41. Some contemporary theologians who are not NAR, including N. T. Wright (Research Professor Emeritus of New Testament and Early Christianity at St. Mary's College in the University of St Andrews) and Tim Mackie (cofounder of the Bible Project), refer to the gospel of the kingdom as including more than just the gospel of forgiveness of sins. But when they use this term, they are not referring to the NAR "gospel of the kingdom" (which emphasizes signs, wonders and "taking dominion"). Rather, they teach that the gospel of the kingdom is the Old Testament message from Isaiah of God's rule that is inaugurated in Christ, which may contain elements of the new era of God's earthly reign.

11. Johnson, *When Heaven Invades Earth*, chapters 8, 9, Kindle.

12. Bethel Church, "Bill and Beni Johnson," Bethel.com, accessed January 1, 2022, https://www.bethel.com/leadership/bill-joh nson/?fbclid=IwAR09W6XgpKvxMpCerknt7-MgGqL2ZXP-X5qb 3WYQxK8J6nWzBsKCi-95UJE.

13. Kris Vallotton, *Poverty, Riches and Wealth: Moving from a Life of Lack into True Kingdom Abundance* (Bloomington, MN: Chosen Books, 2018), chapter 1, Kindle.

14. For an excellent scholarly overview of prosperity gospel teachings, we recommend the book by Kate Bowler, *Blessed: A History of the American Prosperity Gospel* (New York: Oxford University Press, 2013). Also see the full-length film documentary *American Gospel: Christ Alone*.

15. Bill Hamon, *Prophetic Scriptures Yet to Be Fulfilled: During the Third and Final Church Reformation* (Shippensburg, PA: Destiny Image Publishers, 2010), 127–28.

16. C. Peter Wagner and Cindy Jacobs, *The Great Transfer of Wealth: Financial Release for Advancing God's Kingdom* (New Kinsington, PA: Whitaker House, 2014).

17. Jennifer LeClaire, *Releasing the Angels of Abundant Harvest: A Prophetic Word for Radical Increase in 2017* (Lake Mary, FL: Charisma House, 2017), chapter 17, Kindle.

18. This is clearly the case with premillennialists. And although amillennialists believe that apostasy and persecution will be found throughout the history of the church, the standard amillennial view (based on 2 Thess. 2:3) expects an escalation of those things in the days leading up to Christ's return. Robert B. Strimple, representing the amillennialist view, writes: "The idea of the Antichrist in general and

that of the apostasy in particular reminds us that we may not expect an uninterrupted progress of the Christianization of the world until the Parousia. As the reign of truth will be extended, so the forces of evil will gather strength, especially toward the end." See Robert B. Strimple, "An Amillennial Response to Kenneth L. Gentry Jr.," in *Three Views on the Millennium and Beyond*, ed. Darrell L. Bock (Grand Rapids: Zondervan, 1999), 65. Amillennialist Anthony A. Hoekema makes the same general point when he talks about the signs of the times in chapter 11 of his book *The Bible and the Future* (Grand Rapids: William B. Eerdmans, 1979). In his article on amillennialism, Hoekema writes, *"The 'signs of the times' have both present and future relevance.* Amillennialists believe that the return of Christ will be preceded by certain signs: for example, the preaching of the gospel to all the nations, the conversion of the fullness of Israel, the great apostasy, the great tribulation and the coming of the Antichrist." He says, further, "amillennial eschatology looks for a culmination of apostasy and tribulation in the final emergence of a personal Antichrist before Christ comes again. Amillennialists do not expect to see the perfect society realized during this present age" (Anthony Hoekema, "Amillennnialism," Monergism, https://www.monergism.com/amillennialism, accessed February 26, 2022). See also Kim Riddlebarger, *A Case for Amillennialism: Understanding the End Times*, expanded edition (Grand Rapids: Baker Books, 2013), 148, 150, 268–69. About half of Protestant pastors are premillennialists and another third are amillennialists, according to a survey conducted by Lifeway Research. See "Pastors: The End of the World Is Complicated," Lifeway Newsroom, April 26, 2016, accessed February 23, 2022, https://news.lifeway.com/2016/04/26/pastors-the-end-of-the-world-is-complicated. Neither premillennialists nor traditional amillennialists look to establish God's earthly kingdom. But some NAR leaders have recently begun referring to their novel view of the end time as "victorious amillennialism," despite its significant departures from historic amillennialism.

19. See, for example, Kris Vallotton, *Heavy Rain: How to Flood Your World with God's Transforming Power* (Bloomington, MN: Chosen, 2016), chapter 15, Kindle; Bill Johnson, *The Way of Life: Experiencing the Culture of Heaven on Earth*, updated ed. (Shippensburg, PA: Destiny Image, 2019), chapter 10, Kindle.

20. Harold R. Eberle and Martin Trench, *Victorious Eschatology: A Partial Preterist View*, 2nd ed. (Yakima, WA: Worldcast, 2007), 215–18.

21. See, for example, "Study Notes (Word)," document at Teaching Library of Mike Bickle, "Session 1: Introduction and Overview of the

Book of Revelation," Studies in the Book of Revelation, Twelve-part series taught at the International House of Prayer University, Spring Semester 2014, MikeBickle.org, accessed February 22, 2022, http:// mikebickle.org/resource/introduction-and-overview-of-the-book-of-revelation. Bickle's use of the word "loose" references specific NAR teachings about "binding and loosing prayer" (which is carried out by making "prayer declarations").

22. Mike Bickle, "IHOP TV Podcast 3," YouTube video, 10:59, uploaded by Onething TV, December 3, 2008, accessed December 9, 2021, http://www.youtube.com/watch?v=K5FMsDrNyn4. Bickle launched an entire school promoting these NAR teachings about the end time called the Center for Biblical End-Time Studies. He calls his view of the end time "apostolic premillennialism."

23. Bill Johnson describes declarations as more powerful than petitionary prayer, in his book *When Heaven Invades Earth*, chapter 5, Kindle. The NAR practice of making prayer declarations, also known as "positive confessions," stems from prosperity gospel/Word of Faith theology. See Bowler, *Blessed*.

24. Bill Johnson, *Hosting the Presence: Unveiling Heaven's Agenda* (Shippensburg, PA: Destiny Image, 2012), 94; Bill Johnson, *God Is Good: He's Better Than You Think* (Shippensburg, PA: Destiny Image, 2016), 83–84.

25. Johnson, *When Heaven Invades Earth*, 40.

26. A powerful and devotionally rewarding description of how to plead with God, in contrast to making declarations, appears in the classical work *A Guide to Prayer* by Isaac Watts (1716), chapter 1.

27. We shared the story about Olive in chapter 1.

28. Randi Mann, "California's 7th Worst Wildfire Destroyed 1,077 Homes and Spawned a Fire Tornado," Weather Network, July 29, 2021, accessed December 9, 2021, https://www.theweathernetwork.com/ca/news/article/this-day-in-weather-history-july-26-2018-carr-fire-in-california; Heather Sells, "More Than 40 Bethel Members Lose Everything in Carr Fire," *Charisma News*, August 8, 2018, accessed December 9, 2021, https://www.charismanews.com/us/72487-25-bethel-staffers-lose-everything-in-carr-fire.

29. For more on how Bethel Church responded to the Covid-19 outbreak with declarations and decrees (another term often used interchangeably with declarations), see Holly Pivec, "The NAR Antidote to Coronavirus," *HollyPivec.com* (blog), March 21, 2020, accessed December 9, 2021, https://www.hollypivec.com/blog/2020/03/

the-nar-antidote-to-coronavirus/9000. To learn more about the Covid outbreak at Bethel, see Hailey Branson-Potts and Anita Chabria, "God, Masks and Trump: What a Coronavirus Outbreak at a California Church Says about the Election," *Los Angeles Times*, November 1, 2020, accessed December 9, 2021, https://www.latimes.com/california/story/2020-11-01/god-masks-and-trump-what-a-coronavirus-outbreak-at-a-california-church-reveals-about-the-election.

30. Bickle, *Growing in the Prophetic*, 13–15, PDF e-book; Mike Bickle and Sid Roth, "Mike Bickle, Bob Jones, and the International House of Prayer," YouTube video, 4:14, uploaded by God Talk, August 18, 2018, accessed December 9, 2021, https://www.youtube.com/watch?v=bnivpVfkF1Q&t=10s.

31. Mike Bickle, "IHOP TV Podcast 3."

32. Along with Bickle, many Christians believe the Bible teaches that an evil world leader called the Antichrist will rise in the last days and that God will destroy the Antichrist. But they do not believe, as Bickle does, that Christians will "loose" God's judgments against the Antichrist.

33. We describe the Bentley scandal, and explain why it was so damaging to high-profile NAR leaders, in R. Douglas Geivett and Holly Pivec, *A New Apostolic Reformation? A Biblical Response to a Worldwide Movement* (Bellingham, WA: Lexham Press, 2018), Appendix B.

34. See "Bob Jones," Apologetics Index, accessed December 9, 2021, https://www.apologeticsindex.org/3721-bob-jones.

35. Bob Jones, "Bob Jones August 1975 Death Experience," YouTube video, 19:11, uploaded by "NCF Media," January 17, 2019, accessed December 9, 2021, https://www.youtube.com/watch?v=Ta8SL1j0Ya0.

36. See J. Lee Grady, "Prophetic Minister Paul Cain Issues Public Apology for Immoral Lifestyle," *Charisma*, February 28, 2005, accessed December 9, 2021, https://www.charismamag.com/site-archives/154-peopleevents/people-and-events/1514-prophetic-minister-paul-cain-issues-public-apology-for-immoral-lifestyle.

37. Paul Cain, "Paul Cain Stadium Christianity Prophecy," YouTube video, 2:14, uploaded by Contend Global, May 2, 2016, accessed December 9, 2021, https://www.youtube.com/watch?v=nCVSXNsodk0&t=1s.

38. Apologetics Resource Center, "The Apostolic and Prophetic Movement," accessed December 9, 2021, https://arcapologetics.org/the-apostolic-and-prophetic-movement.

39. Bill Johnson, "Eat Meat, Don't Eat the Bones," YouTube video, 57:17, uploaded by Live Forever BJ, March 30, 2015, accessed February

27, 2022, https://www.youtube.com/watch?v=5igclUvzKKI&t=2s; Bill Johnson, "Stewards of Revival," iBethel.TV video, 52:04, accessed February 27, 2022, https://online-sermons.org/billjohnson/4727-bill-johnson-stewards-of-revival.html.

40. Bickle, *Growing in the Prophetic*, 41, 128 PDF e-book. Note that Bickle states that he rarely uses the language of "thus saith the Lord." But he does allow for its use.

41. Vallotton, *Heavy Rain*, chapter 1, Kindle. (Italics are Vallotton's.)

42. We explain and critique their teachings about prophetic illumination in our book: Geivett and Pivec, *A New Apostolic Reformation?*, chapters 11, 13, Kindle.

43. Johnson, *When Heaven Invades Earth*, chapter 11, Kindle. Johnson also writes: "Our study of the Scriptures must take us beyond the historical settings, beyond language studies in the Hebrew and Greek, and at times beyond the context and intent of the human authors as to its content. Our reading of the Word must enable us to hear from God afresh." See Bill and Beni Johnson, *Walking in the Supernatural: Another Cup of Spiritual Java* (Shippensburg, PA: Destiny Image, 2012), chapter 26, Kindle.

44. See some prophetic acts described in Lou Engle, "The Power of Prophetic Acts and Intercessory Warfare," Elijah List, August 30, 2021, accessed December 9, 2021, https://elijahlist.com/words/display_word.html?ID=26032.

45. It is worth noting that just because something *could* be a tell of NAR influence doesn't mean it necessarily *is*. For example, plenty of Christians use "prayer walks" as a way to commit to praying for a community or a neighborhood or a church's ministry without the influence of NAR theology. But when you see these activities, you should at least inquire as to what is meant and intended by them.

46. For example, Johnson makes the following statement: "Jesus lived his earthly life with human limitations. He laid his divinity aside as He sought to fulfill the assignment given to Him by the Father" (our emphasis). See Bill Johnson, *When Heaven Invades Earth: A Practical Guide to a Life of Miracles* (Shippensburg, PA: Destiny Image, 2003), 55, Kindle.

47. Johnson, *God Is Good*, chapter 10, Kindle.

48. We provide an in-depth evaluation of the NAR teaching that Jesus gave up the use of His divine powers when He came to earth in our forthcoming book, Holly Pivec and R. Douglas Geivett, *Reckless Christianity: The Destructive New Teachings and Practices of Bill Johnson,*

Bethel Church, and the Global Movement of Apostles and Prophets (Eugene, OR: Cascade Books).

49. Jennifer LeClaire, *Releasing the Angels of Abundant Harvest: A Prophetic Word for Radical Increase in 2017* (Lake Mary, FL: Charisma House, 2017), Foreword, Kindle.

50. LeClaire, *Releasing the Angels of Abundant Harvest*, 8.

51. See Doughtery, "Paul" and "Morgan," "Why These Christian YouTubers Left the Hyper-Charismatic Movement" (11:00–17:00, 46:00). Paul and Morgan use the term "hyper-charismatics" to refer to the movement we call "NAR."

52. Michael S. Horton, "Bell's Hell: A Review by Michael Horton, Part 1," Westminster Seminary California, March 21, 2011, accessed December 9, 2021, https://www.wscal.edu/blog/bells-hell-a-review-by-michael-horton-part-1. We note that Horton is an amillennialist and, thus, does not look for a future physical kingdom as we do (as premillennialists). But we heartily agree with his assessment that Christians are not tasked with building God's kingdom.

Chapter 7: The Passionately Wrong "Bible"

1. Sid Roth and Brian Simmons, *It's Supernatural!*, video, 28:30, February 2, 2015, accessed May 15, 2022, https://sidroth.org/television/tv-archives/brian-simmons.

2. Roth and Simmons, *It's Supernatural!*

3. "Overview," The Passion Translation, accessed February 22, 2022, https://www.thepassiontranslation.com/book/new-testament-10-book-collection-2020-edition; see also Brian Simmons, *Letters from Heaven by the Apostle Paul*, The Passion Translation (Cicero, NY: 5 Fold Media, 2013), Translator's Introduction, Kindle.

4. Craig Blomberg made this statement while being interviewed by Mike Winger. See Mike Winger and Craig Blomberg, "Dr. Craig Blomberg Reviews *The Passion Translation* Book of 1 Corinthians," YouTube video, 1:39:58, uploaded by Mike Winger, January 13, 2021, accessed December 28, 2021, https://www.youtube.com/watch?v=Fz5GH7UePP0&t=1254s.

5. "Endorsements," The Passion Translation, accessed September 27, 2021, https://www.thepassiontranslation.com/endorsements.

6. "FAQs," The Passion Translation, accessed September 27, 2021, https://www.thepassiontranslation.com/faqs.

7. Those two consultants made those statements in private correspondence with us. Some of the individuals who have "theologically

reviewed" The Passion Translation include Rick Wadholm Jr., Gary S. Greig, Jacqueline Grey, Jeremy Bouma, David Housholder, Stephen D. Renn, and Justin Evans. (See those individuals named in the answer to the question "Is this a single-author translation?" in "FAQs," The Passion Translation.)

8. While being interviewed for the Welton Academy's podcast, Simmons stated, "I had minimal background in biblical languages, so yeah, it was something that, honestly, something the Lord has really helped me with." The podcast has been removed. But the audio of that interview was saved and can be listened to at https://videopress.com/v/dDTilIPH.

9. New Tribes Missions has since been renamed Ethnos360.

10. Mike Winger, "Is Brian Simmons Qualified to Make The Passion Translation?" YouTube video, 1:48, November 20, 2018, accessed December 28, 2021, https://www.youtube.com/watch?v=IBmS5ywXtkY&t=3s.

11. Roth and Simmons, *It's Supernatural.*

12. See, for example, Brian Simmons, Letters from Heaven by the Apostle Paul, The Passion Translation (Cicero, NY: 5 Fold Media, 2013), 2 and Translator's Introduction, Kindle. (Sometimes Simmons calls his Aramaic sources "texts" and sometimes he calls them "manuscripts.")

13. Winger and Blomberg, "Dr. Craig Blomberg Reviews."

14. Winger and Blomberg, "Dr. Craig Blomberg Reviews."

15. "FAQs," The Passion Translation, accessed September 27, 2021, https://www.thepassiontranslation.com/faqs.

16. Craig Keener, "Brief Comments on The Passion Translation," August 27, 2018, accessed December 28, 2021, https://craigkeener.com/brief-comments-on-the-passion-translation. We note that the current FAQ page on the Passion Translation website states that the translation is "based on Greek primacy" and that when Simmons "has resorted to using the alternative Aramaic text, which may vary minimally from the Greek, you will notice an explanatory footnote to let you know." But it is difficult to reconcile those statements—which downplay Simmons's reliance on the Aramaic and the significance of the differences in the Aramaic vs. the Greek texts—with Simmons's other statements, in which he suggests that the New Testament was originally written in Aramaic, that translating from the Aramaic will revolutionize Bible translations, and that his translation makes extensive use of the Aramaic. In addition to his statements we cited in this chapter, he also writes: "I have compared both Greek and Aramaic translations in this monumental project, and have used both in *Letters from Heaven by the Apostle Paul.*

You may consider it as an amalgamation of the two. When there is a vast difference in meaning, many times I have resorted to using the Aramaic alternative." See Brian Simmons, *Letters from Heaven by the Apostle Paul,* Translator's Introduction, Kindle. Notice how different that statement is from the current statement on the Passion Translation website (cited above) in which he refers to the differences between the Greek and Aramaic texts as "minimal" (not "vast") and does not refer to his translation as an "amalgamation" of the Greek and Aramaic. So it seems clear that, on the website, he has felt the need to minimize his reliance on the Aramaic after facing heavy criticism from scholars.

17. "FAQs," The Passion Translation.

18. Simmons has added so many words that some books of the Bible, as they appear in The Passion Translation, stretch far beyond their natural length. For example, the book of Colossians is 38 percent to 48 percent longer than other translations. See Alex D. Hewitson, "Review of *Colossians* in Brian Simmons' The Passion Translation," BibleThinker.org, accessed December 28, 2021, https://biblethinker.org/wp-content/uploads/2021/05/Colossians_-_Alex_Hewitson.pdf. The book of Psalms is at least 50 percent longer than the original. See Andrew G. Shead, "Burning Scripture with Passion: A Review of The Psalms (The Passion Translation), *Themelios* 43, no. 1 (April 2018): 58–71, The Gospel Coalition, accessed December 28, 2021, https://www.thegospelcoalition.org/themelios/article/burning-scripture-with-passion-a-review-of-the-psalms-passion-translation.

19. The examples we show in this chapter all come from the New Testament. Simmons has not completed his work on the Old Testament. The first installment of The Passion Translation, Song of Songs (an Old Testament book), was released in 2011. To date, the entire New Testament has been released along with these other Old Testament books: Genesis, Joshua, Judges, Ruth, The Psalms, Proverbs, and Isaiah.

20. Darrell L. Bock, "Assessment of *The Passion Translation* of Ephesians," BibleThinker.org, accessed December 28, 2021, https://biblethinker.org/wp-content/uploads/2021/05/Darrell-L.-Bock.pdf.

21. Bock, "Assessment of The Passion Translation."

22. Douglas Moo, "A Brief Evaluation of *The Passion Translation* of Romans," BibleThinker.org, accessed November 7, 2021, https://bible-thinker.org/wp-content/uploads/2021/05/Douglas-Moo.pdf.

23. Craig L. Blomberg, "Review of 1 Corinthians in *The Passion Translation*," BibleThinker.org, accessed December 28, 2021, https://biblethinker.org/wp-content/uploads/2021/05/Craig-L.-Blomberg.pdf.

24. Sam Storms, a continuationist who believes that miracles are included among the works alluded to here, acknowledges that "the most popular interpretation in our day is that Jesus's words refer to something other than miraculous deeds and physical healing." See C. Samuel Storms, "Doing the (Miraculous) Works of Jesus—John 14:12," 2016, accessed February 20, 2022, https://www.samstorms.org/all-articles/post/doing-the--miraculous--works-of-jesus---john-1412.

25. D. A. Carson, *The Gospel According to John*, The Pillar New Testament Commentary (Grand Rapids: Eerdmans, 1991), 496.

26. To find out if the Bible translation you use shares these characteristics, take a look at the opening pages. The Preface or Introduction will usually explain the translation strategy—spelling out the credentials of the translators and the principles that have guided their translation decisions. Be sure to look for a church that recommends and uses a standard translation of the Bible. There are many excellent choices (we've mentioned several in this chapter).

Chapter 8: Toxic Worship Music

1. Churches that we identify as overtly NAR accept and teach basic NAR beliefs. These include Bethel Church, Jesus Culture, Gateway Church, and the Forerunner Church at the International House of Prayer in Kansas City, Missouri. Hillsong, if not overtly NAR, has a strong affinity for NAR beliefs. NAR influence on Hillsong is documented in the book by David Cartledge, *The Apostolic Revolution: The Restoration of Apostles and Prophets in the Assemblies of God in Australia* (Chester Hill, NSW: Paraclete Institute, 2000). Hillsong's own leaders, and Brian Houston's ministry associates outside Hillsong, referred to Houston as an apostle. (Houston founded and led Hillsong Church for nearly 40 years until his resignation in 2022, following church investigations into two instances of inappropriate behavior.) For example, the Australian-based evangelist Phil Pringle (while speaking at Hillsong in Australia in 2019) called Brian Houston and his wife, Bobbie, "major apostles in today's Christian world." (See a video clip of this statement preserved by "Churchwatcher," "Phil Pringle Calls Hillsong Leaders Brian and Bobbie Houston 'Major Apostles,'" video, 1:21, uploaded by ChurchWatchCentral.com, July 15, 2019, accessed October 12, 2021, https://churchwatchcentral.com/2019/07/15/phil-pringle-calls-hillsong-leaders-brian-bobbie-houston-major-apostles.) Also, Brian Houston and Bill Johnson have spoken at conferences hosted by each other's churches.

Elevation Church is part of the Southern Baptist Convention, which does not hold to NAR theology. However, Elevation's music label, Elevation Worship, has collaborated with Bethel Music artists. Also, Elevation's founder and lead pastor Steven Furtick spoke together with the "apostle" Bill Johnson and "prophet" Kris Vallotton at Bethel Music's 2019 "Heaven Come" conference in Los Angeles. And NAR buzzwords and concepts are included in the lyrics of many Elevation songs.

2. "Movement Impact," Arise and Build, accessed October 1, 2021, https://ariseandbuild.net/impact.

3. See Larry Sparks, "The Prophetic Message in Hillsong's 'Oceans,'" *Charisma Magazine*, April 25, 2014, accessed December 24, 2021, https://www.charismamag.com/spirit/prophecy/20267-the-prophetic -message-in-hillsong-s-oceans.

4. Barna Group, "Americans Divided on the Importance of Church," March 24, 2014, accessed August 1, 2021, https://www.barna.com/ research/americans-divided-on-the-importance-of-church; "Atheism Doubles Among Generation Z," January 24, 2018, accessed August 1, 2021, https://www.barna.com/research/atheism-doubles-among-generation-z.

5. This view of NAR songs is described by Sparks, "The Prophetic Message in Hillsong's 'Oceans.'" Bethel Music advertisements describe the songs as "declarations." See, for example, "Victory—CD," Bethel Music, accessed February 28, 2022, https://store.bethelmusic.com/ products/victory#:~:text=Mighty%20declarations%20like%2C%20 "I%20raise%20a%20hallelujah%20in,faced%20the%20possible%20 loss%20of%20their%20son%20Jaxon.

6. This is encouraged and taught in books and sermons . . . and music. For a recent book that urges unwise dependence on a burgeon-ing of the miraculous, see J. P. Moreland, *A Simple Guide to Experience Miracles: Instruction and Inspiration for Living Supernaturally in Christ* (Grand Rapids: Zondervan, 2021). This teaching is unwise because it lacks biblical and empirical support, because it distorts the proper and adequate grounds for biblical faith, and because it paints a confused pic-ture of the presence of God's kingdom in the world and the power that is to be associated with it.

7. See the definition of an "open heaven" found under the entry titled "Glory" in Abraham S. Rajah, *Apostolic and Prophetic Dictionary: Language of the End-Time Church* (Bloomington, IN: WestBow Press, 2013), Kindle. *Open Heavens* is also the title of one of Bill Johnson's books.

8. See chapter 6 to learn more about Bob Jones, including the dis-turbing confession he made to abusing his prophetic office.

9. Mike Bickle, "Study Notes (PDF)," document at Teaching Library of Mike Bickle, "Session 12: The Bridal Seal of Mature Love," Studies in the Song of Solomon, Twelve-part series taught at the International House of Prayer University, Spring Semester 2014, MikeBickle.org, accessed May 15, 2022, https://mikebickle.org/resource/the-bridal-seal-of-mature-love.

10. Wendy Griffith, "'The Call' in Kansas City: A Marriage Covenant with Jesus," video, *The 700 Club*, Christian Broadcasting Network, January 3, 2003.

11. To learn more about the problems with viewing one's relationship with God in romantic terms, see Tim L. Anderson, *Into His Presence: A Theology of Intimacy with God* (Grand Rapids: Kregel Academic, 2019), 168–74. We must study to learn intimacy with God on God's terms, and exercise caution regarding the conditions of intimacy that we "feel" should show up in our relationship with God. As J. I. Packer wrote, "Knowledge of God is an experience calculated to thrill a person's heart" (in *Knowing God*). But knowledge of God prepares a person for the kind of thrill that knowing God involves.

12. Bill Johnson and Dann Farrelly, "Episode 1: Bethel's Beliefs about Jesus, God's Sovereignty, and Bible Translations," *Rediscover Bethel*, YouTube video, 1:39:33, uploaded by "Bethel," June 8, 2021, accessed December 24, 2021, https://www.youtube.com/watch?v=XZ2xjnXYfm8&t=28s (1:26:00).

13. See "Katiejoy's" comment posted on September 9, 2019, under the article by Costi Hinn, "Should Your Church Sing Jesus Culture and Bethel Music?," For the Gospel, October 7, 2018, archived at the Wayback Machine October 18, 2019, accessed May 15, 2022, https://web.archive.org/web/20191018204742/http://www.forthegospel.org/should-your-church-sing-jesus-culture-bethel-music/#comments.

14. See "RachelleL's" review at Amazon.com, posted February 15, 2011, accessed October 12, 2021, https://www.amazon.com/Lifted-High-Bethel-Music-2011-07-29/dp/B01JTCD8NA/ref=sr_1_6?dchild=1&keywords=bethel+music&qid=1633161190&sr=8-6.

15. Mike Winger, "Bill Johnson's Theology and Movement Examined Biblically," YouTube video, 1:19:15, uploaded by "Mike Winger," February 13, 2018, accessed October 12, 2021, https://www.youtube.com/watch?v=r3tEv26OMTU (10:00).

16. Jesus Culture worship leader Chris Quilala confirms that the group aims to spread their teachings about miraculous signs and wonders through their music. He said the following about Jesus Culture's

events: "It's not just people showing up to hear some good music. We want people to encounter God's presence obviously in worship, but we also want them to really taste what signs and wonders are and realize that God wants to touch them—and that they can take this out in their cities." (See Marcus Yoars, "The Radical Revivalists," *Charisma Magazine,* June 9, 2011, accessed October 12, 2021, https://www.charismamag.com/site-archives/1447-0611-magazine-articles/features/13785-the-radical-revivalists.)

17. Tim Challies wrote an insightful article arguing this very point. See Tim Challies, "Moroni from the Realms of Glory," Challies.com, December 15, 2014, accessed December 24, 2021, https://www.challies.com/articles/moroni-from-the-realms-of-glory/?fbclid=IwAR2bNmIqUijhoaaOfMzsDOuqX87_zGA3MwXp86KH0y5OB0nnKGI8F96NJIk.

18. This quote by Bill Johnson was posted to the WorshipU Facebook page on September 24, 2019. WorshipU is the online worship school of Bethel Redding. The original WorshipU Facebook page can no longer be found, but a screen capture of the post quoting Johnson was posted to the Bethel Church and Christianity Facebook page, September 24, 2019, accessed October 12, 2021, https://www.facebook.com/BethelChurchandChristianity/photos/a.604267139610313/2363002987070044.

19. Author emphasis.

20. David Henneke, "'Why Our Church No Longer Plays Bethel or Hillsong Music,' Pastor Explains False Teachings," YouTube video, 55:33, uploaded by Doreen Virtue, February 5, 2020, accessed October 12, 2021, https://www.youtube.com/watch?v=C7R6AKFlWhI.

21. Jeannie Ortega Law, "Worship Leader No Longer Supports Hillsong, Elevation, Bethel Music Over 'False Gospel Message,'" *Christian Post,* July 20, 2021, accessed October 12, 2021, https://www.christianpost.com/news/worship-leader-blasts-hillsong-elevation-bethel-music.html.

Chapter 9: Is It Always God's Will to Heal?

1. Author emphasis.

2. Bill Johnson, *God Is Good: He's Better Than You Think* (Shippensburg, PA: Destiny Image, 2016), chapter 8, Kindle.

3. See, for example, Johnson, *God Is Good,* chapter 8, Kindle.

4. See Nabeel Qureshi, "Nabeel's Vlog 012: My Visit to Bethel Church," YouTube video, 25:51, uploaded by Michelle Qureshi Wilson

on December 22, 2016, accessed December 12, 2021, https://www.you-tube.com/watch?v=fwH8C69RWRU.

5. Qureshi estimated that at least 1,700 people "prophesied" his healing when he visited Bethel Church in December 2016. (See note #4 above.) A video on Facebook shows that during his visit many BSSM students, and a leader on the stage, made declarations for his healing during a meeting. This appears to be the incident Qureshi was referring to. (See BSSM, "BSSM: Nabeel Qureshi Testimony," video, 0:15, uploaded to Bethel Church, Redding's Facebook page, December 14, 2016, accessed December 12, 2021, https://www.facebook.com/bethel.church.redding/videos/10154160769191824.

6. Jessica Miller, "The Tragedy of Bethel's #WakeUpOlive: Why It Isn't Always God's Will to Heal," *Premier Christianity*, January 1, 2020, accessed December 12, 2021, https://www.premierchristianity.com/home/the-tragedy-of-bethels-wakeupolive-why-it-isnt-always-gods-will-to-heal/1523.article.

7. Bill Johnson, *Open Heavens: Position Yourself to Encounter the God of Revival* (Shippensburg, PA: Destiny Image Publishers, 2021), chapter 3, Kindle.

8. This testimony is found in the book *The Journey: Stories by Healing Room Directors* (Spokane, WA: Healing Rooms Ministries Publishing, 2020), 319–20, Kindle.

9. This testimony by "J.P." was posted on the Healing Rooms Ministries website on September 28, 2019.

10. "Simple Clues Lead to Treasure," YWAM Frontiers, archived at the Wayback Machine June 24, 2020, accessed May 15, 2022, https://web.archive.org/web/20200624224423/https://ywamfrontiers.com/treasure-hunt.

11. "How 'To' Treasure Hunt," YouTube video, 9:13, uploaded by Jason Chin, October 19, 2013, accessed December 13, 2021, https://www.youtube.com/watch?v=1r7B51EclwE.

12. Molly Hensley-Clancy, "Meet the 'Young Saints' of Bethel Who Go to College to Perform Miracles," *BuzzFeed News*, October 12, 2017, accessed December 12, 2021, https://www.buzzfeednews.com/article/mollyhensleyclancy/meet-the-young-saints-of-bethel-who-go-to-college-to.

13. Dead Raising Team, "Our Director," accessed December 12, 2021, http://deadraisingteam.com/our-director.

14. Bill Johnson, "Eat Meat, Don't Eat the Bones," YouTube video, 57:17, uploaded by Live Forever BJ, March 30, 2015, accessed December 12, 2021, https://www.youtube.com/watch?v=5igclUvzKKI&t=2s.

15. "Bethel Sozo," accessed February 22, 2022, https://www.bethelsozo.com.

16. Relational ties and generational ties refer to common NAR teachings about "soul ties" and "generational curses." A soul tie is a deep spiritual connection that is formed between two people (such as family members, close friends, and spouses) and can sometimes be toxic (thus, such ties need to be broken). A generational curse is a curse that is believed to be passed down in the family line, from one generation to the next, because of sin committed by one or more ancestors. For example, if someone has a lot of divorce in their family, or alcoholism, or poverty, it is believed they may be the victim of a generational curse, which must be broken (by renouncing that sin and making prayer declarations).

17. Studies have shown that false "memories" can be produced during practices associated with recovered memory therapy, and for that reason prominent professional organizations (including the American Medical Association, the American Psychological Association, the Australian Psychological Society, and the British Royal College of Psychiatrists) "have issued strong warnings against [such] practices." See Elizabeth F. Loftus, and Deborah Davis, "Recovered Memories," *Annual Review of Clinical Psychology* 2 (April 27, 2006): 493. According to an entry in the Wikipedia article titled "Inner Healing Movement," the founders of Sozo ministry at Bethel, Dawna De Silva and Teresa Liebscher, denounce the use of memory recovery therapy. The article also states that "practitioners of their methods that have strayed from the standard teaching seem to be the source of these concerning practices." But the sources for those statements are not cited, and we could not find evidence for this alleged denouncement. If it exists, it isn't to be found where you would most expect it, on the Sozo ministry website. Our research strongly suggests that Sozo does rely on recovered memory methodology. A former Sozo practitioner who received formal Sozo training from Bethel describes how memories are recalled during Sozo sessions and reports that, in many cases, false memories were produced. See Doreen Virtue and Oscar Whatmore, "Why Sozo Is Dangerous," YouTube video, 12:16, uploaded by Doreen Virtue, July 9, 2020, accessed January 1, 2022, www.youtube.com/watch?v=rS9KCAOmK7s&t=633s.

18. M. Barbara Hansell, Maria Chadim Kirkpatrick, Joy McCloud, and Oscar Whatmore, *A Hidden Path: Bethel Redding and Beyond* (N.p., Sound Word Ministry Publications, 2019), 108–9.

19. To learn more about Sozo, see "Sozo Prayer Spreading Worldwide, but What Is It?," *Christian Post*, May 19, 2019, accessed

November 7, 2021, https://www.christianpost.com/news/sozo-prayer
-spreading-worldwide-but-what-is-it.html.

20. Bill Johnson, *The Way of Life: Experiencing the Culture of Heaven on Earth*, updated ed. (Shippensburg, PA: Destiny Image, 2019), chapter 19, Kindle. He states, "We believe all can be healed because Jesus demonstrated the Father's will in healing all the sick and demonized He encountered."

21. Johnson, *The Way of Life*, 8, 39–40.

22. Johnson cites Eugene Peterson's *The Message Bible,* a paraphrase of John 20:21. Johnson, *The Way of Life*, 8.

23. "Normal Christianity" is a buzzword in NAR.

24. Bill Johnson, *The Supernatural Power of a Transformed Mind: Access to a Life of Miracles* (Shippensburg, PA: Destiny Image, 2014), chapter 1.

25. In chapter 3, we show that Scripture does not support NAR teachings about the activation of spiritual gifts.

26. Leonardo Blair, "Bethel Church Pastor Beni Johnson Says She's Felt 'So Much Peace' Despite Cancer Diagnosis," *Christian Today*, August 17, 2018, accessed December 15, 2021, https://www.christian-today.com/article/bethel-church-pastor-beni-johnson-says-shes-felt-so-much-peace-despite-cancer-diagnosis/130230.htm; Johnson, *The Way of Life*, chapter 6, Kindle.

27. Eric Johnson and Dan Farrelly, "Revival Chat," YouTube video, 9:59, uploaded by Whizzpopping, August 10, 2009, accessed December 15, 2021, https://www.youtube.com/watch?v=_lO7A8kRpgc (03:00).

28. For example, Bill Johnson says that Jesus never withheld healing because of someone's weak faith, and Christians should never tell a sick person that they did not experience a miracle of healing because of their weak faith. See Johnson, *The Way of Life*, chapter 2, Kindle. Even so, the responsibility does fall on the sick (and maybe even more so on those who could not heal them), as we see in Bill Johnson's other statements on the subject.

29. Johnson, *God Is Good*, chapter 10, Kindle.

30. Johnson, *God Is Good*, chapter 10, Kindle.

31. Bill Johnson and Dann Farrelly, "Episode 1: Bethel's Beliefs about Jesus, God's Sovereignty, and Bible Translations," Rediscover Bethel, YouTube video, 1:39:33, uploaded by Bethel, June 8, 2021, accessed December 24, 2021, https://www.youtube.com/watch?v=XZ2xjnXYfm8&t=5290s (30:00).

32. See Romans 8:18–28.

33. This true prayer of faith contrasts sharply with the so-called "prayer of faith" taught originally by prosperity gospel/Word of Faith teachers and adopted by today's NAR leaders. See Kate Bowler, *Blessed: A History of the American Prosperity Gospel* (New York: Oxford University Press, 2013).

34. "Fake Healing Videos Evaluated: Todd White, Tom Fischer, and More," YouTube video, 57:52, uploaded by Mike Winger, February 6, 2018, accessed December 13, 2021, https://www.youtube.com/watch?v=4_8lT1dJV1k.

35. Derren Brown, "Derren Exposes the Tricks of Faith Healers!," YouTube video, 7:30, September 19, 2020, accessed December 13, 2021, https://www.youtube.com/watch?v=4_8lT1dJV1k (4:00).

36. The unjustified belief that God intends to produce miracles in ever-increasing numbers also creates a temptation for NAR leaders to manufacture miracles.

37. Joni Eareckson Tada, *Joni: An Unforgettable Story* (Grand Rapids: Zondervan, 2021), first published 1976.

38. Robertson McQuilken, "Living by Vows," *Christianity Today*, February 1, 2004, accessed December 18, 2021, https://www.christianitytoday.com/ct/2004/februaryweb-only/2-9-11.0.html.

39. Sarah Eekhoff Zylstra, "Died: Robertson McQuilken, College President Praised for Alzheimer's Resignation," June 2, 2016, accessed December 16, 2021, https://www.christianitytoday.com/news/2016/june/died-robertson-mcquilkin-columbia-president-alzheimers-ciu.html.

40. Robertson McQuilken, *A Promise Kept: The Story of an Unforgettable Love* (Carol Stream, IL: Tyndale House Publishers, 1998).

Chapter 10: Deception-Proofing Your Children

1. Jan Markell, "Wolves Not Sparing the Flock (Part 1)," Audio, 57:00, Olive Tree Ministries, June 16, 2018, accessed November 7, 2021, https://olivetreeviews.org/radio-archives/wolves-not-sparing-the-flock-part-1.

2. Still other parents claim their children recovered false memories after taking part in Sozo. See, for example, "Victims of Johnson's Sozo Ministry Speak Out," *Closing Stages* (blog), July 31, 2012, accessed November 7, 2021, https://closingstages.net/2012/07/31/victims-of-johnsons-sozo-ministry-speak-out.

3. "Women from Bethel Bill Johnson—Disturbing Impartation—Benny Hinn San Jose 2014," YouTube video, 07:00, uploaded by

"Drybones Dead," July 1, 2014, accessed November 7, 2021, https://www.youtube.com/watch?v=VZkgY-bP7yk&t=1s.

4. Incidentally, we make no apology for stressing the importance of this question about each person's eternal destiny, and what to expect after death. This is a centerpiece of New Testament preaching, as amply indicated in the book of Acts. The apostle Paul revels in the fact that, for any believer in Christ, to "be away from the body," which happens when we die, is to be "at home with the Lord" (2 Cor. 5:8).

5. Not all of these practices automatically make an individual or organization NAR, but if more than a couple of these exist, you can bet you're dealing with a church heavily influenced by NAR.

6. Many of these terms are explained elsewhere in this book.

7. Seth Dahl, *Revival Kids 2 Curriculum: Friendship, Freedom, and the Perfect Health Zone*, accessed November 7, 2021, https://shop.bethel.com/products/revival-kids-2-curriculum-friendship-freedom-the-perfect-health-zone?_pos=2&_sid=f8b573dfe&_ss=r.

8. Bill Johnson, and Mike Seth, *Here Comes Heaven! A Kid's Guide to God's Supernatural Power* (Shippensburg, PA: Destiny Image, 2007), chapter 2, Kindle.

9. Holly Pivec, "Is It Too Late to Save This Church from NAR?" HollyPivec.com, September 24, 2019, accessed November 7, 2021, https://www.hollypivec.com/blog/2019/09/is-it-too-late-to-save-this-church-from-nar/8494.

10. Kids in Ministry International, "PowerClubs Are Unique," accessed November 7, 2021, https://kidsinministry.org/powerclubs-are-unique. The website states that these clubs have been designed specifically for Pentecostal and charismatic churches, but it does not mention that they go beyond Pentecostal and charismatic teachings and promote the NAR beliefs and practices of their founder, Becky Fischer.

11. Holly has documented the significant NAR influence on YWAM in an article on her blog. See Holly Pivec, "What Churches Should Know about YWAM Part 2: Partnering with the New Apostolic Reformation," HollyPivec.com, June 7, 2019, accessed November 7, 2021, https://www.hollypivec.com/blog/2019/06/what-churches-should-know-about-ywam-part-2-partnering-with-the-new-apostolic-reformation/8331.

12. See Lindsay Davis, Jeff Durbin, and Jeremiah Roberts, "Defecting from Bethel (Part 1): Interview with Lindsay Davis," *Cultish*, podcast audio, March 23, 2019, accessed November 11, 2021, https://thecultishshow.com/podcast/defecting-from-bethel.

13. Bill Johnson, *When Heaven Invades Earth: A Practical Guide to a Life of Miracles* (Shippensburg, PA: Destiny Image, 2003), chapter 4, Kindle.

14. Douglas Groothuis, *Unmasking the New Age* (Downers Grove, IL: IVP Books, 1986), 172.

15. For example, Duke University professor Kate Bowler—who has carefully researched the prosperity movement—explains that many church leaders who clearly teach the prosperity gospel do not like to be called "prosperity" teachers. They do not want to be associated with the negative connotations people have with that movement. See Kate Bowler, *Blessed: A History of the American Prosperity Gospel* (New York: Oxford University Press, 2013), Appendix B.

16. Natasha Crain has written excellent books designed to help parents teach apologetics to their children. For example, see *Keeping Your Kids on God's Side: 40 Questions to Help Them Build a Lasting Faith* (Eugene, OR: Harvest House Publishers, 2016).

17. Nathaniel Bluedorn and Hans Bluedorn, *The Fallacy Detective: Thirty-Eight Lessons on How to Recognize Bad Reasoning*, Workbook ed. (Christian Logic, 2015).

18. To learn more about how questions can be used effectively to reach nonbelievers with the gospel, we highly recommend the book by Greg Koukl, *Tactics: A Game Plan for Discussing Your Christian Convictions*, updated and expanded ed. (Grand Rapids: Zondervan, 2019). With some thoughtfulness, the tactics described in this book can be adapted for discussion with those who have embraced NAR beliefs. Greg does an excellent job modeling this method of interaction during his regular *Stand to Reason* podcast.

Conclusion: Joining the Resistance

1. For an excellent book refuting progressive Christianity, see Alisa Childers, *Another Gospel? A Lifelong Christian Seeks Truth in Response to Progressive Christianity* (Carol Stream, IL: Tyndale, 2020).

2. We encourage you to see our other books about NAR: R. Douglas Geivett and Holly Pivec, *A New Apostolic Reformation? A Biblical Response to a Worldwide Movement* (Bellingham, WA: Lexham Press, 2018); R. Douglas Geivett, and Holly Pivec, *God's Super-Apostles: Encountering the Worldwide Prophets and Apostles Movement* (Bellingham, WA: Lexham Press, 2018); and, Holly Pivec and R. Douglas Geivett, *Reckless Christianity: The Destructive New Teachings and Practices of Bill Johnson,*

Bethel Church, and the Global Movement of Apostles and Prophets (Eugene, OR: Cascade Books, forthcoming). Throughout this book, we have cited many useful resources produced by other worthy critics of NAR.

3. At the request of a church in the midwestern United States, we crafted a position paper that can be used by any church as a template for its own position paper on NAR. See Holly Pivec, "Protect Your Church from the NAR: Adopt a Position Paper," December 16, 2016, accessed December 20, 2021, https://www.hollypivec.com/blog/2016/12/protect-your-church-from-the-nar-adopt-a-position-paper/6579?rq=position%20paper.

4. Teasi shared this story with us. She included details about the spiritual abuse she experienced in her podcast interview with Alisa Childers: "Spiritual Abuse and the Church: Why Should We Listen? With Teasi Cannon," YouTube video, 47:30, uploaded by Alisa Childers, November 7, 2021, accessed December 23, 2021, https://www.youtube.com/watch?v=dseigzUaGRI.

5. It is common for those introducing divisive teachings into churches to accuse those who speak up against the teachings as divisive. The Center for Biblical Unity—cofounded by Chantal Monique Duson and Krista Bontrager in response to the harmful teachings of critical race theory—is doing excellent work explaining what true biblical unity looks like. See their six-week, small group curriculum, Monique Duson, *Reconciled: A Biblical Approach to Racial Unity* (Center for Biblical Unity).

6. Tertullian, for example, was born in the mid-second century in Carthage, North Africa. He was a brilliant Christian apologist and writer who converted to Montanism—another theologically dangerous movement that, like NAR, promoted authoritative prophets and bizarre manifestations of the Holy Spirit.

Special Appendix: On Miracles and NAR

1. Sometimes we encounter the phrase "signs and miracles," as in Acts 4:16 and 8:13. John's Gospel refers to Jesus's miracles simply as "signs" (see John 2:11; 11:47; 20:30).

2. Clear cases include Moses and the plagues against Egypt, the parting of the Red Sea, and the miraculous provision of food, water, and directional guidance during Israel's Wilderness wanderings (all recounted in Exodus); the miracles of Elijah and Elisha (recorded in

1 and 2 Kings); the earthly ministry of Jesus as reported in the Gospels; and, of course, the miracles described in the book of Acts.

3. For more on miracles, see R. Douglas Geivett and Gary R. Habermas, eds., *In Defense of Miracles: A Comprehensive Case for God's Action in Human History* (Downers Grove, IL: InterVarsity Press, 1997); R. Douglas Geivett, "Why I Believe in the Possibility of Miracles," in *Why I Am a Christian: Leading Thinkers Explain Why They Believe*, ed. Norman L. Geisler and Paul K. Hoffman (Grand Rapids: Baker, 2001), 97–110; and, R. Douglas Geivett, "Miracles," in *The Routledge Companion to the Philosophy of Religion*, ed. Chad Meister and Paul Copan (London and New York: Routledge, 2007), 595–605; Norman L. Geisler, *Miracles and the Modern Mind: A Defense of Biblical Miracles* (Grand Rapids, MI: Baker, 1992); C. S. Lewis, *Miracles* (New York: Macmillan, 1969).